时文速递

云图英语

让/阅/读/更/具/时/事/感

完形填空 | 阅读理解 | 任务型阅读 | 短文填空　　云图分级阅读研究院·编著

强化篇

本书编委

编者（按姓氏音序排列）
李如　刘洁　刘盼　张紫娟

编审（按姓氏音序排列）
陈郅　侯琳　刘倩倩　张欢

北京理工大学出版社
BEIJING INSTITUTE OF TECHNOLOGY PRESS

版权专有　侵权必究

图书在版编目（CIP）数据

云图英语时文速递. 强化篇 / 云图分级阅读研究院
编著. — 北京：北京理工大学出版社，2021.6（2022.6 重印）
　　ISBN 978 – 7 – 5763 – 0012 – 3

Ⅰ. ①云… Ⅱ. ①云… Ⅲ. ①英语—阅读教学—初中
—教学参考资料 Ⅳ. ①G634.413

中国版本图书馆 CIP 数据核字（2021）第 136294 号

出版发行 /	北京理工大学出版社有限责任公司	
社　　址 /	北京市海淀区中关村南大街 5 号	
邮　　编 /	100081	
电　　话 /	（010）68914775（总编室）	
	（010）82562903（教材售后服务热线）	
	（010）68944723（其他图书服务热线）	
网　　址 /	http://www.bitpress.com.cn	
经　　销 /	全国各地新华书店	
印　　刷 /	三河市文阁印刷有限公司	
开　　本 /	889 毫米 × 1194 毫米　1/16	
印　　张 /	11.5	责任编辑 / 武丽娟
字　　数 /	331 千字	文案编辑 / 武丽娟
版　　次 /	2021 年 6 月第 1 版　2022 年 6 月第 3 次印刷	责任校对 / 刘亚男
定　　价 /	36.00 元	责任印制 / 李志强

图书出现印装质量问题，请拨打售后服务热线，本社负责调换

ENGLISH READING

作者的话

一直以来，阅读理解都是中考英语分数占比较高的题型。2022年4月出台的《义务教育英语课程标准（2022年版）》（以下简称"新课标"）中，对阅读"理解性技能"的要求进行了升级，在原来"能理解段落中各句子之间的逻辑关系"的基础上增加了"理解语篇中显性或隐性的逻辑关系"。另外，新课标从"语言能力""文化意识""思维品质""学习能力"四个方面明确了英语学习的目标，其中强调了"对中外文化的理解和对优秀文化的鉴赏"。由此可见，对于阅读理解题型，相比于生硬的解题技巧，学生在新时代表现出的逻辑思维能力以及跨文化认知、态度和行为选择将变得更为重要。

时文阅读作为一种非常有意义的新型阅读模式，不仅可以帮助学生增加阅读量，扩展阅读范围，还能引导学生关注国内外社会热点，关注人类命运和地球家园，帮助学生形成跨文化交际的意识，培养学生跨文化交际的能力，从而进一步拓宽学生的国际视野。现在，越来越多的英语教师选择将英语时文引进课堂教学，让学生接触原汁原味的英文，在培养学生语言能力的同时，还为学生营造了一种英语本土的教学氛围，加深了学生对英语知识、外国文化和风土人情的理解，帮助学生在跨文化交际中克服由于文化背景、交际习惯和思维模式的差异导致的阅读障碍。因此，初中阶段渗透时文阅读具有重要意义。

为了满足广大师生的需求与期望，《云图英语时文速递》在一线名师的共同努力下应运而生。作者精选时文材料，准确把握难易度。全套书共分为基础篇、强化篇和冲刺篇3册，每册设置了14周的阅读内容，每周包括6篇阅读理解题和1篇新闻速递，能满足学生一学期的学习需求。全套书主要包括以下显著特点：

1. 选材新颖，体裁多样

作者依据新课标三大"主题"——人与自我、人与社会、人与自然，从知名新闻网站、杂志刊物广泛选取有关不同国家热点事件的文章，并进一步细分为14个"主题群"，涵盖生活成长、家庭教育、健康饮食、社会人际、文化风俗、科学技术、环境保护等话题。文章结合中学生生活实际情境进行选段，是学生了解国内外信息、提升英语阅读能力的不二之选。同时应用文、记叙文、说明文、议论文等常见文章体裁能让学生着眼于不同体裁文章的思路结构，把握不同文本特点。

2. 贴合学情考情，科学系统设题

本书以新课标为依据，题目设置紧密契合中考要求。题型丰富，既有传统的阅读理解题，也有符合各地区不同需求的完形填空、任务型阅读与短文填空等题型。因此，本书适用于人教

版、仁爱版、外研版、北师大版等多版本初中教材使用者，能满足各地区学生中考阅读的需求。难度的把控是同类书共同的难点。作者在编写本书时，充分考虑并准确把握词汇的丰富度、用语的精准度、句型结构的多样性以及时文的篇幅和词汇量等。全书难度符合新课标7至9年级的目标要求以及初中三个年级学生的认知水平，对学校平时的测验命题也有一定的可借鉴性。

3. 紧跟潮流，时事风向我知道

本书除每周6篇阅读练习外，另新增一篇新闻速递拓展阅读。新闻均出自知名网站与刊物，包括英国广播公司（BBC）、美国之音广播电台（VOA）、《中国日报国际版》《科学美国人》《卫报》《时代周刊》《美国国家地理》《环球时报》。精选最新季度发布且贴合中学生认知兴趣的新闻，同时在改编过程中保留原文特点与风格，帮助学生在掌握新闻类文章阅读技巧的同时，了解国内外最新热点事件，拓宽阅读面。

4. 特色栏目配置，360度全方位攻克阅读

文前小标签给出了词数、难度和建议用时等信息，方便学生进行自我评估。

"答案解析"梳理思路，解答清晰。

"词汇碎片"积累核心词汇。

"重难句讲解"梳理句式，沉淀语法。

"参考译文"单独成册，实现逐句对照精读。

作者期望通过最新的热点和最优质的题文设计，为学生打开探寻国内外热点讯息的一个小小的窗口；作者期望能帮助家长和老师一起把握中考动态，为学生提供训练素材；作者期望能让学生在做题的过程中，有效提高阅读理解能力，并逐渐了解国内外社会动态发展趋势，打开国际视野，把握时代脉搏。

ENGLISH READING

Contents 目录

人与自我

Week One — 生活成长 / 兴趣爱好 — 主题

- 001 Monday   A 完形填空   中国年轻摄影师摘得年度天文摄影师桂冠
- 002 Tuesday   B 阅读理解   马里学生终圆冬奥梦
- 003 Wednesday   C 阅读理解   外国留学生痴迷于太极
- 004 Thursday   D 阅读理解   学生研发电子宠物——虚拟世界的另一个我
- 005 Friday   E 任务型阅读   成骨不全症漫画家的进击之路
- 006 Saturday   F 短文填空   学生克服逆境追求学业梦想

Week Two — 校园生活 — 主题

- 007 Monday   A 完形填空   沉浸式英语：随时随地学英语
- 008 Tuesday   B 阅读理解   主题丰富的项目式学习
- 009 Wednesday   C 阅读理解   传统戏曲走进校园
- 010 Thursday   D 任务型阅读   疫情之下的学与教
- 011 Friday   E 短文填空   香港西贡开展的野外教育
- 012 Saturday   F 短文填空   音乐温暖童心

Week Three — 家庭教育 — 主题

- 013 Monday   A 完形填空   意料之外，孩子改变父母
- 014 Tuesday   B 阅读理解   志愿"火炬"世代相传
- 015 Wednesday   C 阅读理解   姐姐的启发助力创新
- 016 Thursday   D 任务型阅读   兄弟姐妹之间的竞争会结束吗？
- 017 Friday   E 短文填空   监督孩子的游戏时间
- 018 Saturday   F 短文填空   移民父母打破语言障碍

Week Four　　健康饮食　　主题

019	Monday	A 完形填空	淮安美食的历史
020	Tuesday	B 阅读理解	开始健康饮食的四种方法
021	Wednesday	C 阅读理解	食用橄榄油可降低患病风险
022	Thursday	D 阅读理解	关于中风，你需要了解这些
023	Friday	E 任务型阅读	2022最佳饮食榜单公布，地中海饮食实现五连冠
024	Saturday	F 短文填空	基因和黑咖啡之间的那点事儿

人与社会

Week Five　　社会人际　　主题

025	Monday	A 完形填空	如何帮助孩子交友
026	Tuesday	B 阅读理解	帮助听障人士表达自我
027	Wednesday	C 任务型阅读	社区花园
028	Thursday	D 任务型阅读	年轻一代为国内品牌的增长提供了新支点
029	Friday	E 任务型阅读	安全出行服务热线
030	Saturday	F 短文填空	在办公室隔离的48小时

Week Six　　文学艺术　　主题

031	Monday	A 完形填空	冰墩墩为何如此受欢迎
032	Tuesday	B 阅读理解	为什么肖像画让我们着迷数千年
033	Wednesday	C 阅读理解	漫画萌虎
034	Thursday	D 任务型阅读	铺着140吨泥土的地球屋
035	Friday	E 任务型阅读	90后设计师变"废"为宝，制作精美头冠
036	Saturday	F 短文填空	造型惊艳的科幻面具

Week Seven 历史地理 主题

- 037 Monday A 完形填空 上海老旧大院的重生
- 038 Tuesday B 阅读理解 迪拜的另一面：抗击荒漠化
- 039 Wednesday C 任务型阅读 秦始皇帝陵博物院又发现25尊彩绘陶瓷兵马俑
- 040 Thursday D 任务型阅读 时光里的巴黎圣母院
- 041 Friday E 短文填空 马赛："脾气"温和的法国城市
- 042 Saturday F 短文填空 重要考古遗址揭开西藏历史的神秘面纱

Week Eight 文化风俗 主题

- 043 Monday A 完形填空 中国小伙"指尖上的微陶艺"引国内外网友围观
- 044 Tuesday B 阅读理解 大寒
- 045 Wednesday C 阅读理解 虎年说"虎"
- 046 Thursday D 任务型阅读 探寻丽江纳西族文化魅力
- 047 Friday E 任务型阅读 腊八节的由来和习俗
- 048 Saturday F 短文填空 舞狮表演点亮疫情下的悉尼唐人街

Week Nine 科学技术 主题

- 049 Monday A 完形填空 奶牛试图隐藏的缺陷逃不过人工智能的"法眼"？
- 050 Tuesday B 阅读理解 最佳安卓新款应用程序，助力解决生活小问题
- 051 Wednesday C 阅读理解 日本科学家研发新型口罩，新冠病毒"露出马脚"
- 052 Thursday D 阅读理解 小行星撞击地球致死的概率有多大？
- 053 Friday E 短文填空 世界各地奋力阻止变化无常的全球气候破坏道路
- 054 Saturday F 短文填空 又是不想做饭的一天？机器人厨师来帮你忙

Week Ten　人物传奇　　主题

055	Monday	A 完形填空	徐诗晓：以勇气为浪，推动皮划艇前行
056	Tuesday	B 阅读理解	毕比安·蒙特尔-斯皮：残奥会的传奇人物
057	Wednesday	C 阅读理解	拉斐尔·纳达尔获21次大满贯冠军的背后
058	Thursday	D 阅读理解	天才发型师将头发编成盛放的花朵
059	Friday	E 阅读理解	拉塔·曼吉茜卡：宝莱坞的"夜莺"
060	Saturday	F 任务型阅读	谷爱凌：我承认，我爱上了恐惧

Week Eleven　旅行交通　　主题

061	Monday	A 完形填空	三个不可错过的人文、美食、自然旅行胜地
062	Tuesday	B 阅读理解	伺"季"而动，国内冰雪季的推荐去处
063	Wednesday	C 阅读理解	瑞典旅游胜地达拉纳偷走了我的心
064	Thursday	D 阅读理解	加拿大最难驾驶的道路
065	Friday	E 任务型阅读	西藏旅游业蓬勃发展，收入翻倍
066	Saturday	F 短文填空	加利福尼亚州值得一去的湖泊

Week Twelve　异国风情　　主题

067	Monday	A 完形填空	不可错过的传统西班牙美食
068	Tuesday	B 阅读理解	你对弗拉明戈舞了解多少？
069	Wednesday	C 阅读理解	参加2022年威尼斯狂欢节：你需要注意些什么？
070	Thursday	D 阅读理解	走近濒临消失的北印度游牧民族
071	Friday	E 任务型阅读	世界各地过新年的奇异传统
072	Saturday	F 短文填空	印度排灯节：光明的节日

人与自然

Week Thirteen — 自然生态 — 主题

073	Monday	A 完形填空	北冰洋饥肠辘辘的海绵以化石为食
074	Tuesday	B 阅读理解	生物多样性的丧失可能造成"生态崩溃"
075	Wednesday	C 阅读理解	新西兰南露脊鲸异常的迁徙模式
076	Thursday	D 任务型阅读	受人喜爱的海牛再次以惊人的数量死亡
077	Friday	E 任务型阅读	南太平洋一处不同寻常的珊瑚礁
078	Saturday	F 短文填空	非洲壮观的动物大迁徙

Week Fourteen — 环境保护 — 主题

079	Monday	A 完形填空	中国年轻人引领"绿色"行动
080	Tuesday	B 阅读理解	如何减少节日垃圾，让庆祝体面散场？
081	Wednesday	C 阅读理解	保护生物多样性，中国年轻一代在行动
082	Thursday	D 任务型阅读	中国谱写"绿化"奇迹，筑起生态屏障
083	Friday	E 短文填空	中国的植物"诺亚方舟"
084	Saturday	F 短文填空	美国少年让蝴蝶回归

答案解析 085

Week One 生活成长／兴趣爱好

Monday A 完形填空

| 体　裁 | 记叙文 | 题　材 | 兴趣爱好 | 正 确 率 | ＿＿＿／10 | 词　数 | 229 |
| 难　度 | ★★★☆☆ | 建议用时 | 10 分钟 | 实际用时 | | 答案页码 | 085 |

Dong Shuchang, a 23-year-old photographer (摄影师), became the winner of the Astronomy (天文学) Photographer of the Year in mid-September for his photograph "The Golden Ring". This masterpiece (杰作) was taken in Ali, southwest China's Tibet Autonomous Region last year. It __1__ the moon blocking out (挡住) most of the solar disc (太阳圆面) and leaving only a __2__ ring of sunlight shining through.

The __3__ received 4,500 works from 75 countries and areas. Dong started to __4__ the trip to take photos at the end of 2019. However, that didn't go as he expected. The COVID-19 pandemic (新冠肺炎疫情) made his plans stop in early 2020. All of a sudden, everything became uncertain. Thanks to the successful pandemic control in China, Dong moved with his plan in the middle of 2020.

He says that __5__ he uses a telephoto lens (长焦镜头) to take photos, he can see the details (细节) of the Milky Way (银河), as well as its red, green and blue colors that can be __6__ sharp relief (鲜明的轮廓) through photography. Dong's self-confidence (自信心) increased __7__ winning the best newcomer award (最佳新人奖) with his work "Sky and Ground, Stars and Sand". Dong says over three years of chasing (追逐) the stars has __8__ brought excitement and achievement to him, although the process was often mixed with sweat (汗水) and __9__ .

Speaking about his future plan, Dong says he will find new photography fields and __10__ ways to integrate (整合) science and art.

1. A. waits　　B. shows
   C. has　　　D. gets
2. A. thin　　　B. long
   C. fat　　　　D. tall
3. A. park　　　B. vacation
   C. school　　D. competition
4. A. get up　　B. prepare for
   C. fall down　D. pass by
5. A. until　　　B. although
   C. when　　　D. where
6. A. made into　B. made up
   C. made sure　D. made from
7. A. for　　　　B. from
   C. after　　　D. before
8. A. easily　　　B. finally
   C. normally　　D. quickly
9. A. feelings　　B. changes
   C. smiles　　　D. tears
10. A. better　　　B. kinder
    C. stricter　　　D. cheaper

词汇碎片

area n. 地区；地域　　uncertain adj. 不确定的　　process n. 过程；步骤　　mix with 和……混合

重难句讲解

Dong Shuchang, a 23-year-old photographer, became the winner of the Astronomy Photographer of the Year in mid-September for his photograph "The Golden Ring". 23 岁的摄影师董书畅因其拍摄的《金环》，于 9 月中旬荣膺年度天文摄影师总冠军。

本句是简单句。a 23-year-old photographer 是 Dong Shuchang 的同位语，对其身份信息进行补充说明；of the Astronomy Photographer of the Year 为后置定语，修饰 winner。

Tuesday B 阅读理解

When the 2022 Winter Olympics opened on Friday night in Beijing, Komani Mayentao, an international student at the Beijing International Studies University, walked proudly onto the glittering (闪闪发光的) stage of the National Stadium, also known as the Bird's Nest, together with other foreign students and professors (教授).

Interested in Chinese culture and kung fu since childhood, Mayentao took part in Chinese Bridge, a worldwide Chinese proficiency competition (世界性汉语水平竞赛) for foreign students, and won a scholarship (奖学金) to study in China when he was 18 years old.

Mayentao, who speaks Chinese well, was picked as a performer for the opening ceremony (仪式). "Although I did not get to serve as a volunteer, it's a great honor (荣誉) to be able to perform at the opening ceremony. I achieved my Winter Olympic dream in Beijing," he says.

Since being chosen last year as a performer at the opening ceremony of the Winter Olympics, Mayentao, the 24-year-old student from Mali, has visited the Bird's Nest for rehearsals (排练) no matter rain or shine. He made friends with performers from other countries when they rehearsed at the National Stadium.

Mayentao believes that people with different languages and cultural backgrounds working together shows exactly the cultural diversity (多样性) of Beijing, which will be a valued experience for his future life and job. After the Olympic fire was lit at the Bird's Nest, Mayentao said, "I'm so excited. We've been working very hard to perform at the amazing (令人惊叹的) opening ceremony."

1. What did Mayentao want to do at first for the 2022 Winter Olympics?
   A. To dance with other foreign students.
   B. To sing a Chinese song.
   C. To serve as a volunteer.
   D. To light the Olympic fire.

2. Which word can best describe Mayentao?
   A. Lazy.
   B. Smart.
   C. Hardworking.
   D. Strong.

3. What can we know according to the passage?
   A. Mayentao will work in China after graduation.
   B. Mayentao won a gold medal in the 2022 Winter Olympics.
   C. Mayentao was very excited about performing at the opening ceremony.
   D. Mayentao came to study in China for free when he was 24.

词汇碎片
achieve v. 实现   choose v. 选择

重难句讲解
Mayentao, who speaks Chinese well, was picked as a performer for the opening ceremony. 中文说得不错的张衣笙被选为开幕式的表演者。

本句是复合句。who引导非限制性定语从句，修饰先行词Mayentao；was picked为被动语态；opening ceremony 意为"开幕式"。

Wednesday C 阅读理解

Practicing a series (系列) of gentle tai chi (太极) moves, Khamisi Ally Abdi feels his body warm up in the cold morning. The 25-year-old student at Cangzhou Technical College, in northern China's Hebei Province, has practiced the slow-moving traditional Chinese martial art (武术) for two years and is now a huge fan.

The college offers the tai chi course to all its foreign students. Abdi has already developed the balance and deep rhythmic (有节奏的) breathing that tai chi requires. This allows him to fully experience the discipline (训练方法), which calms the mind while building and toning (使更健壮) muscles (肌肉). While learning tai chi, Abdi has met many kung fu fans from Africa and Asia. As a result of its rich history in martial arts, Cangzhou was named the "Hometown of Martial Arts" by sports authorities in 1992.

Through practicing tai chi, Abdi has got a comprehensive (全面的) knowledge of Chinese culture and now prefers that people call him by his Chinese name. "When I return home, I will use my Chinese name to teach tai chi in my country, so that more people can benefit from (受益于) this magical kung fu," he said.

1. Why does Abdi feel warm in the cold morning?
   A. Because he wears lots of clothes.
   B. Because he finishes a long run.
   C. Because he plays basketball.
   D. Because he practices tai chi.
2. What does a person need to do if he or she wants to do tai chi well?
   A. To have a strong body and a good mind in daily life.
   B. To do exercise in the morning and keep healthy.
   C. To develop the balance and deep rhythmic breathing.
   D. To prepare suitable clothes and comfortable shoes.
3. We can infer (推断) from the passage that _____.
   A. tai chi is very difficult to learn for foreigners
   B. more people in Abdi's hometown will learn of tai chi
   C. every school in China will teach tai chi in the future
   D. sports authorities will call on people to learn tai chi
4. What's the main idea of the passage?
   A. How to practice tai chi at school.
   B. Tai chi is welcomed by foreign students.
   C. A college in Hebei teaches tai chi.
   D. Practicing tai chi is good for health.

词汇碎片
province *n.* 省份　　course *n.* 课程　　develop *v.* 培养；发展　　magical *adj.* 神奇的；魔法的

重难句讲解
This allows him to fully experience the discipline, which calms the mind while building and toning muscles. 这让他能够充分体验到这一训练方法，在锻炼和强健肌肉的同时，还能让头脑平静下来。
本句是复合句。allow sb. to do sth. 意为"允许某人做某事"；which 引导非限制性定语从句。

Thursday D 阅读理解

Chinese students are showing their love and creative thinking about mobile apps (应用软件) by coming up with a group of creative apps to solve social issues (社会问题) and help improve the quality of life. Li Xiang, a student at Zhejiang University, developed a mobile app with two schoolmates that can help users develop good habits by building and feeding virtual electronic pets (虚拟电子宠物).

The special digital pet is created in the app Weier, which sounds similar to the English word "well". A user's daily behavior is used to help it grow. When users complete their daily exercise goals, their special electronic pets will also be full of energy, and when they go to bed too late at night, their pets will have black circles under their eyes. The digital pet is like a projection (形象化) of the user in the virtual world. But unlike other digital pets that focused on the similarity (相似性) with the user's appearance (外表), the app is more of a projection of the user's inner (内心的) character and behavior. The app is made to enable users to better know themselves and help them form good habits.

The app is one of over 1,400 projects developed by students from more than 500 universities that were submitted (提交) to the 2021 Mobile Application Innovation Contest, co-organized by Zhejiang University and tech company Apple of the United States. The contest ended in mid-December.

At the contest, students also designed apps to help solve social difficulties like protecting traditional culture and caring for family members.

1. To make their digital pets energetic, what should the users do?
   A. The users should feed their pets more food.
   B. The users should finish their daily exercise goals.
   C. The users should do exercise with their pets together.
   D. The users should make their pets have a good sleep.

2. Why do the digital pets have black circles under their eyes?
   A. Because they don't have a good sleep.
   B. Because their users are too lazy to feed them.
   C. Because their users don't have enough sleep.
   D. Because their users don't finish their daily work.

3. What are other digital pets like?
   A. They have a similar look with their users.
   B. They have a similar character with their users.
   C. They have similar hobbies with their users.
   D. They have similar behaviors with their users.

4. The app Weier is designed _____.
   A. to make a lot of money from users
   B. to help users form good habits
   C. to solve learning problems
   D. to care for family members

5. We can infer from the passage that _____.
   A. by feeding the digital pets, people will pay more attention to their health
   B. Li Xiang and his schoolmates won the first prize in the contest
   C. all racers (参赛者) came from universities in China
   D. many social difficulties have been solved through the contest

---

solve v. 解决　　create v. 创建；创造　　behavior n. 行为，举止　　care for 照顾，照料

The special digital pet is created in the app Weier, which sounds similar to the English word "well". 这一独特的数字宠物创建于应用程序"谓尔"（发音与英语单词"well"相似）中。

本句是复合句。which 引导非限制性定语从句，修饰先行词 Weier；(be) similar to 意为"与……相似"。

Friday E 任务型阅读

体裁	记叙文	题材	兴趣爱好	正确率	___/4	词数	240
难度	★★★☆☆	建议用时	5分钟	实际用时	___	答案页码	086

Caricature (漫画) artist Zhai Jin is finding creative ways to fully enjoy life and encourage his creativity. From the age of 18 to 32, caricaturist Zhai Jin hardly left his own home in Anhui Province. He was diagnosed (诊断) with osteogenesis imperfecta (成骨不全症), an illness that makes his bones (骨头) break easily.

Zhai's interest in painting started at an early age. At about 3 years old, he liked to scribble (乱画) on pieces of paper. It was an activity encouraged by his parents because it required him to stay still and avoid injury.

Influenced by animated TV series (动画电视连续剧) and graphic novels (漫画小说), he started copying characters, designing those of his own and imagining new stories for them in his mind. To improve his ability in character design, he practiced creating manga characters (漫画角色) that were based on real people, a style that he later learned was quite similar to Japanese caricature art.

Knowing that there was a need for such drawings, and confident in his own abilities, in 2019, he launched (推出) his own brand Gene's Caricature, offering personalized (个性化的) caricatures, both in person and online. He often sets up his stall (摊位) in a market, and sits in front of customers, asking and learning what they would like to be created. He says painting for a customer always gives him a sense of achievement.

He also opened an account (账户) on Bilibili, which now has around 7,000 fans. He posts video blogs of himself creating caricatures and about his everyday life.

1题找出并写下第二段的主题句；2题简略回答问题；3、4题完成句子。

1. _____

2. Why did Zhai Jin's parents encourage him to paint?
_____

3. Zhai Jin began copying characters and created his own characters influenced by _____.

4. _____ gives a sense of achievement to Zhai Jin.

词汇碎片

avoid v. 避免；防止   copy v. 模仿；复制   brand n. 品牌；类型   customer n. 顾客

重难句讲解

Knowing that there was a need for such drawings, and confident in his own abilities, in 2019, he launched his own brand Gene's Caricature, offering personalized caricatures, both in person and online. 他了解到对此类漫画的需求，并对自己的能力充满信心，于是2019年推出了自己的品牌"阿进似颜绘"，在现场或网上提供个性化的漫画创作。

本句是复合句。主句的主干是 he launched his own brand Gene's Caricature, 为主谓宾结构；Knowing that there was a need..., and confident in his own abilities 为现在分词短语作状语，其中 that 引导宾语从句作 Knowing 的宾语；offering personalized caricatures 为现在分词短语作伴随状语。

Saturday F 短文填空

| 体裁 | 记叙文 | 题材 | 生活成长 | 正确率 | ___/10 | 词数 | 258 |
| 难度 | ★★★☆☆ | 建议用时 | 10分钟 | 实际用时 | | 答案页码 | 087 |

Zhou Yibing, a college student from Tsinghua University in Beijing, encouraged people across the country after realizing her academic (学术的) dream in June 2021.

She realized her dream, although she was unable to take part in the 2020 *gaokao* due to having two spinal surgeries (脊柱手术). After (1) _____ (care) thought, Zhou chose to major in instrumentation and control systems technology (测控技术与仪器). She wanted to spend her life (2) _____ (serve) her country's development and innovation (创新).

In April 2020, Zhou suddenly felt (3) _____ (she) body go numb (麻木的), with no more than two months left before the *gaokao*. At first, she did not pay much attention. (4) _____ the pain in her lumbar spine (腰脊柱) quickly became noticeable. Zhou was diagnosed with a congenital isthmic fissure (先天性峡部裂). Doctors suggested that Zhou (5) _____ (leave) school for surgery.

In May 2020, Zhou had surgery, believing that (6) _____ operation would be enough to solve her spinal problems. However, post-surgery complications (术后并发症) caused her to experience all kinds of side effects (副作用). One month later, Zhou returned to the operating room. The (7) _____ (two) surgery was a success and she could get out of bed after two weeks. She immersed (沉浸于) herself in rehabilitation (康复) at (8) _____ and took every opportunity to catch up on her studies. Three months later, Zhou (9) _____ (return) to her senior classroom at the Affiliated High School of Shanghai Jiaotong University.

She built her confidence again and started making (10) _____ (prepare) for the 2021 *gaokao* with the support of her teachers and classmates. "As long as you haven't lost the courage to live, everything can start from zero," Zhou said.

阅读短文，在短文空缺处填入适当的单词，或用括号内所给单词的适当形式填空。每空限填一词。

(1) _____
(2) _____
(3) _____
(4) _____
(5) _____
(6) _____
(7) _____
(8) _____
(9) _____
(10) _____

词汇碎片
encourage v. 激励；鼓舞　　major in 主修；专攻　　operation n. 手术　　catch up on 赶上

重难句讲解
"As long as you haven't lost the courage to live, everything can start from zero," Zhou said. 周怡冰说："只要还没有失去生活的勇气，所有的事情都能从头再来。"

本句是复合句。双引号内的内容为直接引语，其中 everything can start from zero 是主句，为主谓结构；As long as you haven't lost the courage to live 为 As long as 引导的条件状语从句。

Week Two 校园生活

Monday A 完形填空

| 体裁 | 说明文 | 题材 | 校园生活 | 正确率 | ___/15 | 词数 | 241 |
| 难度 | ★★★☆☆ | 建议用时 | 15分钟 | 实际用时 | ___ | 答案页码 | 088 |

Have you ever heard of a language immersion (沉浸) program? These programs can __1__ in a school or other location (位置) where a learner can practice using their second language in a natural setting. Here are some ideas for helping you __2__ the four language skills in English.

Listening

• Listen to English-speaking artists __3__ your favorite style of music. Sing along if you like hearing yourself sing.

• Watch __4__ English movies and television programs online. Turn off the subtitles (字幕) to make it __5__.

Speaking

• Talk with __6__ in English. This may feel strange at first. __7__, the more you do it, the more you will begin to think in English, __8__ is a big step towards becoming fluent (流利的).

• Play online games in English. Having fun while you learn makes it much easier to remember what you are learning.

Reading

• __9__ your social (社交的) media language to English. Follow English speakers and make __10__ in English.

• Put small signs around your __11__ with the name of common things in English. After you __12__ the words, you can act __13__ a broadcaster (节目主持人) who is telling about your movements through your house.

Writing

• Write your to-do list or marketing (营销) list in English.

• __14__ a diary or daily journal in English. Writing about your own __15__ will help you learn words important to your life.

Let's look for ways to make your immersion program fun!

试题原创

1. A. take off B. take place
   C. take away D. take on
2. A. get B. introduce
   C. practice D. realize
3. A. performing B. talking
   C. reading D. discovering
4. A. traditional B. excellent
   C. extra D. particular
5. A. easier B. simpler
   C. harder D. better
6. A. you B. yourself
   C. myself D. themselves
7. A. Recently B. Therefore
   C. However D. And
8. A. which B. what
   C. that D. when
9. A. Choose B. Agree
   C. Move D. Change
10. A. statements B. themes
    C. comments D. guesses
11. A. house B. company
    C. charity D. hometown
12. A. beat B. learn
    C. use D. meet
13. A. into B. before
    C. like D. except
14. A. Write B. Have
    C. Make D. Give
15. A. knowledge B. entertainment
    C. experiences D. predictions

词汇碎片

setting n. 环境　　have fun 玩得高兴；过得快乐　　common adj. 常见的；共同的；普通的

重难句讲解

Having fun while you learn makes it much easier to remember what you are learning. 在学习的同时获得乐趣可以让你更轻松地记住所学的内容。

本句是复合句。Having fun while you learn 作主句的主语，其中包含 while 引导的时间状语从句；what 引导宾语从句，作 remember 的宾语。

Tuesday B 阅读理解

体 裁	应用文	题 材	校园生活	正确率	___/5	词 数	200
难 度	★★★☆☆	建议用时	6分钟	实际用时	___	答案页码	088

A video of children playing *baduanjin* (八段锦) is very popular online. It was created by a group of third-graders as a result of their project-based learning plan. The video was praised by students and parents who shared it on their social website accounts (账户). The following is some information about the project-based learning.

Aim	To let students take part in special courses to encourage them to explore (探索) the world by themselves on specific themes	
Topics	Spring	plants and flower exhibitions
	Summer	work in high-temperature environments
	Autumn	foodstuffs like dishes and desserts or health care (医疗保健)
	Winter	the Winter Olympics
The ways of participation (参与)	Students of different age groups receive different tasks. Pupils in grade one or two can paint or draw. Pupils in grade three to six may show their research in more complex (复杂的) ways.	
Time limit	One or two months to finish the tasks	
Requirements	Think deeply. Do research. Communicate with others. Present findings with cross-disciplinary (跨学科的) skills.	
Importance	Help students: adapt to (适应) the new high school entrance exam; get independent-study (独立学习) skills; deal with complex problems with what they have learned; arouse (引起) curiosity (好奇心) and motivation (动力) for learning; work in groups and learn from their classmates by communicating; find a balance between basic education and key abilities.	

1. What is parents' view on children playing *baduanjin*?
   A. Negative.
   B. Not clear.
   C. Positive.
   D. Neutral (不含褒贬义的).
2. Which topic will students choose in autumn if they want to take part in the project-based learning?
   A. Interviewing a policeman who directs traffic in the hot weather.
   B. Making delicious moon cakes together with family members.
   C. Knowing and learning some interesting winter sports.
   D. Enjoying beautiful red roses in a big garden.
3. How do a group of students in the second grade take part in the course?
   A. By drawing a fantastic picture.
   B. By writing an English story.
   C. By making an excellent video.
   D. By making a speech in class.
4. If your teacher gives you a project-based learning task on January 21st, when can you finish your work?
   A. On April 1st.
   B. On March 25th.
   C. On May 21st.
   D. On February 15th.
5. Students can't learn _____ through the project-based learning plan.
   A. writing skills
   B. to work in groups
   C. communication skills
   D. to deal with difficult problems

词汇碎片

special *adj.* 特殊的；独具特色的   basic *adj.* 基础的；初级的   ability *n.* 能力

重难句讲解

The video was praised by students and parents who shared it on their social website accounts. 这段视频受到了学生和家长的称赞，他们在自己的社交网站账户上进行了分享。

本句是复合句。主句为被动句，The video 在句中作主语，was praised 作谓语；其中 who shared it on their social website accounts 是 who 引导的定语从句，修饰先行词 students and parents。

Wednesday C 阅读理解

The 2021 Operas Entering Campuses (2021 "戏曲进校园"), an opera program organized by the Shenzhen Theater, has once again proved to be a success. Different types of traditional operas drew attention among students in colleges, primary and middle schools.

The organizers have invited famous opera actors and actresses to perform, educate and show classic opera scenes from Peking opera, Kun opera, Henan opera, Cantonese opera (粤剧) and Huangmei opera to create an environment for students to learn age-old performing arts. According to the organizers, the program includes lectures (讲座) on opera history, costume exhibition, opera makeup experience, opera performance, and opera theater classes, through which students could get a deep understanding of operas and so develop a strong interest in traditional cultures of our nation.

At Shenzhen No.3 Vocational School of Technology (深圳市第三职业技术学校), Jiang Wenrui, a national class-A actress, gave a lecture on Cantonese opera. Nearly 2,600 students listened to the lecture. Besides, the modern Peking opera "A New Era" was popular at the Southern University of Science and Technology (南方科技大学) and Shenzhen Middle School. A student in Shenzhen Middle School said, "It was quite a surprise for us. I'm so happy to see opera actors come to our school and share with us the stories and cultures behind the opera. I think it's very wonderful."

Shenzhen is actively finding new ways to use new media technologies to promote (促进) traditional Chinese culture. For example, Shenzhen Theater livestreamed (直播) all the performances in schools, and had 420,000 views, according to a report.

1. How many types of traditional operas were showed in the program organized by the Shenzhen Theater?
   A. Three.   B. Five.
   C. Six.   D. Seven.

2. Why was the opera program The 2021 Operas Entering Campuses organized?
   A. To invite students to perform classic operas in the program.
   B. To introduce basic knowledge of classic operas to the public.
   C. To draw students' interest in our country's traditional cultures.
   D. To make students understand opera history.

3. Which way wasn't used in the opera program according to the passage?
   A. Shows presented by famous opera actors and actresses.
   B. Lectures made by artists on opera history.
   C. All the performances livestreamed in schools.
   D. Discussion with students who know well classic operas.

4. The underlined word "It" in the third paragraph probably refers to (指的是) _____.
   A. the lecture on Cantonese opera
   B. the opera history
   C. the modern Peking opera "A New Era"
   D. the national class-A actress

词汇碎片

according to 根据；按照   costume n. 特定场合穿的成套服装或戏装   actively adv. 积极地；活跃地

重难句讲解

According to the organizers, the program includes lectures on opera history, costume exhibition, opera makeup experience, opera performance, and opera theater classes, through which students could get a deep understanding of operas and so develop a strong interest in traditional cultures of our nation. 据承办单位介绍，该活动包括戏曲历史讲座、服饰展览、戏曲化妆体验、戏曲表演和戏曲剧场课堂，通过这些，学生们可以深入地了解戏曲，从而培养对我国传统文化的浓厚兴趣。

本句是复合句。on opera history 为介词短语作后置定语修饰 lectures；through which... our nation 为"介词＋关系代词"引导的一个定语从句，which 指代 lectures on opera history, costume exhibition... opera theater classes；develop a strong interest in 为固定搭配，意为"培养对……的浓厚兴趣"。

Thursday D 任务型阅读

阅读短文，从下列选项中选出能填入文中空白处的最佳选项。

How to keep students learning during school closures (封锁) has been one of the most difficult questions of the pandemic (流行病).

But inequality (不平等) among families, schools, and countries means that some students were better prepared to succeed during the pandemic than others. When schools closed, countries' teaching and learning methods were greatly different around the world. __1__, but others were simply not able to make that change.

__2__. But in the African countries of Burkina Faso (布基纳法索) and Kenya (肯尼亚), fewer than 10 percent of students had laptops (笔记本电脑). Countries that did not have digital resources (资源) had other ways to reach students outside the classroom. __3__. But when schools closed, many students didn't have any schooling at all. Most students in Burkina Faso and about one-fifth of students in Kenya did not do any schoolwork for at least four months.

__4__. In India, for example, 85 percent of teachers said they needed additional mental (精神上的) health support. __5__. And many teachers in some countries were afraid of being infected (感染的) with COVID-19 while working. Many school leaders reported an increase in the use of mental health resources during the pandemic.

A. Teachers also felt the emotional influences of the pandemic
B. Some countries were able to quickly move to online learning
C. In Russia, 64 percent of teachers reported feeling tired most of the time
D. Educational television and radio broadcasts increased in some places, including Kenya and Russia
E. In European countries like Denmark, more than 95 percent of students had laptop computers for schoolwork

词汇碎片

succeed v. 成功；达到   digital adj. 数字的；数码的   be afraid of 害怕

重难句讲解

Countries that did not have digital resources had other ways to reach students outside the classroom. 没有数字资源的国家有其他方式让学生在课堂之外进行学习。

本句是复合句。that did not have digital resources 是 that 引导的定语从句，修饰先行词 Countries；to reach students outside the classroom 为动词不定式短语作后置定语修饰 ways。

Friday　E 短文填空

| 体　裁 | 记叙文 | 题　材 | 校园生活 | 正确率 | ___/10 | 词　数 | 204 |
| 难　度 | ★★★☆☆ | 建议用时 | 10 分钟 | 实际用时 | | 答案页码 | 090 |

阅读短文，从方框中选择合适的单词并用其正确形式填空，使短文通顺，意思完整。

plant　down　skill　get　see　song　and　what　at　them

In Sai Kung (西贡), a neighborhood in Hong Kong, a group of school children are running up and (1) _____ a tree-covered slope (斜坡), singing a (2) _____ in English: "I love the mountains, I love the sun so bright."

Here, under the maple trees (枫树), the children and their teachers are experimenting with a new learning style that is becoming more (3) _____ more popular—forest school. It is a way of connecting (联系) children with nature and educating a child-led way of learning. "This can help my son (4) _____ more outdoor knowledge, and stay curious (好奇的). It's good for developing their different abilities," says a mother, looking (5) _____ her four-year-old son mixing mud (泥) with water under the trees. Forest school makes children confident and develops their problem-solving (6) _____. For example, one time they wanted to do something after (7) _____ so much litter on the beach.

Looking at children filling their buckets (水桶) with seawater or sand on the beach in Sai Kung, the teacher blew her whistle (口哨) to gather (聚集，集合) (8) _____ for the next activity. Asked what the next part should be about, the children said they wanted (9) _____ flowers. That settled (确定) it because the children decide (10) _____ they wish to learn each time.

---

cover v. 覆盖；遮掩　　　experiment v. 尝试；实验　　　fill v. 装满；填满

重难句讲解

It is a way of connecting children with nature and educating a child-led way of learning. 这是一种将孩子与自然联系起来、培养孩子主导学习的方式。

本句是简单句。句子的主干是 It is a way，为主系表结构；of connecting children with nature and educating a child-led way of learning 作后置定语修饰 a way；connect... with... 为固定搭配，意为"将……与……联系（或连接）起来"。

Saturday F 短文填空

| 体裁 | 记叙文 | 题材 | 校园生活 | 正确率 | ___/5 | 词数 | 218 |
| 难度 | ★★★☆☆ | 建议用时 | 6分钟 | 实际用时 | ___ | 答案页码 | 090 |

Caopu Primary School (草埔小学) recently was named one of the 10 model (示范) schools in art education in Shenzhen, thanks (1) _____ its successful teaching of recorder (竖笛) playing.

Music brings out energy, says Xu Chunsheng, headmaster of the school. He also believes that art education can warm children's hearts, as these children sometimes are neglected (忽视) by their parents (2) _____ are too busy trying to make a living. The school has chosen to teach the recorder, since this instrument is easy to learn and affordable. All students at the school can play the recorder, with first- and second-graders taking part (3) _____ the instrument training each week and three- to six-graders playing the recorder for 15 minutes of each music class.

More importantly, music has enriched (丰富) the lives of students and planted confidence in them. A student, a shy boy, had been a loner (独来独往的人) and somehow unhappy. He has become more confident since joining the recorder playing club and winning a prize (4) _____ his classmates.

The effort is also recognized (认可) by parents. "My son plays the recorder after finishing his homework every day," a mother said. "It is like we have our own family concert now. His practice has also set (5) _____ good example for his baby sister, who became interested in music too."

阅读短文,根据语篇要求填空,使短文通顺,意思完整。每空限填一词。

(1) _____

(2) _____

(3) _____

(4) _____

(5) _____

词汇碎片

make a living 谋生   instrument n. 乐器；器具   confidence n. 自信，信心

重难句讲解

The school has chosen to teach the recorder, since this instrument is easy to learn and affordable. 学校之所以选择教竖笛，是因为竖笛比较容易学，而且价格便宜。

本句是复合句。主句是 The school has chosen to teach the recorder；since 引导原因状语从句；easy to learn 和 affordable 并列，作 is 的表语。

Week Three 家庭教育

Monday A 完形填空

体裁	记叙文	题材	家庭教育	正确率	___/10	词数	235
难度	★★★★☆	建议用时	12分钟	实际用时		答案页码	091

I never thought that at four years old, our daughter would still bother us when we are sleeping, which feels especially unfair __1__ her younger brother sleeps well. I once tried to tell her not to wake us up, explaining that it would make us tired the next day. She thought about this for a moment and then replied: "But that's OK if you are tired because you can drink coffee tomorrow."

See? She has changed my __2__, including my increasing coffee consumption (消耗量). In fact, she may be __3__ me on a much deeper level, far beyond my sleep.

Children begin influencing us even before they are born: we plan __4__ their arrival and change our lives to welcome them. As babies, they direct our sleep and our moods (情绪). Staying calm is not always easy, however. Getting two unhappy children __5__ and ready to leave the house, as one cries about the wrong socks or shoes, can make parents __6__, especially when trying to get to work __7__. In such stressful (压力大的) __8__, it can help to realize that children have their own sense of agency (能动性). They want to act __9__ and make their own choices.

Finally, we are all learning from each other. Accepting this, and responding (回应) to children's needs, makes life go well—even if it __10__ having that extra cup of coffee after another night of broken sleep.

1. A. though   B. if
   C. because   D. unless
2. A. habits   B. solutions
   C. problems D. strategies
3. A. stopping   B. influencing
   C. depending D. pushing
4. A. from   B. for
   C. in   D. of
5. A. dressed   B. caught
   C. destroyed D. cleaned
6. A. lucky   B. annoyed
   C. pleased   D. creative
7. A. in particular B. at first
   C. on time   D. in general
8. A. situations B. projects
   C. decisions D. mistakes
9. A. sincerely   B. casually
   C. politely   D. freely
10. A. saves   B. suggests
    C. starts   D. means

词汇碎片

wake sb. up 唤醒某人   explain v. 解释；说明   in fact 事实上   extra adj. 额外的；附加的

重难句讲解

I once tried to tell her not to wake us up, explaining that it would make us tired the next day. 我曾经试着告诉她不要叫醒我们，解释说这会让我们第二天感到疲倦。

本句是复合句。explaining that it would make us tired the next day 为现在分词短语作伴随状语；that 引导宾语从句作 explaining 的逻辑宾语；make sb.+adj. 意为"使某人……"。

Tuesday B 阅读理解

Dear friends,

The 2022 Winter Games ended in a memorable (难忘的) way after International Olympic Committee President Thomas Bach declared (宣告) its closing. Today I want to talk about the important role of volunteers in the Olympics.

Tao Zhenguo was a good example. As Tao Zhenguo prepared to work as a volunteer for the Beijing Olympics in 2008, he became a grandfather. His daughter gave birth to a boy baby, Guo Xiaoyu, just days ahead of the opening ceremony (开幕式) in August. Tao was so happy about his grandson's arrival, but he didn't have much time to spend with Guo that month. He was very busy with his volunteer work. Tao didn't speak English, but he was clear that "as an Olympics volunteer, I have to learn it to at least be able to communicate with foreign guests". Tao said, "I hope that I can say 'Welcome to Beijing' when I meet with foreign athletes and guests."

Later, Guo Xiaoyu has also become an Olympics volunteer. He was helping with garbage sorting (分类), traffic guidance and information inquiries (查询) in a community that was home to the Olympic Village. Guo said he learned a lot from his grandfather. He listened to Tao's volunteer experience and began doing community work.

Both grandfather and grandson were volunteering at the Beijing 2022 Winter Olympics. They were so helpful and lovely. I'm very proud of my country and so many excellent volunteers. Thank you!

1. Why didn't Tao Zhenguo have enough time to stay with his grandson in 2008?
   A. Because he was busy with his company's work.
   B. Because he lived far away from his daughter's house.
   C. Because he didn't want to take care of his grandson.
   D. Because he worked on his volunteer work during the Olympics.

2. How old is Guo Xiaoyu in 2022?
   A. Twelve years old.   B. Thirteen years old.
   C. Fourteen years old. D. Twenty years old.

3. Why did Tao Zhenguo want to learn English during the Olympics?
   A. To improve his English level and get a high mark.
   B. To become an English-language master.
   C. To communicate with foreign athletes and guests well.
   D. To show his hard work to others.

4. What did Guo Xiaoyu do at the 2022 Winter Olympics?
   A. He shared his experiences with foreigners.
   B. He learned English together with his grandfather.
   C. He helped to sort litter and direct traffic.
   D. He taught other visitors English.

5. How many times has Tao Zhenguo volunteered for the Olympics?
   A. Once.   B. Twice.
   C. Three times. D. Four times.

词汇碎片

volunteer n. 志愿者 v. 自愿；无偿做   garbage n. 垃圾；废料   guidance n. 引导，指导

重难句讲解

He was helping with garbage sorting, traffic guidance and information inquiries in a community that was home to the Olympic Village. 他在奥运村所在的社区帮忙进行垃圾分类、交通引导和信息查询。

本句是复合句。that was home to the Olympic Village 是 that 引导的定语从句，修饰先行词 a community；be home to 为固定短语，意为"……的所在地"。

Wednesday C 阅读理解

Estrella Salazar, a 17-year-old science talent from a town near Mexico City, was inspired (启发) by her sister to develop an application (应用程序) to help deaf and hard-of-hearing Mexicans communicate more easily.

Salazar's older sister, Perla, was born with a serious illness that influences mobility (移动的能力) and hearing, called MERRF syndrome (综合征). The 25-year-old has had a lot of surgeries (手术) followed by years of therapy (治疗). And she was told by one sign language school that she would be unable to learn to sign because of her condition. Salazar's study abilities allowed her to graduate three years early from high school. After seeing the discrimination (歧视) Perla faced, she asked herself: "What am I doing to help my sister?"

Later, she started developing an application to connect Mexican Sign Language (MSL) speakers with hearing users—allowing people to change from sign language to text or voice, and vice versa (反之亦然). Salazar built an organization of nearly 90 participants (参与者)—including native speakers and interpreters (口译员)—to develop the app, called Hands with Voice, which she hopes to put into the market this year. In recent months, the family has started to learn signs as Perla's mobility has improved. "I take pride in my sister," said Perla. "And I've liked finding a community along the way."

Now, Salazar is looking for a US university that will allow her to continue her study.

1. Salazar developed the application inspired by _____.
   A. her friend's illness
   B. her sister's illness
   C. sign language lessons
   D. her study of sign language

2. Why couldn't Perla go to a sign language school to learn to sign?
   A. Because she was unable to leave home alone.
   B. Because she was born with a serious illness.
   C. Because she couldn't understand what the teacher said.
   D. Because she didn't have study abilities at all.

3. What does the underlined word "discrimination" in the second paragraph refer to?
   A. Salazar was refused by a university.
   B. Perla was laughed at in public.
   C. Salazar was laughed at for her hearing problem.
   D. Perla was refused by a sign language school.

4. How did Perla feel after Salazar developed the useful application?
   A. Worried.   B. Relaxed.
   C. Proud.   D. Upset.

5. What can we know from the passage?
   A. Salazar developed an application that allowed the change from sign language to pictures.
   B. Salazar could go to a US university to continue her study thanks to her invention.
   C. Perla could move freely at her home with the help of the application.
   D. Salazar was very talented and cared for her family.

Thursday D任务型阅读

Roseanne, a 46-year-old mom who lives in New Jersey, US, has a 16-year-old son and a 14-year-old daughter who haven't gotten along since they were young. "There was a lot of conflict (冲突) between them. __1__. They're each always worried about the other person, making comments, making the other angry," Roseanne says.

As almost anyone who has a sibling (兄弟姐妹) knows, a rivalry (竞争) is common. In many families, bickering (争吵) among siblings is helpful. __2__. As human beings, we love to compare. For example, it's easy for siblings to compare their academic (学业的) or athletic (体育的) success, or argue over who is the "favourite" child, since siblings often have similar experiences. __3__.

Another major driver of sibling rivalry is fairness (公平). Parents are more likely to give privileges (特权) to younger children sooner than they did the older kids. When younger children get permission earlier than an older sibling did, that can cause the older one to feel things are unfair. __4__.

Experts suggest parents encourage siblings to develop close relationships into adulthood. "__5__," says Roseanne. "But now, we're together at family parties, we chat about my mom—even though it took until much later in life."

阅读短文，从下列选项中选出能填入文中空白处的最佳选项，使短文通顺，意思完整。选项中有两项为多余选项。

A. And the closer in age kids are, the more intense (激烈的) the rivalry can be
B. That creates conflict
C. It helps children learn to deal with conflict and makes them better at communicating with others
D. Sibling rivalry may not seem surprising in childhood years
E. There was a lot of tension (矛盾) between me and my brothers in our house growing up
F. They can't sit at the dinner table for 10 minutes without fighting
G. Many people know that siblings fight with each other

Friday E 短文填空

体 裁	议论文	题 材	家庭教育	正确率	___/10	词 数	218
难 度	★★★☆☆	建议用时	10分钟	实际用时	___	答案页码	092

阅读短文，用方框中所给单词或短语的适当形式填空。

| positive | worry about | holiday | all the time | agree | be supposed to | child | problem | play | too much |

Tencent (腾讯) allowed only 14 hours in total for children to play its video games over the 14 days of the 2022 Spring Festival (1) _____. Can any child resist (抵制) the seduction (诱惑) of playing video games? Not one that I know of. In fact, they (2) _____ play outside with their friends and classmates. But what I see is that with a mobile phone or a tablet (平板电脑) at hand, young people can lose themselves in the gaming world (3) _____, without noticing the call of anyone.

Why are parents (4) _____ the situation? In my view, I see there is (5) _____ violence (暴力) in some popular games. They are bad, no matter for children or adults. Such things are not in games only—but in books and films. But the idea of limiting (限制) video game time in the hope of saving (6) _____ from harm is not so smart. What if children make full use of this one hour and enjoy (7) _____ such games? One hour each day is enough to cause (8) _____.

What should be done is to offer (9) _____ things, and allow children to play as they wish, while making sure they keep healthy. For my 13-year-old son, we have (10) _____ on a 20-minute break after playing games, with time set aside for study, exercise and sleep.

词汇碎片

lose oneself in sth. 使某人沉迷于……　　notice v. 注意；察觉　　what if 如果……将会……
make full use of 充分利用

重难句讲解

Such things are not in games only—but in books and films. 此类内容不仅存在于游戏中，还存在于书籍和电影中。
本句是简单句。not... but... 结构作表语，表示"不仅……而且……；不是……而是……"，连接的前后内容在意义上表示转折，在结构上表示并列。

Saturday F 短文填空

| 体　裁 | 记叙文 | 题　材 | 家庭教育 | 正确率 | ___/10 | 词　数 | 228 |
| 难　度 | ★★★★☆ | 建议用时 | 11 分钟 | 实际用时 | ___ | 答案页码 | 093 |

As the number of English learners in American schools continues to rise, it is not just students that are going to (1) n_____ more help. Parents and families that do not (2) s_____ English also need support. Parents need to feel like they can be actively involved in (参与) their children's schooling, regardless of (不管) any language difficulties.

It is important (3) f_____ parents and families to be able to communicate in their own language. Janet Huger-Johnson is the principal (校长) of the East New York Elementary School of Excellence. She said her school, for (4) e_____, uses a phone app that allows teachers to send (5) m_____ in English that will be translated into the parent's language. And when the parent replies, the message is (6) t_____ back into English. Sometimes the school will need to hire (雇用) people in the community to help with translation.

A recent study (7) f_____ that schools in the city of Philadelphia often provide little support to immigrant (移民的) parents. Some parents said the school offered poor translation services. Mandy is a parent in Philadelphia who speaks Mandarin (普通话). Her child has special needs. During a school meeting, a telephone translator (译员) said she did not know anything (8) a_____ special education and refused to translate. Recently, she had to bring a friend to the school to translate during a school (9) m_____.

Creating a space for (10) p_____ and families to be involved without language difficulties is important.

阅读短文，根据首字母提示用单词的适当形式填空。

(1) _____
(2) _____
(3) _____
(4) _____
(5) _____
(6) _____
(7) _____
(8) _____
(9) _____
(10) _____

词汇碎片

support n. 支持；维持　　translate v. 翻译；（使）转变　　provide v. 提供；供应

重难句讲解

Parents need to feel like they can be actively involved in their children's schooling, regardless of any language difficulties. 家长想要他们可以积极参与孩子的学校教育，即使有语言困难。

本句是复合句。they can be actively involved in their children's schooling 为省略引导词 that 的宾语从句，作 feel like 的宾语，feel like 意为"想要"；be involved in 为固定搭配，意为"参与；涉及"；regardless of 为固定搭配，意为"不管；不顾"。

Week Four 健康饮食

Monday A 完形填空

体 裁	说明文	题 材	健康饮食	正确率	___/15	词 数	222
难 度	★★★★☆	建议用时	16 分钟	实际用时		答案页码	094

Huai'an is in East China's Jiangsu Province. As the __1__ of the late Premier Zhou Enlai, it has been __2__ as one of the new cities to be added to the UNESCO (联合国教育、科学及文化组织) Creative Cities Network, thanks __3__ its rich history of food.

Sitting on the North-South divide of the country, the geographical location (地理位置) has __4__ the city both northern and southern Chinese cuisine (菜肴).

The city lies alongside the Beijing-Hangzhou Grand Canal (京杭大运河), making it an important water __5__ port (港口). It is also one of the __6__ birthplaces of Huaiyang cuisine—a term for dishes from Huai'an and Yangzhou. Huai'an food has been __7__ by the 2,500-year history of the canal. As early as the Spring and Autumn Period (春秋时期), the canal was __8__ around Huai'an. In the Qing Dynasty, with the development of water transportation, Huai'an cuisine spread to northern parts of China __9__ Beijing. The city's cuisine also started to __10__ cooking ways from across the __11__.

Fish is another star ingredient of Huai'an cuisine, __12__ often has a sweet flavor (味道) and keeps the __13__ taste of the ingredient. Local __14__ often feature in national banquets (国宴). Based on a book recording the __15__ of Beijing Hotel where the first national banquet was held after the establishment (建立) of the People's Republic of China in 1949, the "grand national banquet was completely based on Huaiyang cuisine."

1. A. market B. airport C. station D. hometown
2. A. chosen B. decided C. followed D. praised
3. A. at B. in C. to D. on
4. A. celebrated B. given C. put D. took
5. A. transportation B. achievement C. exchange D. management
6. A. similar B. single C. main D. possible
7. A. organized B. stored C. imagined D. influenced
8. A. built B. carried C. set D. collected
9. A. before B. between C. including D. from
10. A. turn on B. take in C. take away D. turn off
11. A. city B. world C. village D. country
12. A. which B. what C. where D. that
13. A. opposite B. careful C. original D. upset
14. A. relishes B. sauces C. recipes D. dishes
15. A. temperature B. history C. cruise D. advantage

词汇碎片

ingredient n.（烹调用的）材料；原料，成分　　feature v. 占重要地位，起重要作用

重难句讲解

Based on a book recording the history of Beijing Hotel where the first national banquet was held after the establishment of the People's Republic of China in 1949, the "grand national banquet was completely based on Huaiyang cuisine." 根据1949年中华人民共和国成立后首次举行国宴的北京饭店的历史记载，"盛大的国宴完全以淮扬菜为基础"。

本句是复合句。主句是 the "grand national banquet was completely based on Huaiyang cuisine"，其中的固定搭配 be based on 意为"以……为基础"；Based on a book... in 1949 作状语，其中 where 引导定语从句，修饰先行词 Beijing Hotel。

Tuesday B 阅读理解

One of the most important things to keep healthy is to eat a balanced and nutritious (营养丰富的) diet. What is "healthy eating"? How can you start eating healthily and make it stick for a long time? Here are the best strategies for doing that.

Start slow

If you don't know everything about healthy eating, one way is to try a new vegetable each week. Pick a vegetable you've never tried before and research a new recipe to make it a meal. That's a way to eat healthily in a manner that won't overwhelm (压垮) you.

Log (记录) your intake (摄入)

If you don't plan your meals before eating them, you might find that you're eating less healthfully than you plan to. Write down your reasons for wanting to eat healthily (lose weight, increase energy, etc.), and read your list every day. You might be surprised when you really record what you're eating.

Eat fewer ultra-processed (超加工的) foods

Pre-made foods can be super convenient, especially when you're busy with working. Some foods like store-bought cookies, frozen (冷冻的) corn dogs, and similar convenience foods are often high in added sugar and calories (卡路里). So instead, make your whole foods and meals by yourself.

Balance your plate

Think according to what's on your plate. Fruits and vegetables should be the foundation (基础) of your meal. You should have fruit at each mealtime and lean protein (蛋白质), like eggs, chicken breast or fish.

1. How many positive ways are there to help you eat healthily according to the passage?
   A. Two. B. Three.
   C. Four. D. Five.

2. Which strategy especially suits you if you are not good at planning your foods before eating?
   A. Start slow.
   B. Log your intake.
   C. Eat fewer ultra-processed foods.
   D. Balance your plate.

3. What can you do if some convenience foods are high in added sugar and calories according to the passage?
   A. Buy other healthy foods.
   B. Make foods by yourself.
   C. Eat them after doing exercises.
   D. Eat more fruits.

4. Which of the following is NOT advised according to the passage?
   A. Make your meal balanced.
   B. Drink much water if possible.
   C. Eat fewer convenience foods.
   D. Try a new vegetable each week.

5. From which is the passage most probably taken?
   A. A travel guidebook.
   B. A science report.
   C. A health magazine.
   D. A medicine instruction.

---

strategy *n.* 策略   research *v.* 研究；调查   convenient *adj.* 方便的，便利的

That's a way to eat healthily in a manner that won't overwhelm you. 这是一种健康饮食的方式，而且不会让你不堪重负。
本句是复合句。to eat healthily 是动词不定式作后置定语，修饰 a way；that won't overwhelm you 是 that 引导的定语从句，修饰先行词 a manner；manner 意为"方式"，overwhelm 意为"压垮；打败"。

Wednesday C 阅读理解

For years, nutritionists (营养学家) have suggested using olive oil (橄榄油) in your diet instead of butter and other dairy fats (乳脂). The new research finds that people who take in 10 grams a day of olive oil have an up to 34% lower risk of dying. People who consume (消耗) more olive oil in their meals have lower risks of getting serious health conditions, including Alzheimer's disease (阿尔茨海默病), cardiovascular disease (心血管疾病), and cancer.

Could it be that people in the study who consumed more olive oil were just healthier? Researchers pointed out that people who had more olive oil on a regular basis were usually more physically (身体上) active, less likely (有可能的) to smoke, and more likely to eat more fruits and vegetables compared with people who ate less olive oil. All of those reasons can lower your disease risk.

"Doctors should be advising patients not to use certain fats, such as margarine (人造黄油) and butter, and they can have olive oil to improve their health," an expert (专家) Guasch-Ferré said. About this, Dr. Tadwalkar agrees, "When fats are needed, plant oils from seeds, nuts, fruits, are the way to go," he says. "Olive oil, especially extra virgin (初榨的) olive oil, has been shown to be important when people are looking to improve their health."

Should you consider replacing certain fats in your diet with olive oil? Even if olive oil is good for lowering certain health risks, a lot of questions remain. It's unclear, for example, how much people should consume for a protective effect.

1. What does the new research find according to Paragraph 1?
   A. Some diseases are caused by butter and other dairy fats.
   B. All of us should consume more olive oil every day for health.
   C. People using butter and other dairy fats have an up to 34% lower risk of dying.
   D. People having more olive oil have lower risks of getting serious health conditions.

2. Which way is NOT mentioned to lower your disease risk?
   A. Taking in olive oil.
   B. Keeping your body active.
   C. Eating more fruits and vegetables.
   D. Going out for dinner.

3. According to Dr. Tadwalkar, we can get plant oils from the followings except _____.
   A. seeds   B. butter   C. nuts   D. fruits

4. What is talked about in Paragraph 3?
   A. The reason why doctors should advise patients not to use certain fats.
   B. Ways to get enough fats when needed.
   C. Opinions from different experts on taking in olive oil.
   D. The importance of improving your health.

5. Which of the following will Dr. Tadwalkar most agree with according to the passage?
   A. It's good to consume olive oil rather than butter.
   B. It's unclear how much olive oil people should consume to keep healthy.
   C. Extra virgin olive oil has been proven not healthy for your body.
   D. Patients shouldn't consume more olive oil and fats.

词汇碎片

cancer n. 癌症   regular adj. 频繁的；定期的   improve v. 改善，改进   even if 即使

重难句讲解

Researchers pointed out that people who had more olive oil on a regular basis were usually more physically active, less likely to smoke, and more likely to eat more fruits and vegetables compared with people who ate less olive oil. 研究人员指出，与那些食用橄榄油较少的人相比，那些经常食用较多橄榄油的人通常身体更有活力，不太可能吸烟，而且更可能吃较多的水果和蔬菜。

本句是复合句。that 引导宾语从句作 pointed out 的宾语；在宾语从句中，who had more olive oil on a regular basis 是一个定语从句，修饰第一个 people；and 连接三个并列的形容词短语作表语，be likely to do sth. 为固定句型，意为"有可能做某事"；who ate less olive oil 是一个定语从句，修饰第二个 people；on a regular basis 为固定短语，意为"经常地；定期地"。

Thursday D 阅读理解

New research has found that diets with fat from vegetables instead of from meat are connected with a lower risk of stroke (中风), according to reports.

In the study, people who ate the most vegetables and polyunsaturated fats (多不饱和脂肪) were 12 percent less likely to have ischemic strokes (缺血性中风) compared with those who ate the least. People who ate the most animal fats—excluding dairy fat—were 16 percent more likely to have strokes than those who ate the least. Dairy fat was not connected with increased risk of stroke. About 87 percent of all strokes are ischemic strokes when blood flow becomes blocked (堵住的).

Symptoms (症状) of a stroke include sudden confusion, serious headache, trouble walking, trouble seeing and weakness or numbness (麻木) in the face, arm or leg. Chances of survival (存活) are greater when emergency (紧急状况) treatment is gotten quickly.

Transient ischemic attacks (TIA) and hemorrhagic strokes are other types of strokes. "A TIA is a sign of a serious condition that will not go away without medical help," a medical professor notes. Hemorrhagic strokes happen when an artery (动脉) in the brain leaks (渗漏) blood, which could hurt brain cells. While stroke risk increases with age, strokes can happen at any age. High blood pressure, smoking, diabetes (糖尿病) and high cholesterol (胆固醇) are the leading causes of stroke.

1. According to reports, diets with fat from _____ are closely connected with a lower risk of stroke.
   A. rice   B. meat
   C. cream   D. vegetables
2. Which of the following is TRUE according to the passage?
   A. Dairy fat is connected with increased risk of stroke.
   B. Transient ischemic attacks are signs of serious diseases.
   C. It is more likely to have ischemic strokes for eating polyunsaturated fats.
   D. Hemorrhagic strokes don't hurt brain cells.
3. What is talked about in Paragraph 3?
   A. Major causes of stroke.
   B. The diets of cutting down chances of getting a stroke.
   C. Some symptoms of getting a stroke.
   D. Different types of strokes.
4. Which one is NOT the leading causes of stroke?
   A. High blood pressure.
   B. Lack of exercises.
   C. Smoking.
   D. High cholesterol.
5. What's the writer's purpose of writing the passage?
   A. To show us two different types of strokes.
   B. To tell us symptoms of getting a stroke.
   C. To share some information about stroke.
   D. To tell us a new research about fats.

词汇碎片
instead of 而不是；代替   type n. 类型，种类   medical adj. 医学的，医疗的   cause n. 原因，理由

重难句讲解
About 87 percent of all strokes are ischemic strokes when blood flow becomes blocked. 大约87%的中风是血流受阻引发的缺血性中风。

本句是复合句。主句为主系表结构，其中 About 87 percent of all strokes 在句中作主语，are 为系动词，ischemic strokes 作表语；when 引导状语从句。

Friday E 任务型阅读

体裁	说明文	题材	健康饮食	正确率	___/5	词数	213
难度	★★★★☆	建议用时	7分钟	实际用时		答案页码	096

For the fifth year in a row, the Mediterranean diet (地中海饮食) was first across the finish line in the annual (年度的) race for the best diet, according to a report by *U.S. News & World Report*. __1__ And the third is the flexitarian diet (弹性素食饮食), which encourages being a vegetarian (素食主义者) most of the time, but allows a burger at times. __2__

Generally speaking, the top diets are decided by what you can eat, not what you can't eat. And right now—during these hard times of the pandemic (流行病)—that's especially helpful for people. We want food we can enjoy. __3__ The top diets offer this. The Mediterranean diet is simple, plant-based cooking, in every meal with fruits and vegetables, whole grains, a few nuts, and olive oil. __4__

__5__ The diet can help reduce (降低) the risk for illnesses like memory loss, depression (抑郁症) and cancer. The diet has also been connected with stronger bones, a healthier heart and longer life.

阅读短文，从下列选项中选出能填入文中空白处的最佳选项，选项中有两项为多余选项。

A. And we want food that will keep us healthy.
B. All the diets that perform well are safe and supported by science.
C. Lots of studies have found the Mediterranean diet has many advantages.
D. The diet winner also provides much added sugar.
E. The DASH diet which stresses less salt intake comes in second.
F. Eating healthy fish is also encouraged, while eggs are eaten in much smaller portions (部分).
G. All three of these diets stress less processed foods and packing your plate with fruits, vegetables, beans and nuts.

词汇碎片

at times 偶尔，有时候   decide v. 决定   offer v. 提供   be connected with 与……有关

重难句讲解

And the third is the flexitarian diet, which encourages being a vegetarian most of the time, but allows a burger at times. 排名第三的是弹性素食饮食，鼓励在大多数时间当一个素食主义者，但偶尔可以吃个汉堡。

本句是复合句。主句是 the third is the flexitarian diet，为主系表结构。which 引导非限制性定语从句修饰 the flexitarian diet，该定语从句中的 but 连接两个并列的谓宾结构。

Saturday F 短文填空

Prefer your coffee black? Then you (1) _____ like dark, bitter chocolate, according to a new research.

Studies find moderate (适中的) amounts of black coffee—between 3 and 5 cups daily—have been shown to lower the risk of some serious illnesses such as cancers. (2) _____ the research, Cornelis and her team (3) _____ that a genetic variant (基因变体) may explain why some people (4) _____ so many cups of coffee a day, while others do not like it. People with the gene metabolize (代谢) caffeine (咖啡因) faster, so the stimulating (刺激的) effects wear off (逐渐消失) faster, and they need to (5) _____ more coffee. This could (6) _____ why some people seem to be fine drinking a lot of coffee, while someone else might get nervous or become very (7) _____.

"When they think of coffee, they think of a bitter taste, so they also enjoy dark (8) _____," Cornelis said. "It's possible these people are just very sensitive (敏感的) to the effects of caffeine and they also have that learned behavior with other bitter (9) _____."

Future studies will try to deal (10) _____ the genetic preference for other bitter foods which are generally connected with more health problems.

阅读短文，从方框中选择合适的单词填空，使短文通顺，意思完整。每空限填一词，每词限用一次。

enjoy

drink

foods

chocolate

probably

discovered

with

anxious

In

explain

词汇碎片

prefer v. 更喜爱，更喜欢   bitter adj. 味苦的   serious adj. 严重的；严肃的   taste n. 味道；品味

重难句讲解

Studies find moderate amounts of black coffee—between 3 and 5 cups daily—have been shown to lower the risk of some serious illnesses such as cancers. 研究发现，适量的黑咖啡——每天3到5杯——已被证明可以降低患某些严重疾病的风险，比如癌症。

本句是复合句。moderate amounts of black coffee... some serious illnesses such as cancers 为省略引导词 that 的宾语从句，作 find 的宾语；破折号中间的内容 between 3 and 5 cups daily 作插入语，对 moderate amounts of black coffee 进行补充说明；lower the risk of 意为"降低……的风险"。

Week Five 社会人际

Monday A 完形填空

| 体 裁 | 议论文 | 题 材 | 社会人际 | 正确率 | ___/8 | 词 数 | 238 |
| 难 度 | ★★★☆☆ | 建议用时 | 8分钟 | 实际用时 | | 答案页码 | 097 |

For many of us, the COVID-19 revealed who our closest friends are. Many children missed their social (社交的) circle—especially their best friends, because they didn't have enough social __1__ to communicate with a wider group due to the COVID-19. These friends aren't just people we enjoy __2__. Instead, they are the ones we believe completely. Having healthy friendships is often seen as an __3__ skill for a child. Close friendships in childhood help kids practice the skills they need in close relationships (关系) throughout their lives, such as dealing __4__ feelings like loneliness (孤独), fear and failure.

Kids usually make friends by doing fun things together, so parents may need to think about their children's interests and find out __5__ that could be done with other children. Parents can also teach their children __6__ to join in with games and activities.

Besides, having close friends can help children out of difficult situations. Friendships change all the time throughout childhood. When best friends move away, it can be __7__ difficult for young children, who aren't used to relationships ending. It is important that parents discuss this with their children and __8__ them.

For children who have not yet found that special friend, there are still a lot of chances ahead. It is never too late to make new friends, but it's a great idea to start early.

1. A. chances   B. invitations   C. organizations
2. A. coming up with   B. putting up with   C. hanging out with
3. A. honest   B. important   C. easy
4. A. on   B. in   C. with
5. A. interviews   B. activities   C. habits
6. A. how   B. why   C. what
7. A. simply   B. impossibly   C. extremely
8. A. support   B. save   C. criticize

词汇碎片

find out 找出   situation n. 情景；形势

重难句讲解

Besides, having close friends can help children out of difficult situations. 另外，拥有亲密的朋友可以帮助孩子走出困境。
本句是简单句。动名词短语 having close friends 在句中作主语，can help 作谓语，children 作宾语，介词短语 out of difficult situations 作宾语补足语。help... out of... 为固定搭配，意为"帮助……脱离……"。

Tuesday B 阅读理解

体裁	记叙文	题材	社会人际	正确率	___/5	词数	242
难度	★★★☆☆	建议用时	6分钟	实际用时		答案页码	097

When Peng Linqian was 7 years old, she had a fever that made her lose her hearing. She remembered that her world had gone completely quiet then. The hearing impairment (障碍) influenced her ability to express herself, which led her to fall into self-isolation (自我孤立). When she grew up, she has been working to give a voice to the hearing-impaired because she knew the importance of self-expression (自我表达).

Then, she joined a project of performing workshops (讲习班) for children with hearing difficulties. For each day, they designed many writing, storytelling and theater activities that aimed to make children exercise their imagination (想象力), find their own voices, in the end, perform the stories with both sign and body language. Under the suggestion of Peng, they also designed a few activities, for example, taking off their hearing aids (助听器) or shouting.

However, they experienced all kinds of difficulties. The children were either too shy or too <u>unwilling</u> to take part in the activities. One of the girls spent the whole day practicing paper folding. Later, the team changed their plan and took the children to a creative place, with the task of finding a shop they like and watching the people and things in it. The group ended up having a pleasant day together, even the girl who liked paper folding left a message in the postcard shop she chose. She wrote: "Today, I had a wonderful time."

They finally established friendships with the children through the project.

1. Why has Peng Linqian been working to help children with hearing impairment?
   A. To show her love.
   B. To be praised by others.
   C. To help them have the ability of self-expression.
   D. To recommend (推荐) the performing workshop.

2. Which is NOT used by Peng Linqian to help children with hearing difficulties in the project?
   A. Telling stories.
   B. Taking regular exercise.
   C. Designing theater activities.
   D. Taking off kids' hearing aids.

3. What does the underlined word "unwilling" in Paragraph 3 most probably mean in Chinese?
   A. 喜欢的   B. 果断的
   C. 不愿意的 D. 恼怒的

4. How did the girl who liked paper folding feel at last in Paragraph 3?
   A. Pleased.   B. Angry.
   C. Bored.   D. Confident.

5. What's the writer's purpose of writing the passage?
   A. To tell us how to get along well with teenagers who have hearing difficulties.
   B. To introduce Peng Linqian's efforts to help children with hearing difficulties.
   C. To encourage children with hearing impairment to take part in the project.
   D. To show us how to help children with hearing impairment.

词汇碎片

completely *adv.* 完全地；彻底地   design *v.* 设计；构思   pleasant *adj.* 令人愉快的；合意的
establish *v.* 建立；设立

重难句讲解

Later, the team changed their plan and took the children to a creative place, with the task of finding a shop they like and watching the people and things in it. 后来，团队成员改变了他们的计划，带着孩子们去了一个有创意的地方，孩子们的任务是找到一家他们喜欢的商店，并观察里面的人和物。

本句是复合句。并列连词 and 连接 changed their plan 和 took the children to a creative place 两个动宾结构；they like 是省略引导词 that 的定语从句，修饰 a shop。

City Blossoms is a non-profit (非营利的) organization with the aim of bringing nature to children who might not have green spaces. The organization has helped to create green spaces at seven elementary schools, two high schools and 18 early childhood centers across Washington, D.C.

City Blossoms' lessons center on environmental (生态环境的) science, healthy living skills like cooking, and artistic expression. In the garden, students can learn environmental ideas like plant lifecycles (生命周期) or ecosystems (生态系统). But teachers can also use the green space for reading lessons by reading a garden-related book or learning nature words. Young children and older adults have gotten involved with the community green spaces. During cooking lessons, for example, people will tell about meals that are special to their culture. The community gardens represent the diversity (多样性) of D.C. It's like putting pieces together of so many different people and cultures and neighborhoods.

Healthy food is hard to find in some parts of Washington, D.C., especially in poorer areas. About 15 percent of D.C. is a "food desert". Part of the organization's task is to grow in spaces that might not have green spaces, and might not have fresh, healthy food. For older students at schools, students learn how to grow and harvest (收割) crops through the organization of City Blossoms' program. They also sell their vegetables and herbs at local farmers markets.

People have really woken up to the fact that green spaces are of great importance in our communities. And, they want to spend more time outside experiencing nature.

阅读短文，根据短文内容，在方框内的缩写文章中，填入与短文意思最符合的单词，每空一词。

City Blossoms is an organization which is (1)_____ at bringing nature to children who don't have green spaces. There are many (2)_____ organized by City Blossoms, including environmental science, healthy living skills and artistic expression. Besides, teachers can also (3)_____ students to read some books using green spaces and learn new words about nature. Both children and adults have the chance to join the community green spaces.

It's difficult to find healthy food, particularly in some poor parts of Washington, D.C. So, in order to have fresh and healthy food, students at school are (4)_____ by City Blossom's program to learn how to grow and harvest crops.

People have realized that green spaces are really (5)_____ in our own communities.

词汇碎片

expression n. 表达；词语   community n. 社区；团体   represent v. 代表；表示
local adj. 当地的；地方的

重难句讲解

People have really woken up to the fact that green spaces are of great importance in our communities. 人们已经意识到绿色空间在我们的社区中是非常重要的。

本句是复合句。that green spaces are of great importance in our communities 为 that 引导的同位语从句，解释说明抽象名词 fact 的具体内容，that 在从句中不充当任何成分；wake up to 为固定搭配，意为"意识到；认识到"。

Thursday D任务型阅读

It seems that the younger generation (一代人) has become more welcoming to domestic (国内的) brands, preferring to pay for the product's design and quality. __1__

__2__ The company supported flood-hit (遭受洪灾的) Zhengzhou, Henan Province, in July last year. The sports and lifestyle company donated (捐赠) supplies worth 50 million yuan, despite (尽管) having a loss of 220 million yuan before. The generosity (慷慨) shown has given other domestic brands the opportunity to let Chinese customers (消费者) know that they also have fine products and a deep love for the country.

I used to be among the group that preferred foreign brands, especially cosmetics (化妆品). __3__ I was also worried about the out-of-style designs and poor quality of domestic goods. I dropped my prejudice (偏见) later when I tried some domestically made clothes by Chinese designers. __4__

I think people's confidence in the nation's development and the improved designs and quality of domestic products are the main reasons for the growth of these new national products. __5__

阅读短文，从下列选项中选出能填入文中空白处的最佳选项，选项中有一项为多余选项。

A. I was impressed by the great efforts (努力) ERKE made.
B. They have changed our shopping habits thanks to their good quality.
C. The quality is as good as that of foreign things, while the prices are much nicer.
D. I always believed that using foreign goods made me look very trendy.
E. Young people don't just pay for big-name brands reading "Made in Italy".
F. The change in attitude is more noticeable among the younger generation, who have grown up in an environment in which China's economy has boomed (繁荣).

brand n. 品牌；类型   product n. 产品   quality n. 质量；品质

The generosity shown has given other domestic brands the opportunity to let Chinese customers know that they also have fine products and a deep love for the country. 这种慷慨的行为给了其他国内品牌一个机会，可以让中国消费者知道，他们也有优质的产品和对国家深深的爱。

本句是复合句。在主句中，The generosity 作主语，has given 作谓语，other domestic brands 作间接宾语，the opportunity 作直接宾语；其中 shown 是过去分词作后置定语修饰 The generosity；that 引导宾语从句作 know 的宾语；a deep love for 意为"深爱……"。

Friday E 任务型阅读

Women's safety is once again in the spotlight (公众注意的中心), and they are afraid of walking home at night. A telephone helpline called Strut Safe, launched in Edinburgh (爱丁堡) last year, is keeping people company when they walk home alone.

Alice Jackson, 22, and her friend Rachel Chung came up with the idea of a telephone helpline that people can call if they're walking home alone at night. Alice says, "We bought a cheap phone, asked people to volunteer to answer it, and posted (公布) the number in community groups."

The volunteers who answer calls are there to chat and to provide reassurance (安慰), but sometimes callers worry for their own safety.

If a caller thinks she is not safe, she can give her name, her age, her birthday, her address, and a full description of what she looks like and every item of clothing that she is wearing. Volunteers like Alice are ready to alert (向……报警) the police or call an ambulance (救护车) if needs be.

Alice says, "Every time a caller gets home safely, it's a relief (慰藉). They'll say, 'I can see my house now,' or, 'I'm only a minute away,' but I always say, 'Don't worry. It's OK. I'll stay on the phone. Just let me know when you're in the door.'"

She'll hear the clatter (咔嗒声) of keys, someone's mum calling, "Where have you been?" or a dog bark (犬吠).

Strut Safe's free helpline works from 7 pm—3 am on Fridays and Saturdays, and 7 pm—1 am on Sundays.

阅读短文,完成下面1~6小题。

1. According to the passage, who came up with the idea of a telephone helpline?
   _____

2. Alice and her friend bought a cheap phone, _____ people to volunteer to answer it, and posted _____ in community groups.

3. Please translate the underlined sentence into Chinese.
   _____

4. What can volunteers answering calls do if the caller thinks she is not safe?
   _____

5. For Alice, it's a relief when a caller gets home _____ (safe).

6. When can you call Strut Safe's free helpline if you need?
   _____

in the spotlight 处于公众注意的中心 be afraid of 害怕 provide v. 提供;供给

A telephone helpline called Strut Safe, launched in Edinburgh last year, is keeping people company when they walk home alone.
去年在爱丁堡开通的名为 Strut Safe 的热线电话可以在人们独自步行回家时陪伴他们。
本句是复合句。called Strut Safe 和 launched in Edinburgh last year 都是过去分词短语作后置定语,修饰 A telephone helpline;when 引导时间状语从句。

Saturday F 短文填空

What should you do if you are locked down (封锁) for 48 hours in an office building?

This sounds (1) _____. But Allen, a director (2) _____ at a company who was trapped (困住) in the company's building in Shanghai, felt calm and (3) _____. "There was no panic; our first reaction (反应) was to get daily things in the office," (4) _____ remembered. "We were told there was a positive case (阳性病例) in our building and we needed to take nucleic acid testing (核酸检测) in the morning. Then there was a lockdown in the office for 48 hours," she said. Someone ordered things online, and others called family members (5) _____ things to them. The government and companies bought bedding sets and sent them (6) _____ bedtime. Meal allowances (津贴) (7) _____ to order food.

Would it be embarrassing to sleep in the same room with co-workers (同事)? Allen said they were divided into small groups, and the office room was divided into several areas. "So we had enough space to put the beds. The only (8) _____ was that we could not shower during the 48-hour lockdown." All food was sent to the office, so the lockdown turned into a kind of dinner party.

Most office workers under lockdown showed (9) _____ and gave a thumbs-up (竖起大拇指；称赞) for the quick reply and quick (10) _____.

阅读短文，从方框中选择合适的单词并用其正确形式填空，使短文通顺，意思完整。有两个词为多余项。

she
work
send
behave
understand
before
give
terrible
problem
after
peace
bring

---

order v. 订购；点（酒、菜等）　　embarrassing adj. 令人尴尬的；令人为难的
divide v. （使）分开；使分离

Allen said they were divided into small groups, and the office room was divided into several areas. 艾伦说，大家被分成好几个小组，并且办公室被分成了好几个区域。

本句是复合句。said 后面为省略引导词 that 的宾语从句，作 said 的宾语；宾语从句中，连词 and 连接两个并列句；divide... into... 为固定搭配，表示"把……分成……"。

Week Six 文学艺术

Monday A 完形填空

体 裁	记叙文	题 材	文学艺术	正确率	___/10	词 数	210
难 度	★★★☆☆	建议用时	10 分钟	实际用时	___	答案页码	100

Bing Dwen Dwen, the cute mascot (吉祥物) of the Beijing 2022 Winter Olympics, has been selling like hotcakes (畅销). Why is this panda so __1__? What are the ideas __2__ its design? Guangzhou Academy of Fine Arts (广州美术学院) professor (教授) Cao Xue, who leads the mascot design team, __3__ the story.

Cao Xue __4__ remembers the exciting day of September 17th, 2019. On that day, the Organizing Committee of the Winter Olympic Games (冬季奥运会组委会) announced the mascot __5__ by Guangzhou Academy of Fine Arts as the mascot of the Beijing Winter Olympic Games. After a __6__ by many experts (专家), the mascot got a new name—"Bing Dwen Dwen".

Bing Dwen Dwen is a panda with a high sense of science and technology (技术). It catches attention with its full-body "shell" made out of ice. Cao said the idea came from __7__ Chinese food *tanghulu*, while the shell is also like a spacesuit (航天服). In order to make the panda look more pleasant, Cao and his team members __8__ to China Wolong Daxiongmao Museum for field observation (实地观察).

As for Bing Dwen Dwen's popularity (流行), Cao said, "Its ice shell is cold, __9__ the image looks warm and lovely. I believe this kind of __10__ can be something everybody feels. I hope it will become an impressive (给人印象深刻的) memory in Olympic history."

1. A. popular   B. common   C. natural
2. A. among   B. of   C. with
3. A. told   B. spoke   C. said
4. A. casually   B. weakly   C. clearly
5. A. reviewed   B. designed   C. received
6. A. performance   B. discussion   C. management
7. A. clean   B. modern   C. traditional
8. A. failed   B. jumped   C. flew
9. A. but   B. and   C. or
10. A. culture   B. talent   C. warmth

词汇碎片

sense *n.* 感觉，意识；感官   pleasant *adj.* 令人愉快的   lovely *adj.* 可爱的

重难句讲解

Guangzhou Academy of Fine Arts professor Cao Xue, who leads the mascot design team, told the story. 广州美术学院教授、吉祥物设计团队负责人曹雪讲述了这个故事。

本句是复合句。who leads the mascot design team 是由 who 引导的非限制性定语从句，修饰先行词 Cao Xue。

From ancient times to today, portraiture (肖像画) has told us elementary truths about human nature and identity (身份), whoever the subject. By looking at who was drawn, and how, we are able to know more about social and cultural history that no other type of painting can offer.

Self-portrait by Catharina van Hemessen	The famous self-portrait by Catharina van Hemessen focuses on her identity as an artist. The self-portrait has of course also been an important part of artistic (艺术的) expression. Portraits record, celebrate, and show us who we were and who we are now.
Self-portrait with Bandaged Ear by Van Gogh	Van Gogh's *Self-portrait with Bandaged Ear*, painted after he cut off part of his ear following an argument (争论) with Gauguin, shows his great determination (决心) to continue painting despite the hurt. It takes centre stage at the Courtauld's current exhibition of his self-portraits.
James Hunter Black Draftee by Alice Neel	Although Alice Neel did not get praise for her particular portraits until late in her career (职业生涯), their documentary and democratic (民主的) nature shows many functions (功能) that portraits can serve. In the past portraiture was really a mark of rank or status (地位) or famous people.

You are welcomed to make comments on the passage online and can also message us about your opinions.

1. Which of the following is NOT told by the portraiture according to the passage?
   A. Identity of the person in portraiture.
   B. Cultural history.
   C. Hobbies of the person in portraiture.
   D. Social history.

2. What can we infer through the description of *Self-portrait with Bandaged Ear*?
   A. An argument with our friends is not advised.
   B. Van Gogh loves painting very much.
   C. We shouldn't continue painting if we get hurt.
   D. Gauguin learns painting from Van Gogh.

3. From which is the passage most probably taken?
   A. A postcard.
   B. A storybook.
   C. A research paper.
   D. An art website.

In Chinese culture, the tiger stands for energy and vitality (活力). But the big cats created by a cartoonist (漫画家) who goes by the pen name Bu2ma are not so. His tigers are fat and lazy, often with interesting and foolish expressions, which has made Bu2ma's cute Panghu tiger popular on the Internet, especially in this Year of the Tiger.

"I saw pictures of tigers in a zoo, and they were really, really fat," he remembered. "I drew them as I saw them and posted (发布) them online. I didn't expect them to become so popular." One of Bu2ma's most popular works is named "Cub Calling for Its Mother". It shows a little tiger with flat, little ears and closed eyes shouting out "Mom!" Another drawing is called "Fierce Tiger Descending the Mountain". Instead of the traditional strong tiger, Bu2ma's tiger is fat with a kind of funny grimace (鬼脸). "Those works were created soon after the COVID-19 pandemic (流行病) broke out in China, when people were in lockdown (封闭) and in need of some cute things for comfort," he said. "I think that's why Panghu is popular."

"My biggest trouble at present is that Panghu is so popular that I don't have enough time to learn new things and improve myself, which is a dangerous sign for me," he said. "I hope that in this Year of the Tiger, I can make some positive changes."

1. What is the tiger like in Chinese culture according to the passage?
   A. Cute and lovely.
   B. Energetic and strong.
   C. Funny and fat.
2. Which of the following is NOT the reason for Panghu tiger's popularity (流行) on the Internet?
   A. The Panghu tiger has interesting and foolish expressions.
   B. This year is the Year of the Tiger.
   C. The tiger is full of energy and vitality.
3. How many drawings of Bu2ma are mentioned in the passage?
   A. One.
   B. Two.
   C. Three.
4. What does the underlined phrase "broke out" in Paragraph 2 most probably mean in Chinese?
   A. 暴发
   B. 泄露
   C. 举报
5. What is Bu2ma worried about according to the passage?
   A. He has no time to try something new.
   B. Too many people like his drawings.
   C. He can't draw other popular paintings.

energy n. 力量；能源   trouble n. 忧虑；苦恼   at present 目前，现在

Those works were created soon after the COVID-19 pandemic broke out in China, when people were in lockdown and in need of some cute things for comfort. 这些作品是新冠肺炎疫情在中国暴发不久后创作的，当时人们处于疫情封锁期，需要通过一些可爱的东西来获得安慰。

本句是复合句。主句为 Those works were created；after the COVID-19 pandemic broke out in China 为 after 引导的时间状语从句；when 引导时间状语从句；in need of 意为"需要"。

Thursday D任务型阅读

With about 250 cubic (立方的) meters of fertile (肥沃的) dirt (泥土) covering the floor, the New York Earth Room is one of New York City's most unusual art attractions. The Dia Art Foundation invited the local artist Walter De Maria to create it in 1977. __1__

Art lovers can visit the unusual attraction, enjoy the mass (堆) of dirt and take in its earthy fragrance (泥土的芬芳). __2__ Believe it or not, keeping 140 tons of dirt in pristine (原始的) condition for over 40 years is a lot harder than it sounds. They water the soil from time to time, rake (耙平) it, and make sure to remove any mushrooms (蘑菇) that sprout (出现) out of the dirt.

__3__ He spends his days sitting at a desk, counting visitors, answering questions, and looking mysterious. "__4__ So I think what I really want people to know is that they don't have to know anything about the work," Dilworth, an artist himself, said.

You might think that few people would happily go to see a large loft filled with dirt, but you would be wrong. __5__

阅读短文，从下列选项中选出能填入文中空白处的最佳选项。

A. However, they are forbidden from stepping on the dirt or even touching it.

B. And it was opened to the general public in 1980 after three-year efforts.

C. Up to 100 people visit the unusual artwork every day when the room is open.

D. Bill Dilworth, the room's caretaker, has been answering visitors' questions since 1989.

E. People always wonder what it means, but the artist never gives any meaning to it.

词汇碎片
unusual adj. 不寻常的；独特的   attraction n. 有吸引力的人或物   from time to time 偶尔；有时候

重难句讲解
With about 250 cubic meters of fertile dirt covering the floor, the New York Earth Room is one of New York City's most unusual art attractions. 纽约地球屋的地板上铺着约250立方米的肥沃泥土，是纽约市最不寻常的艺术景点之一。
本句是简单句。With... covering the floor 作伴随状语，其中现在分词短语 covering the floor 作后置定语修饰 fertile dirt。

Friday E 任务型阅读

Do you know dried turnips (萝卜干) can also be turned into a beautiful "flower" used to decorate (装饰) headdresses (头饰)? Wang Ping, a photographer and stylist, has "the magic" to make this happen.

The 26-year-old man, who owns two photography studios (工作室), became interested in crafting (精心制作) headdresses in 2020. He found that there wasn't any headdress (头饰) that fitted with the studio's costumes. As an industrial art major, Wang is skilled at drawing. So he decided to make them on his own. To craft a headdress there are three steps. "Firstly, I do a design drawing. Then, I prepare all the materials needed and make the framework (框架) of the headwear," Wang said. "The last step is to assemble (组装) all materials and paint." Surprisingly, almost all of them are "waste" as they come from waste clothes. Wang said, "I decided to make the most out of these 'waste materials'. I try my best to design and make the headdresses in an environment-friendly (环保型的) way."

He prefers to make traditional Chinese phoenix coronets (凤冠). Making one often takes from one week to up to several months as it uses up to over 30 types of materials. Now, Wang is making clothing featuring a dragon. Wang said, "It takes about one year to complete."

As people are embracing (欣然接受) the growing trend of *guochao*, it is no wonder that Wang's work has been very popular. "I'll keep to blending (使……融合) traditional Chinese culture and fashionable elements (元素) to craft finer headdresses," Wang said.

阅读短文,回答下面1~5小题。
1. Why did Wang Ping decide to make headdresses on his own?
2. What is the first step to make a headdress?
3. Why are the headdresses environment-friendly?
4. What kind of headdress does Wang Ping prefer to make?
5. How long does it take to make clothing featuring a dragon?

词汇碎片
major *n.* 主修学生；专业   be skilled at 擅长   material *n.* 材料；原料   keep to 坚持

重难句讲解
As people are embracing the growing trend of *guochao*, it is no wonder that Wang's work has been very popular. 随着人们欣然接受"国潮"风的兴起,王平的作品深受大众喜爱也就不足为奇了。
本句是复合句。As引导时间状语从句；主句的主干为it is no wonder that... 结构,意为"……不足为奇",it作形式主语,真正的主语为that从句。

Saturday F 短文填空

Dmitry Bragin is a Ukrainian artist who is good (1)_____ making steampunk masks (蒸汽朋克面具) that make the wearer look more machine (机器) (2)_____ man.

While Bragin's fantastic-looking masks (3)_____ (main) aren't technically (在技术上) steampunk, as they include no moving parts, it's clear that the sci-fi style served as the major inspiration for them. The talented artist starts off with a light plastic mask that is easy to shape as the base and adds all (4)_____ (type) of decorative (装饰性的) parts to it in order (5)_____ (change) it into the wearable (可穿戴的) wonders you see. The materials in (6)_____ (he) basement (地下室) include motorcycle parts, useless camera lenses, metallic (金属制的) children's toys and so on, although you couldn't really tell by (7)_____ (look) at the finished product.

Bragin's steampunk masks look 100% metallic, but, that is only an illusion (错觉) created with the help of metallic paint. To be (8)_____ (honest), many of the parts in the mask are actually light, making it a lot easier and more comfortable to wear. The paint that (9)_____ (give) the impressive-looking accessory its heavy, vintage (古色古香的) look can be seen.

Dmitry Bragin shares his newest mask with his fans (10)_____ are interested in this kind of design on social media platforms (平台).

阅读短文，在短文空缺处填入适当的单词，或用括号内所给单词的适当形式填空。

(1) _____
(2) _____
(3) _____
(4) _____
(5) _____
(6) _____
(7) _____
(8) _____
(9) _____
(10) _____

词汇碎片

inspiration *n.* 灵感；启发　　paint *n.* 涂料；油漆　　be interested in 对……感兴趣

重难句讲解

Bragin's steampunk masks look 100% metallic, but, that is only an illusion created with the help of metallic paint. 布拉金的蒸汽朋克面具看起来100%是金属的，但这只是在金属涂料的帮助下产生的错觉。

本句是but连接的并列句。created with the help of metallic paint 作后置定语，修饰illusion；with the help of 意为"在……的帮助下"。

Week Seven 历史地理

Monday A 完形填空

体裁	记叙文	题材	历史地理	正确率	___/15	词数	239
难度	★★★★☆	建议用时	16分钟	实际用时	___	答案页码	103

The INLET, the latest place in Shanghai's arts and cultural center, opened to the public after three years of renovation (翻新). Located (位于) near one of Shanghai's major business __1__, North Sichuan Road, the place was __2__ from a century-old compound (建筑群) __3__ 60 *shikumen*-Shanghai-style houses and eight stand-alone buildings.

The area has been __4__ to many famous persons throughout history, such as the translator Qu Qiubai, and the writer and poet Lu Xun. The road is also where the country's first cinema and the private (私立的) Shanghai Academy of Fine Arts (上海美术学院) were __5__ located.

It was clear from the __6__ that the compound would be restored (修复) to serve as a public space for art and culture. The other focus (重点) of the project was to show Shanghai-style culture __7__ combining traditional and __8__ design. Old bricks (砖块) were __9__ to restore the buildings __10__ developers (开发商) want to keep the original look. The developers also restored the doors of the old houses using stones __11__ to the original.

The In-Shanghai Art festival is the first art activity to take place in The INLET and will see artists from __12__ fields (领域), including opera, jazz and modern dance, perform through Sunday. The festival __13__ to bring art closer to the public. Zheng Bingze, CEO of the Chongbang Group who is responsible for (为……负责) the renovation project, __14__ that he hopes young people in Shanghai will __15__ cultural activities there.

1. A. playgrounds B. houses C. streets D. factories
2. A. seen B. given C. controlled D. changed
3. A. except B. including C. among D. through
4. A. home B. place C. earth D. company
5. A. once B. never C. always D. probably
6. A. middle B. end C. beginning D. top
7. A. by B. across C. before D. under
8. A. modern B. strange C. dangerous D. dull
9. A. borrowed B. bought C. used D. compared
10. A. although B. while C. so D. because
11. A. lazy B. similar C. crazy D. nervous
12. A. clean B. polite C. brave D. different
13. A. refuses B. fails C. aims D. behaves
14. A. says B. discusses C. argues D. cries
15. A. take out B. take part in C. take away D. take care of

---

place *n.* 地点，场所　　**translator** *n.* 翻译家，译者　　**original** *adj.* 原有的；新颖的

词汇碎片

The INLET, the latest place in Shanghai's arts and cultural center, opened to the public after three years of renovation. 上海的艺术和文化中心的一处新场所今潮8弄(The INLET)经过三年的翻新后向公众开放了。

本句是简单句。the latest place in Shanghai's arts and cultural center 作 The INLET 的同位语，对其进行补充说明；after three years of renovation 为时间状语。

重难句讲解

Tuesday B 阅读理解

Over the last 50 years, Dubai (迪拜) has become a mysterious success story, <u>transforming</u> from a sleepy fishing port to an energetic and big city. But the city is faced with a major challenge: desertification (荒漠化) makes the remaining rich land dangerous. With an increase in population and food consumption (消耗量), desertification is becoming extremely serious.

Desertification is a type of land degradation (退化), making rich land in dry areas unproductive (产量少的). It usually happens when natural resources (资源) such as water and soil are overburdened (负担过重的). While it can happen naturally, desertification is more and more serious both in the Dubai and in the world because of human activities such as overgrazing (过度放牧), modern farming and building development. "Desertification happens when rich land, usually at the borders of deserts, is overburdened," says William H. Schlesinger, a scientist.

Finding useful solutions has become important. The aim is not to conquer (征服) the desert, but to restore areas of land that are no longer productive. An old environmental solution is simply planting more trees. Trees fix the soil, take in carbon (碳), improve soil fertility (肥沃) and also improve recharge (补给) of groundwater. Choosing the right trees, especially natives, is important for tree planting projects in dry areas. In 2010, Sheikh Mohammed started the One Million Trees Project, aiming to plant a million trees to stop desertification.

1. What does the underlined word "transforming" in Paragraph 1 probably mean in Chinese?
   A. 转变   B. 下降
   C. 穿梭   D. 浮动

2. Which one of the following is NOT the reason why desertification happens according to the passage?
   A. Modern farming and building development.
   B. Overburdened water resources.
   C. Overburdened rich land in dry areas.
   D. Extremely hot weather.

3. The advantages of planting more trees in dry areas don't include _____.
   A. fixing the soil
   B. taking in carbon
   C. improving soil fertility
   D. feeding more animals

4. What is the last paragraph mainly about?
   A. Planting more trees can be a helpful solution.
   B. Choosing the right trees is important for tree planting projects.
   C. The One Million Trees Project was started.
   D. Desertification is becoming serious in Dubai.

---

energetic *adj.* 有活力的   population *n.* 人口   solution *n.* 解决办法   fix *v.* 固定；维修

词汇碎片

In 2010, Sheikh Mohammed started the One Million Trees Project, aiming to plant a million trees to stop desertification. 2010年，谢赫·穆罕默德开启了"一百万棵树项目"，旨在种植一百万棵树来阻止荒漠化。

本句是简单句。Sheikh Mohammed started the One Million Trees Project 为句子的主干；aiming to plant a million trees to stop desertification 为现在分词短语作目的状语；aim to do sth. 为固定搭配，意为"旨在做某事"。

重难句讲解

Wednesday C 任务型阅读

体 裁	记叙文	题 材	历史地理	正确率	/5	词 数	185
难 度	★★★☆☆	建议用时	6分钟	实际用时		答案页码	104

The Terracotta Warriors (兵马俑) are unusual burial (埋葬的) things for China's first Emperor Qinshihuang, the founder (创建人) of China's Qin Dynasty. The mausoleum (陵墓) of Emperor Qinshihuang was found in 1974 and listed on the World Cultural Heritage List in 1987.

Located in northwest China's Shaanxi Province, the Emperor Qinshihuang's Mausoleum Site Museum including the burial site of Qinshihuang, is famous for the Terracotta Warriors, which are called a wonder of the world. The 25 pottery figurines (陶俑) were newly found in Pit (坑) No.1 of the well-known museum. Among the cultural relics (文物), one figurine is of a general and another one of a medium-ranking (中级的) officer. The 25 painted pottery figurines are in good condition, and are being stored in the protection room in order to make them safe. They are very important for understanding and studying the military (军事的) arrays (排列) of the pit, said Chinese archaeologists (考古学家).

At present, archaeologists have restored some cultural relics including three chariots (二轮战车) and horses, and gold-, silver- and bronze-made figurines, which all show the rich life of nobles (贵族) during the Qin Dynasty.

阅读短文，回答下面 1~5 小题。

1. Who is the founder of China's Qin Dynasty?
   _____
   _____

2. What is the Emperor Qinshihuang's Mausoleum Site Museum famous for?
   _____
   _____

3. How many pottery figurines were found recently?
   _____
   _____

4. Where were the pottery figurines found?
   _____
   _____

5. Why are the pottery figurines being stored in the protection room?
   _____
   _____

词汇碎片
find v. 发现　　wonder n. 奇迹；奇观　　store v. 储藏；保存　　in order to 为了

重难句讲解
At present, archaeologists have restored some cultural relics including three chariots and horses, and gold-, silver- and bronze-made figurines, which all show the rich life of nobles during the Qin Dynasty. 目前，考古学家已经修复了一些文物，包括三辆二轮战车、马匹和多件金、银、铜制的俑，所有这些都展现了秦朝贵族的奢华生活。
　　本句是复合句。主句的主干是 archaeologists have restored some cultural relics；including... figurines 为介词短语作后置定语，修饰 cultural relics；which 引导非限制性定语从句，修饰前面的 some cultural relics... figurines。

Thursday D 任务型阅读

We are able to get new knowledge of the past and the place that we learned through photography. And you'll see the first photograph ever taken of Notre Dame Cathedral (巴黎圣母院) in Paris. That photo, taken in 1838 or 1839 by Louis Daguerre, shows a great similarity (相似性) to the church as it looks today, after the serious 2019 fire: There's no spire (尖顶).

The spire that burned in 2019, (A) along with Notre Dame Cathedral's whole roof and its attic (阁楼), did not yet appear in 1839. It (B) _____ (build) during a twenty-year-long restoration (修复) of the cathedral that began in 1844. Led by the great architect (建筑师) Eugène Emmanuel Viollet-le-Duc, that first restoration became a pioneering (先锋的) embodiment (体现) of historic preservation.

(C) 今天，巴黎圣母院正在重建。Recording that effort for the February cover story, Paris photographer Tomas van Houtryve was inspired (赋予灵感) by a portrait (肖像) made by the (D) famous photographer Nadar. "I wanted to take a photo of the present architect and team of workers using the same technique (技术), linking (连接) all these guardians (守卫者) of the cathedral across time," van Houtryve says. His choice to work with the old technique honors (尊重) not just the present workers but the spirit of their project.

阅读短文，然后按要求完成1~5小题。

1. 写出文中画线部分（A）和（D）的同义词或近义词。
   _____；_____

2. 写出文中（B）空格后括号内单词的正确形式。
   _____

3. 将文中画线部分（C）译成英语。
   _____
   _____
   _____

4. Who recorded the image (影像) of the present architect and team of workers?
   _____
   _____

5. 从文中找出两个与建筑有关的名词。
   _____；_____

Friday E 短文填空

体　裁	记叙文	题　材	历史地理	正确率	___/7	词　数	251
难　度	★★★★☆	建议用时	9分钟	实际用时		答案页码	105

阅读短文，用括号内所给单词的适当形式填空。

As the train from Paris ran towards the southern part, I thought about Marseille (马赛), which is different from the rest of the country. It's a big city both geographically (在地理上) and culturally, and its people are made up of waves of migrants (移民), making it one of the (1) _____ (old) cities in France and the most multicultural (多元文化的) one.

(2) _____ (arrive) at the Marseille-Saint-Charles station, visitors can have a good view from its lavish (奢华的), high forecourt (前院). My eyes followed the Boulevard d'Athènes (雅典大道), a sloping (倾斜的) street. There, the Notre-Dame de La Garde (圣母加德大教堂)—the city's highest point, (3) _____ (shine) like a holy (神圣的) lighthouse out to sea. The Vieux Port (旧港) still is the city's center, and there (4) _____ (be) some yachts (游艇) like swans (天鹅) on a lake.

There are 300 days of sunshine in the city each year. To run away from the heat, I headed to the Plage des Catalans (加泰罗尼亚海滩). In the late-afternoon sun, the beach was covered in a mysterious amber (琥珀) color. I (5) _____ (walk) past a group playing volleyball, and locals sunbathed and talked. The city's "good-natured" was easy to (6) _____ (feel). It was here that I (7) _____ (clear) noticed Marseille's "Frenchness". It reminded me of some great port cities like Shanghai or New York, which were ever caught between the state and the sea.

I had a point about Marseille: the city is just another expression of a country, culturally more different and particular than it often likes to admit.

(1) _____

(2) _____

(3) _____

(4) _____

(5) _____

(6) _____

(7) _____

词汇碎片

be different from 与……不同　　station n. 车站　　follow v. 跟随　　mysterious adj. 神秘的

重难句讲解

As the train from Paris ran towards the southern part, I thought about Marseille, which is different from the rest of the country. 当从巴黎出发的火车向南部区域行驶时，我想起了马赛，它与法国的其他地区不同。

本句是复合句。As引导时间状语从句；I thought about Marseille 为主句的主干；which引导非限制性定语从句，修饰Marseille。

Saturday F 短文填空

According to research by Chinese archaeologists in recent years, the cultural communication between the Central Plains and the Tibet plateau (高原) can (1) _____ to the Paleolithic period (旧石器时期). China's National Cultural Heritage Administration (国家文物局) announced the latest research results on the most representative (代表性的) archaeological sites (考古遗址) with great importance to the history of Tibet and its people.

More than 500 relics, mainly made of stone and earth, have been discovered at the first site, the Qiere Site (切热遗址) in Tibetan Gar County. The relics and (2) _____ stone tools show that ancient people in Tibet had (3) _____ with other areas. At the same time, the site has provided valuable materials for research into the origin and migration (迁徙) routes of ancient people.

Besides, in the Mabucuo Site (玛不错遗址) in Kangmar County, archaeological evidences of human activity (4) _____ fire pits, tombs (墓) and pottery have been found there.

The Gebusailu Site (格布赛鲁遗址) in Zanda County was home to a relatively (相对地) independent (独立的) culture. Interestingly, the tombs in the site (5) _____ tombs from the same period in Xinjiang Uygur Autonomous Region (新疆维吾尔自治区).

This work report shows that the history and culture of Tibet are not independent, but were formed from different areas and rich cultural backgrounds.

阅读短文，从方框中选出可以填入文中空白处的短语。

cultural communication

are similar to

such as

date back

all types of

词汇碎片

latest *adj.* 最近的；最新的   ancient *adj.* 古代的；古老的   origin *n.* 起源；出身   evidence *n.* 证据

重难句讲解

The Gebusailu Site in Zanda County was home to a relatively independent culture. 札达县的格布赛鲁遗址拥有相对独立的文化。本句是简单句。be home to 意为"……的所在地"。

Week Eight 文化风俗

Monday A 完形填空

体 裁	记叙文	题 材	文化风俗	正 确 率	___/10	词 数	222
难 度	★★★☆☆	建议用时	10分钟	实际用时		答案页码	106

As the founder (创办者) of a miniature ceramics studio (微型陶瓷工作室), Wang Wenhua never __1__ that his work would surprise viewers (观众) in China and abroad. His short videos have gotten over 45 million views and 4.2 million likes on Douyin, the Chinese version (版本) of Tik Tok.

Wang said he had once seen the world's biggest ceramic but he had never seen the __2__, so he decided one day to try something __3__—making miniature ceramics.

Things were not easy in the beginning, and many people __4__ him. However, Wang did not __5__. Eventually (最终) he figured out how to make this new idea a reality on __6__ own.

__7__ Wang, the key to making a miniature ceramic work is concentration (专注). After trying many times, Wang found that the smallest he could get were works about 2 millimeters (毫米) in size, or he would need to use a microscope (显微镜).

"Sometimes, my followers or fans tell me some __8__ ideas. We have a very good relationship," said Wang. He often talked a lot with his fans on livestreams (直播).

Now, Wang can produce about 100 mini vases (花瓶) per day, but more creative works may __9__ one or two days.

"The works I created are like my children, and I am not willing to sell them __10__ the buyer is also a pottery (陶艺；陶器) lover or they really like my work," said Wang.

1. A. appeared   B. expected
   C. cared   D. shared
2. A. smallest   B. longest
   C. biggest   D. lightest
3. A. successful B. dangerous
   C. different D. stupid
4. A. believed   B. loved
   C. understood D. doubted
5. A. look up   B. set up
   C. put up   D. give up
6. A. its   B. his
   C. her   D. their
7. A. As for   B. According to
   C. In order to D. In case of
8. A. educational B. unhealthy
   C. creative   D. weak
9. A. take   B. spend
   C. pay   D. bring
10. A. because   B. so
    C. but   D. unless

---

figure out 想出；弄明白   be willing to 愿意，乐意   **词汇碎片**

After trying many times, Wang found that the smallest he could get were works about 2 millimeters in size, or he would need to use a microscope. 无数次的尝试之后，王文化发现他能做出的最小号的作品在2毫米左右，否则他就要用显微镜了。

本句是复合句。that引导宾语从句，作 found 的宾语，该宾语从句是一个由 or 连接的并列句，or 意为"否则"；其中 he could get 是一个省略引导词的定语从句，修饰 the smallest。

重难句讲解

Tuesday B 阅读理解

Major Cold (大寒), the last solar term (节气) in 24 solar terms, comes around January 20th each year, marking the end of winter.

During Major Cold, the weather is very cold. Although in some regions (地区) of China the weather during Major Cold is not colder than Minor Cold (小寒), the lowest temperatures of the whole year still occur (出现) in the Major Cold period in some coastal (沿海的) areas.

During Major Cold, people in Beijing have a habit of eating "dispelling (驱除) cold cake", a kind of rice cake. In Chinese, the word "rice cake" has the same pronunciation as the word "higher in a new year", which symbolizes good luck and continual promotion (提升). In Anqing of Anhui Province, people traditionally eat fried spring rolls during Major Cold. The stuffing (馅) inside the spring roll contains (包含) meat or vegetables. The rolls can be salty or sweet. People in Nanjing of Jiangsu Province enjoy chicken soup during the Major Cold period. Chicken soup can keep us warm and help <u>prevent</u> colds.

In various regions of China, Major Cold is the perfect time for winter sports such as skiing and ice skating.

1. Of 24 solar terms, Major Cold is _____.
   A. the first one   B. the 20th one
   C. the 22nd one   D. the 24th one
2. The weather during Major Cold is _____.
   A. always warmer than Minor Cold
   B. always colder than Minor Cold
   C. the coldest of the year in some regions of China
   D. the warmest of the year in some regions of China
3. The salty food we can learn from this passage is _____.
   A. dispelling cold cake
   B. fried rice cake
   C. fried spring rolls
   D. tomato sauce
4. What does "prevent" in the third paragraph mean in Chinese?
   A. 预防   B. 感染
   C. 保持   D. 发生
5. Which of the following statements is NOT TRUE?
   A. People in Beijing traditionally eat a kind of rice cake during Major Cold.
   B. The pronunciation of "rice cake" in Chinese is the same as "good luck".
   C. People in Nanjing enjoy chicken soup during Major Cold.
   D. People can do a lot of winter sports during Major Cold.

---

temperature n. 温度   pronunciation n. 发音   salty adj. 咸的；含盐的

Major Cold, the last solar term in 24 solar terms, comes around January 20th each year, marking the end of winter. 大寒是二十四节气中的最后一个节气，通常是在每年的1月20日前后到来，标志着冬天的结束。

本句是简单句。句子的主干是 Major Cold comes around January 20th each year；the last solar term in 24 solar terms 是 Major Cold 的同位语，marking the end of winter 是状语。

Wednesday C 阅读理解

体裁	说明文	题材	文化风俗	正确率	___/5	词数	224
难度	★★★☆☆	建议用时	6分钟	实际用时		答案页码	106

In Chinese culture, tigers are considered as the king of all beasts. They symbolize (象征) energy, protection, generosity (慷慨) and unpredictability (不可预测性). Tigers are seen as fearless creatures. That's why in China you can see images (形象) of tigers on the walls of temples and houses to <u>ward off</u> disasters (灾难) and danger.

Tigers have an important cultural meaning not just in China, but across Asia.

As they mostly live in Asia, for many people in the West, tigers have become a cultural symbol of Eastern countries. For example, strong economies (经济体) in the East—Singapore, Republic of Korea, China's Hong Kong and Taiwan—were called "The Four Asian Tigers". In the book *Life of Pi*, Canadian writer Yann Martel chose a Bengal (孟加拉) tiger as the partner for Indian boy Pi on his adventure (冒险) in the Pacific Ocean.

Instead of tigers, lions are considered as the king of all beasts in the West. Brave soldiers were given the name "the lion". In Europe, the animal is a national emblem (国徽) for the UK and 13 other countries. But in the West, tigers are also seen as very powerful (强大的) animals. In English, if you want someone to calm down, you can say "easy tiger".

Tigers are also one of my favorite animals. As a young animal lover, I felt so sad that they were an endangered species (濒危物种) and I wanted to help protect them.

1. The underlined phrase "ward off" in the first paragraph could be replaced (替换) by _____.
   A. put off
   B. take up
   C. come from
   D. keep away from

2. Which of the following countries or districts was not one of "The Four Asian Tigers"?
   A. Singapore.
   B. Republic of Korea.
   C. India.
   D. China's Hong Kong.

3. Which of the following statements is TRUE?
   A. Tigers are of cultural importance only in China.
   B. Tigers are the king of all beasts for people in the West.
   C. Brave soldiers were called "the lion" in the East.
   D. Tigers have become an important cultural symbol in the East.

4. When someone was told "easy tiger", it was probably because _____.
   A. he was angry
   B. he was hungry
   C. he was happy
   D. he was calm

5. What was the author's attitude towards the fact that tigers were endangered?
   A. Excited. B. Sorry.
   C. Bored.   D. Happy.

词汇碎片

consider v. 认为；考虑   energy n. 活力；能量   creature n. 生物

重难句讲解

Instead of tigers, lions are considered as the king of all beasts in the West. 在西方，公认的百兽之王不是老虎，而是狮子。本句是简单句。Instead of 意为"而不是；代替"；be considered as 意为"被认为是……，被看作……"。

The ancient city of Lijiang, in southwestern China's Yunnan Province, is home to ancient architecture (建筑) and rich ethnic (民族的) culture. __1__.

The Lijiang basin (流域) has rich water resources (资源) and pleasant weather. __2__. Once settled (定居), the Naxi built towns and transported water into villages by creating wells. The wells had three openings. __3__. Water in the first opening at the high level comes from the spring (泉水). __4__. The water that flows (流动) down into the second opening is clean and designated (指定) for washing vegetables, fruit, and kitchen utensils (厨房用具); while the water that flows down into the third opening is designated for washing daily used items like clothing.

Today, modern running water facilities (设施) have been installed (安装) in every home for many years. It puts an end to using water from the well for daily needs. __5__. You will still never see young or elderly Naxi washing food in the first well opening.

阅读短文，从下列选项中选出能填入文中空白处的最佳选项，选项中有两项为多余选项。

A. They were used for different purposes to help save water resources

B. It is also home to the Chinese ethnic minority (少数民族) Naxi people

C. The ancestors of the Naxi people decided to live in the area and take up farming

D. The ancestors of the Naxi people left behind their old way of living

E. However, the ancient tradition is still in the memory of every local person

F. Therefore it is designated as drinking water

G. This is a view of the Old Town of Lijiang

---

ancient adj. 古老的   create v. 创建；创造

词汇碎片

The ancient city of Lijiang, in southwestern China's Yunnan Province, is home to ancient architecture and rich ethnic culture. 丽江古城位于中国西南部的云南省，拥有古建筑和丰富的民族文化。

本句是简单句。in southwestern China's Yunnan Province 是地点状语；ancient city 意为"古城"；be home to 是固定短语，意为"是……的所在地"；ethnic culture 意为"民族文化"。

重难句讲解

Friday E 任务型阅读

体裁	说明文	题材	文化风俗	正确率	___/5	词数	216
难度	★★★★☆	建议用时	7分钟	实际用时	___	答案页码	107

The 12th lunar (农历的) month in Chinese is called *la yue*. The eighth day of this lunar month is *la yue chu ba*, or *laba*. The day is also known as the Laba Rice Porridge Festival.

Three major customs on Laba are ancestor worship (祭祖), eating Laba rice porridge and making Laba garlic (蒜).

In ancient times, the Chinese called the act of making sacrifices (献祭) to their ancestors *la*. And they called the day of sacrifice for wishing for safety, harvest (丰收), and health "the day of *la*". The Laba Festival was on the 12th lunar month, as a result, this month was called "month of *la*".

There are several stories about the beginning of eating rice porridge on Laba. Some say it is from Buddhists (佛教徒); some say the porridge, made of red beans (红豆), can keep evil (魔鬼) away from children. Others say the porridge is in memory of a poor couple.

The main ingredients (食材) of the Laba rice porridge are rice and sticky rice (糯米). People also add sugar, walnuts, red beans, peanuts and other various materials to make the porridge special.

In northern China, people like to make Laba garlic. They put the garlic into vinegar (醋) in a sealed (密封的) glass bottle. The vinegar makes the garlic green, while the vinegar itself is infused (充满) with the good taste of the garlic.

阅读短文,回答下面1~5小题。

1. When is the Laba Rice Porridge Festival?
   ___

2. What are the three major customs on Laba?
   ___

3. What does *la* mean?
   ___

4. What are the main ingredients of the Laba rice porridge?
   ___

5. How do people in northern China make Laba garlic?
   ___

词汇碎片

custom *n.* 习俗   ancestor *n.* 祖先,祖宗   in memory of 纪念……

重难句讲解

And they called the day of sacrifice for wishing for safety, harvest, and health "the day of *la*". 他们也把祈求平安、丰收和健康的祭祀日称为"腊日"。

本句是简单句。句子的主干是 they called the day "the day of *la*";call 意作 "称呼;认为……是" 时,可接名词或形容词作宾语补足语。

Saturday F 短文填空

体裁：记叙文　题材：文化风俗　正确率：___/10　词数：237
难度：★★★★☆　建议用时：11分钟　实际用时：___　答案页码：108

On the three past Sundays, Sydney Choy Lee Fut lion dance team performed in both hot weather and rain in (1)_____ to promote (宣传) Chinatown (唐人街) and attract people to return.

"The COVID-19 pandemic (新冠肺炎疫情) has taken everyone out of Chinatown. A lot of businesses have shut (2)_____, and everyone's spirits are a little bit low because (3)_____ last year," the director Paul Nomchong says. "So this is a way to (4)_____ their spirits and also bring people (5)_____ into Chinatown."

Choy Lee Fut, which runs Chinese kung fu and lion dance classes, has been part of the Chinatown community (6)_____ over 40 years.

Nomchong says many people have firstly come to them to learn Chinese kung fu and then started liking lion dance, as the two are related (相关的).

Anna Lamont is a lion (7)_____ team member. "Since I was a child, I've always wanted to do kung fu... I've been training at the school (8)_____ 2017, and started lion dance pretty much straight away," she says. Lamont has found that learning lion dance can be both challenging and rewarding (值得的，有收获的).

"In the beginning, it is challenging, (9)_____ your body is not used to moving that way. Apart from remembering the steps, it is also about learning (10)_____ to handle (处理) the weight of the lion's head," she says. "But you can learn so many skills through doing lion dance... and it makes you feel like you're part of a big family."

阅读短文，在短文空缺处填入适当的单词，使短文通顺，意思完整。

(1)_____
(2)_____
(3)_____
(4)_____
(5)_____
(6)_____
(7)_____
(8)_____
(9)_____
(10)_____

词汇碎片

director n. 负责人；导演　　community n. 社区　　weight n. 重量

重难句讲解

Nomchong says many people have firstly come to them to learn Chinese kung fu and then started liking lion dance, as the two are related. 纳木钟说，很多人是先来他们这里学习中国功夫，然后开始喜欢上舞狮的，因为这两者是相关的。

本句是复合句。主语是 Nomchong，谓语是 says。many people... the two are related 是省略引导词 that 的宾语从句，作 says 的宾语。as 表示原因，引导原因状语从句。

Week Nine 科学技术

Monday A 完形填空

| 体 裁 | 记叙文 | 题 材 | 科学技术 | 正确率 | ___/15 | 词 数 | 250 |
| 难 度 | ★★★☆☆ | 建议用时 | 15 分钟 | 实际用时 | ___ | 答案页码 | 109 |

Cows have evolved (进化) to hide lameness (跛足). As cow number 2073 makes her way out of the milking shed (棚屋) and passes in front of a nearby camera, the computer watches her every __1__.

She is only on screen for a short time but there is a little unevenness (不平衡) to her step, which she is trying to __2__. A human might not notice that something is wrong __3__ the machine picks it up.

"AI can replace __4__ watching cows," says Terry Canning, co-founder and chief executive (联合创始人兼首席执行官) of CattleEye. His firm's technology automatically (自动地) detects (检测) __5__ signs of lameness in cattle (牛). It is only available in milking sheds, for now, but is already being rolled out on dairy (生产乳品的) farms. About 20,000 cows now are under the system's (系统) watch. Lame cows __6__ less milk. If they cannot be treated in time, they will end up being __7__.

Yet, there are lots of farms that have not yet used these __8__. Dr. Sarah Lloyd, her husband and her family, __9__ a farm with about 400 cows. All of the __10__ they produce goes for cheese (奶酪) production.

"The __11__ of the technology just can't be covered by our milk price," Sarah says. Her husband prefers to work "with his sleeves (袖子) rolled up" __12__ depend on machines.

Others take a __13__ view. Dr. Jeffrey Bewley said that lameness is something that cows naturally try to hide __14__ they have evolved as prey (猎物) animals. So technology that helps the farmer find the earliest signs of lameness could be __15__.

原创试题

1. A. business   B. road
   C. look   D. step
2. A. hide   B. change
   C. treat   D. move
3. A. but   B. so
   C. if   D. and
4. A. cows   B. animals
   C. human   D. machines
5. A. late   B. early
   C. natural   D. popular
6. A. improve   B. study
   C. produce   D. try
7. A. put out   B. taken out
   C. knocked out D. found out
8. A. inventions B. technologies
   C. firms   D. activities
9. A. run   B. develop
   C. give   D. invite
10. A. meat   B. water
    C. juice   D. milk
11. A. money   B. cost
    C. sign   D. idea
12. A. more than B. rather than
    C. other than D. less than
13. A. same   B. different
    C. perfect   D. terrible
14. A. yet   B. though
    C. or   D. because
15. A. interesting B. strict
    C. useful   D. wrong

词汇碎片

nearby *adj.* 附近的；近处的   **replace** *v.* 替代   **sign** *n.* 迹象；标志   **prefer** *v.* 更喜爱；宁可

重难句讲解

It is only available in milking sheds, for now, but is already being rolled out on dairy farms. 目前，这项技术只适用于挤奶棚，但已经在奶牛场进行推广。

本句是 but 连接的并列句。but 后句子的主语为 it，被省略；roll out 意为"正式推出（新产品）；把……展开"；dairy farm 意为"奶牛场"。

Tuesday B 阅读理解

Are you looking for some new apps (应用程序)? We got you covered with the best new Android apps in February!

Auto Redial Price: Free / Up to $3.49 ★★★★☆ 3.3 7516 Ratings	What's cool: It basically (基本上) auto redials (自动重拨) a number for you if the number you were trying to dial was busy or wasn't picked up. The app saves numbers you've redialed, and you can stop it at any time. The app size isn't too ridiculous (荒谬的).
Celebrations Passport Price: Free / $19.99 per year ★★★★☆ 3.7 45 Ratings	What's cool: Celebrations Passport is a new app. It lets you put together gift baskets or other things like that for different occasions (场合) like Mother's Day. You can add flowers, cookies and other pretty things. The app is generally free to use. However, there is a $19.99 per year subscription (订阅费) that gives you things like free shipping and other benefits (福利).
Magic Photo Editor Price: Free ★★★★☆ 3.4 5 Ratings	What's cool: Magic Photo Editor is a basic photo editor (编辑器). It lets you edit various photo things on your phone. However, the app does have a rather aggressive advertising strategy that a lot of people won't like. If the developers (开发者) give users an option (选择) to pay to remove (除去) ads, this could be a really great photo editor.

If we missed any great new Android apps, tell us about them in the comments area! You can also click (点击) here to check out our latest Android apps and game lists!

Thank you for reading!

1. What does the underlined phrase "picked up" mean in Chinese?
   A. 接收   B. 捡起
   C. 接听   D. 学会
2. Which app is completely free?
   A. Auto Redial.
   B. Celebrations Passport.
   C. Magic Photo Editor.
   D. All of the above.
3. Which of the following is TRUE about the app Celebrations Passport?
   A. It is very popular.
   B. It has a regular size.
   C. It is usually used for festivals.
   D. It has an aggressive advertising strategy.
4. According to the material, we can know that _____.
   A. the author is introducing the best three Android apps in 2022
   B. the author has missed out some great Android apps
   C. the author likes Magic Photo Editor best
   D. the author is giving a full description of these apps
5. What is this material probably chosen from?
   A. An official website.
   B. A piece of newspaper.
   C. An advertisement.
   D. A book report.

cover v. 覆盖；掩护 basket n. 篮子 aggressive adj. 气势汹汹的；侵略的 advertising n. 广告活动；广告业

However, the app does have a rather aggressive advertising strategy that a lot of people won't like. 但是，该应用程序的广告策略确实比较激进，很多人都不喜欢这一点。

本句是复合句。主句是 the app does have a rather aggressive advertising strategy。that 引导定语从句，修饰 advertising strategy。本句中 does 表强调，其单复数形式与主语保持一致。

A team of Japanese scientists has created a new face mask (口罩). It will glow (发光) under UV light (紫外线) and show traces (踪迹) of the COVID-19 virus (病毒) if the wearer is infected (感染).

Scientists from the Kyoto Prefectural University say that the masks they've made have an additional filter (过滤片) inside them. When sprayed (喷) with a fluorescent dye (荧光染料) with antibodies (抗体), the filter will glow when placed under UV light if traces of the COVID-19 virus are discovered.

The team developed this method by first injecting (注射) an inactive (灭活的) form of the COVID-19 virus into ostriches (鸵鸟). From there, they worked to get antibodies from the eggs of these ostriches, putting these antibodies into the fluorescent spray.

A Japanese researcher said that his team did some experiments with 32 people who had COVID-19. They found that the masks worn by these 32 testers glowed brightly and showed traces of the COVID-19 virus after being sprayed with the antibody spray and held under a UV light. His team also noted that the glow was gone over time as the patients got better and their viral load (病毒载量) decreased.

The researcher plans to try the mask on 150 testers in the team's next round of testing and hopes to get the green light from the Japanese government to sell the masks in 2022.

1. The wearer in Paragraph 1 refers to _____.
   A. people who get a cold
   B. people who are not infected
   C. people who wear the new face mask
   D. people who wear the normal mask
2. Which of the following statements is NOT TRUE?
   A. The new mask will glow under UV light if the wearer is healthy.
   B. The team tried to inject an active form of the virus into ostriches.
   C. The antibodies were taken out from ostriches.
   D. All of the above.
3. The underlined word "decreased" in Paragraph 4 probably means "_____" in Chinese.
   A. 降低   B. 升高
   C. 正常   D. 活跃
4. What does "get the green light" in the last paragraph mean?
   A. Get destroyed.
   B. Get suspended (暂停).
   C. Get hurt.
   D. Get approved (批准).
5. What is the purpose of the passage ?
   A. To show how the new mask works.
   B. To find out how to prevent the virus.
   C. To study the influences of the COVID-19 virus.
   D. To introduce a new mask made by Japanese scientists.

researcher n. 研究者   experiment n. 试验；实验   patient n. 病人   government n. 政府

It will glow under UV light and show traces of the COVID-19 virus if the wearer is infected. 如果佩戴者感染了新型冠状病毒，这款口罩就会在紫外线下发光，并且显示病毒的踪迹。

本句是复合句。主句是 It will glow under UV light and show traces of the COVID-19 virus，是 and 连接的并列句。if the wearer is infected 是 if 引导的条件状语从句。

Thursday D 阅读理解

Small rocks impact (撞击) all the time. Something the size of a small car hits Earth's atmosphere (大气层) about once a year, according to NASA, but they burn up in the atmosphere and explode (爆炸) well before they hit the ground. When this happens, no one really notices. Some people may even think that the scene is really cool, since these rocks cause what we call meteors (流星)—the "shooting stars" we enjoy watching on a dark, clear night.

NASA is testing a new technique (技术) called Double Asteroid Redirection Test (双小行星重定向测试), or DART. It might be used if a large asteroid is going to hit Earth. It's expected to test whether hitting an asteroid with a spacecraft (航天器) can change the rock's <u>trajectory</u> enough to avoid an impact with the earth, given enough time.

An American scientist compares Americans' risk of dying from different causes. Dying from an asteroid impact is about 1 in 75,000. However, the chances of being killed in an asteroid impact shouldn't keep you up at night. The chances that an American would die from a plane crash (坠毁) are 1 in 30,000, and 1 in 60,000 die from a tornado (龙卷风); either of those fates (命运) is much more likely to be the cause of your death than an asteroid impact.

1. In the first paragraph, it is clear that _____.
   A. most rocks can reach Earth's ground
   B. asteroids hit Earth's atmosphere regularly
   C. small rocks never hit Earth before
   D. rocks impact is caused by meteors

2. The underlined word "trajectory" in Paragraph 2 probably means "_____" in Chinese.
   A. 轨道   B. 面积
   C. 重量   D. 成分

3. Which of the following statements is NOT TRUE about DART?
   A. It has already gone into service.
   B. It aims to avoid an asteroid impact.
   C. It is being tested by NASA.
   D. It is a new technology.

4. Which of the following is TRUE according to Paragraph 3?
   A. No one has yet been killed in an asteroid impact.
   B. American could more probably die from a tornado than from a plane crash.
   C. There will be no more asteroid impacts.
   D. The risk of dying from an asteroid impact is very low.

5. What does the writer mainly want to tell us?
   A. The small rocks cause meteors.
   B. An asteroid impact always causes many problems.
   C. American could die from different causes.
   D. We shouldn't worry too much about the asteroid impact.

scene *n.* 景象；场景   avoid *v.* 避免   risk *n.* 风险

However, the chances of being killed in an asteroid impact shouldn't keep you up at night. 然而，被小行星撞击致死的概率不应该让你夜不能寐。

本句是简单句。However 是副词，表示转折，位于句首时，需用逗号将其与句子隔开；keep sb. up at night 意为"使某人夜不能寐"。

Friday E 短文填空

The (1) _____ global climate (全球气候) is an increasing threat (威胁) to transportation. Queensland's floods (洪水) of 2010 destroyed 19,000 km of roads, including those needed for emergency vehicles.

Since then, Queensland has been using foamed bitumen (泡沫沥青). It injects (注入) a small (2) _____ of air and cold water into hot bitumen. The bitumen then expands (扩大) and forms a water-resistant layer (防水层). The result is a stronger yet flexible (柔韧的) road surface that is better (3) _____ to withstand (承受) flooding.

One of the biggest (4) _____ with roads is that they are easily destroyed by high temperatures. Extreme heat can soften roads, (5) _____ more cracks (裂缝) or surface depressions (凹地). One solution is heat shields (隔热层). They can lighten the color of streets and reflect (反射) solar radiation (太阳辐射). Some of these heat-shield roads could reduce (降低) the surface temperature by up to 10°C.

Ahead of the 2020 Olympics, Tokyo tried solar-blocking paint (防晒涂料). By the end of 2020, solar-blocking paint had been used on nearly three million square meters of the country's road surfaces. While such paint might protect the road surface, it could make life more uncomfortable for people passing by.

阅读短文，从下列选项中选出能填入文中空白处的最佳选项，选项中有两项为多余选项。

A. changeable

B. able

C. up to

D. chances

E. problems

F. leading to

G. amount

Saturday F 短文填空

If you don't want to cook your family's Christmas Day dinner, now you can get a robot chef to do everything. A (1) n_____ of tech firms are now developing robots that can cook, both in commercial and home kitchens.

To help develop the robot, Moley employed (雇用) the services of professional chef Tim Anderson, who back in 2011 (2) w_____ the BBC's MasterChef TV competition. He explains how he would make (3) d_____, and the robot would be programmed to copy his movement.

"I would (4) c_____ through the recipe in a kitchen with a layout (布局) to that of the Moley kitchen, and my movements would be recorded, and then transferred (转移) onto the robotic hands and arms," says Mr. Anderson.

"Those (5) m_____ would then be streamlined (精简) by the robotics team, and in the end, we ended up with a consistent (一致的) program that would produce the (6) s_____ dish every time."

Mikaela Pisani Leal is a scientist in machine learning. She says robot chefs offer restaurants lots of benefits (好处). "These robots could reduce viruses (减少病毒) in food, (7) i_____ cleanliness and hygiene (卫生)... they could turn the industry on its head." But she also warns they could (8) r_____ in job losses.

Wesley Smalley, an owner and head chef of a fine dining restaurant, says that (9) w_____ kitchen robots offer convenience, they won't be of interest to the higher end of the market (高端市场).

Yet for many of us who (10) w_____ like to do the cooking at home on Christmas Day, kitchen robots are a good thought.

词汇碎片
chef n. 厨师　　industry n. 行业；产业　　convenience n. 便利

重难句讲解
To help develop the robot, Moley employed the services of professional chef Tim Anderson, who back in 2011 who the BBC's MasterChef TV competition. 为了帮助开发这款机器人，莫雷公司聘请了专业厨师蒂姆·安德森，他在2011年赢得了BBC《厨艺大师》电视比赛的冠军。

本句是复合句。who引导定语从句，修饰Tim Anderson；不定式短语To help develop the robot 在句首表目的；help do sth. 意为"帮助做某事"。

Week Ten 人物传奇

Monday A 完形填空

| 体裁 | 记叙文 | 题材 | 人物传奇 | 正确率 | ___/10 | 词数 | 233 |
| 难度 | ★★★★☆ | 建议用时 | 12分钟 | 实际用时 | ___ | 答案页码 | 112 |

  Xu Shixiao was born in a small county in a mountainous (多山的) area in Jiangxi. Before becoming a __1__, Xu couldn't even swim since her hometown is surrounded (围绕) by __2__.

  In 2005, a rowing coach came to __3__ potential (有潜力的) paddlers (皮划艇运动员) in her school. The 13-year-old Xu, who was much taller than her friends, attracted his __4__. "Every day my canoe (皮划艇) __5__ many times. I drank lots of water in rivers," recalls (回忆) Xu of her first canoeing training.

  In 2013, the news that women's canoeing was still not an Olympic event (赛事) gave her a heavy __6__. There were no Olympic Games and no competitions. Xu's coach suggested she should either change to another sport or __7__. It was __8__ for her to change the sport at age 21. Xu gave up on canoeing and found her first job as a saleswoman in a furniture company.

  Five years ago, she was surprised to get a __9__ from her former coach, asking about her willingness (意愿) to return to canoeing and compete in the Tokyo Olympic Games. Xu quickly made her decision and went back to training three days later.

  On August 7th, 2021, Xu and her __10__, Sun Mengya, won gold in the women's canoe double 500m event at the Tokyo Games. It was also the first Olympic gold medal for China in the event.

1. A. paddler   B. swimmer
 C. runner   D. high jumper
2. A. rivers   B. lakes
 C. mountains   D. clouds
3. A. look around   B. look up
 C. look for   D. look back
4. A. attention   B. discussion
 C. interest   D. conversation
5. A. got over   B. came over
 C. took over   D. turned over
6. A. blow   B. sigh
 C. hand   D. project
7. A. continue   B. retire
 C. decide   D. celebrate
8. A. possible   B. impossible
 C. enjoyable   D. believable
9. A. call   B. gift
 C. secret   D. look
10. A. sister   B. brother
 C. partner   D. mother

词汇碎片

rowing n. 划艇运动；划船　　coach n. 教练　　compete in 参加（比赛、竞赛）

重难句讲解

Xu quickly made her decision and went back to training three days later. 徐诗晓很快就做出了决定，三天后她就重返训练场了。
本句是and连接的并列句。make one's decision 意为"做决定"；go back to 中的 to 在这里是介词，故 train 要用 -ing 形式。

Tuesday B 阅读理解

To the students of Class 3:

English writing test will be on June 22nd, 8:30 am-10:00 am. The test is based on (基于) Passage One, Unit Two.

Passage One:

Bibian Mentel-Spee was a snowboarder (单板滑雪者) who died in March 2021 at the age of 48. She was also a pioneer (先驱), one of the driving forces behind the inclusion (包含) of her sport in the Winter Paralympics (残奥会).

Mentel-Spee's journey to becoming a Paralympic legend (传奇人物) began during her campaign (战役；运动) to qualify (取得资格) for the Winter Olympics of 2002 in Salt Lake City. She was a successful snowboarder and on course for the Games when she was diagnosed with bone cancer in her lower right leg at the age of 29. They had to cut her leg off.

The sport was then in its infancy (初期). There was little infrastructure (基础设施), no common rules, and no global (全球的) competitions. So with a group of other para-snowboarders from around the world, she set to work. Together they organized a World Cup circuit (巡回赛), arranged sponsorship (赞助), lobbied officials (游说官员) and tried to keep the sport in the public eye. She decided to prove that her sport belonged to the top table. After more than eight years of campaigning, she got a phone call to say that snowboarding would be on the schedule (日程安排) at the 2014 Paralympic Games in Sochi.

After you complete the writing task, you will be given 5-10 minutes to read it and check for mistakes. In particular, pay attention to:

incorrect use of tenses;
wrong expressions

1. When will the English writing test be held?

   A. On March 22nd.
   B. On June 22nd.
   C. On March 23rd.
   D. On June 23rd.

2. What does the underlined word "diagnosed" mean in Chinese?

   A. 合格
   B. 对话
   C. 计算
   D. 诊断

3. What difficulties did Mentel-Spee and her friends have during the campaign?

   A. Little infrastructure.
   B. No common rules.
   C. No global competitions.
   D. All of the above.

---

complete v. 完成   mistake n. 错误   in particular 尤其，特别   incorrect adj. 错误的

She decided to prove that her sport belonged to the top table. 她下决心要证明单板滑雪运动属于顶级赛事。
本句是复合句。that 引导宾语从句，作 prove 的宾语；belong to 意为"属于"。

Wednesday C 阅读理解

Rafael Nadal won 16 of his 21 Grand Slam titles (大满贯冠军) with his uncle Toni as head coach. From the first ball Toni Nadal threw to his three-year-old nephew (侄子), he could see there was something different about this kid. "Normally, when I sent a ball to a small kid, he stood and waited until the ball arrived. But my nephew went looking for it. This was special." Toni shaped him as a player and a person. As Rafael has so often acknowledged (承认), it is doubtful he would have achieved success without his uncle Toni.

"I demanded (要求) a lot from Rafael because I cared a lot," says Toni. Rafael has said his uncle used to shout and try to frighten (使害怕) him. If the young boy's mind <u>drifted off</u> while they were on the court, Toni used to knock balls towards him. At the end of practice, Toni asked Rafael to pick up all the balls and sweep the red dirt (尘土). If he forgot his water bottle, he had to train without drinking any water in the hot sun. In his book, Rafael wrote, "(Even though) Toni was making me nervous, I knew I had a good thing going with him. Toni was right. So often infuriating (令人生气的) but, in the long run, right."

When Rafael won his 10th French Open title (法国网球公开赛冠军)—Toni's final French Open as his coach—this uncle came to court to present the trophy (奖杯). Pride shone across his face, and love between the pair showed as they shared a tight hug (紧紧的拥抱).

1. What is the second paragraph mainly about?
   A. Achievements Toni has made.
   B. Bad feelings Rafael had for his uncle.
   C. Difficulties Toni has been through.
   D. The way Toni trained the young Rafael.

2. What does the underlined phrase "drifted off" in Paragraph 2 mean in Chinese?
   A. 渐渐离去
   B. 匆匆而来
   C. 兴奋起来
   D. 困惑不已

3. Which of the following can best describe uncle Toni?
   A. Brave.
   B. Strict.
   C. Smart.
   D. Scary.

词汇碎片

different *adj.* 不同的   doubtful *adj.* 怀疑的，不确定的   court *n.* 球场

重难句讲解

Normally, when I sent a ball to a small kid, he stood and waited until the ball arrived. 通常情况下，当我给一个小孩扔球时，他会站着等球被送到他身边。

本句是复合句。when 引导时间状语从句，主句是 he stood and waited；until 也引导时间状语从句，意为"直到……才"。

Thursday D 阅读理解

Nguyen Phat Tri, a young hairstylist (发型师) from Vietnam, has been getting a lot of attention for his eye-catching floral (花卉的) hair designs.

The 28-year-old Nguyen Phat Tri graduated from An Giang University, with a degree in biotechnology (生物技术), in 2015. As he was always into the arts, he decided to go to Ho Chi Minh City (胡志明市) to study makeup and hairdressing. He made a name for himself on the Vietnamese hairstyling scene, thanks to some truly creative techniques and designs.

Nguyen Phat Tri's designs have millions of views on social media, but few people can realize just how much work goes into each one of them. The simplest design takes 1 to 2 days to complete, but the most complex (复杂的) of them can take 2 to 3 months to complete.

Despite the lucrative (获利多的) business, Nguyen Phat Tri usually turns down more requests than he accepts (接受), because he prefers to spend his time researching new designs and techniques. "I want to inspire (激发) creativity in people who share my passion (热情), and I hope to help Vietnam's hair industry grow and reach the world," he said.

Asked what advice he would offer to young stylists, the Vietnamese artist said that the most important thing for them is to assess (评估) their talent because this is a field that requires an "artistic eye". Then, they need to have passion, perseverance (毅力) and determination (决心) to go after their dream.

1. Nguyen Phat Tri studied makeup and hair-dressing after graduation because _____.
   A. his parents asked him to do so
   B. he wanted to make good money
   C. he was really interested in the art
   D. biotechnology was too hard for him

2. The underlined phrase "made a name for himself" in Paragraph 2 is closest to _____ in meaning.
   A. looking for help
   B. achieving nothing
   C. donating a lot of money
   D. becoming well-known

3. What do we know about Nguyen Phat Tri's designs?
   A. There are only a few views of his designs on social media.
   B. Most people have a clear idea about his work.
   C. The simplest design takes a few hours to complete.
   D. The most complex design can take months to complete.

4. Why does Nguyen Phat Tri turn down a lot of requests?
   A. Because he has not prepared well.
   B. Because he wants to ask for more money.
   C. Because he wants to spend more time on video games.
   D. Because he wants to spend more time researching new designs.

词汇碎片

design n. 设计   request n. 请求；需求   research v. 研究，探索

重难句讲解

As he was always into the arts, he decided to go to Ho Chi Minh City to study makeup and hairdressing. 由于他一直对艺术有浓厚的兴趣，他决定去胡志明市学习化妆和美发。

本句是复合句。As 引导原因状语从句，表示原因；be into something/somebody 表示"对某事物/某人很感兴趣；喜欢某事物/某人"。

Lata Mangeshkar, who has died on February 6th, 2022. She was an Indian cultural icon (标志) and national treasure who made her name in Bollywood (宝莱坞). For decades (几十年), the "nightingale (夜莺) of Bollywood" was the country's most popular singer. Every top actress wanted her to sing their songs.

Lata Mangeshkar was born in the central Indian city of Indore in 1929. She was never formally (正式地) educated. Since there wasn't enough singing in films in the early 1940s, young Lata turned to acting to earn a living. By 1947, she has been making her living acting in films, but she wasn't happy. "I never liked it—the makeup (化妆), the lights. People ordering you about, say this dialogue, say that dialogue, I felt so uncomfortable," she told one interviewer later. Lata sang her first full song in the film *Mahal* in 1949 and was noticed right away. Over the next four decades, she sang memorable and popular songs in a lot of films.

Lata was good enough to challenge the top male (男性的) singers. "I am a self-made (白手起家的) person. I have learned how to fight. I am quite fearless. But I never imagined I would get as much as I have," she once said. Her everlasting (永恒的) music certainly brought happiness to millions of Indians and became the soundtrack (电影配音) to their lives.

1. Lata Mangeshkar died at the age of _____.
   A. 80   B. 85
   C. 90   D. 93
2. What can we learn from the passage?
   A. Mangeshkar loved acting.
   B. Mangeshkar was well-educated.
   C. Mangeshkar was famous for her acting.
   D. Mangeshkar was important for many Indian people.
3. Paragraph 2 is written in the order of _____.
   A. space
   B. time
   C. persons
   D. direction
4. What can we infer (推断) from "became the soundtrack to their lives" in the last paragraph?
   A. Mangeshkar was a good actress.
   B. Mangeshkar sang for many films.
   C. Mangeshkar set a good example for Indians.
   D. Mangeshkar's music had a great influence on Indian people's lives.

Saturday F 任务型阅读

I'm a professional freeskier (自由式滑雪者). Or the last 10 of my 18 years, I've gone after a love affair (事情) with fear.

Like all fascinating (迷人的) lovers, this important other can be… changeable. "Fear" is really a term for three different feelings: excitement, uncertainty (无把握), and pressure. I've learned that the small signs of each of these feelings can be helpful to success when noticed and positively used.

It's easy to think of extreme sports athletes as fearless or capricious (任性的). It's biologically counterintuitive (违反直觉的) for us to place ourselves in positions of risk. Instead of running away from fear, we build a particular relationship with it by developing a sense of self-awareness (自我意识) and making risk assessments (评估).

As I become a big girl, I'm proud of the work I've done to deal with the pressure of "prove yourself" by boosting my self-esteem (增强自尊) and making my need for expectations weaker. I focus on the joy this sport brings me.

Though my views of myself and the world are changing, one thing is for certain: no matter how much time passes, I'll always be a hopeless romantic (浪漫主义者) when it comes to fear.

阅读短文，回答下面1~3小题。

1. What feelings does "fear" have in the writer's opinion?

_____

2. What do people usually think of extreme sports athletes?

_____

3. How does the writer deal with the pressure?

_____

词汇碎片

extreme adj. 极端的；极度的   risk n. 风险   particular adj. 特殊的；独特的

重难句讲解

I've learned that the small signs of each of these feelings can be helpful to success when noticed and positively used. 我了解到，当你注意到这些迹象并积极运用这些感觉时，它们能够帮助你成功。

本句是复合句。that 引导宾语从句，作 learned 的宾语，其中 the small signs of each of these feelings 是宾语从句的主语；when noticed and positively used 是宾语从句中的状语；be helpful to 意为"对……有帮助"。

Week Eleven 旅行交通

Monday A 完形填空

| 体裁 | 说明文 | 题材 | 旅行交通 | 正确率 | ___/10 | 词数 | 192 |
| 难度 | ★★★☆☆ | 建议用时 | 10分钟 | 实际用时 | ___ | 答案页码 | 114 |

Chioggia, Italy

Chioggia was built on a __1__ of islands in the Venetian Lagoon (威尼斯潟湖), with centuries-old buildings rising from the rivers. Today, Chioggia is popular with Italian and German __2__. They are attracted both by the architectural (建筑的) beauties in the historic center and the family-friendly beaches of Sottomarina. The city can serve as a __3__ base for bicycle tours.

Queens, New York

Queens wants you to show up __4__. It may be the only place where you can try the home cooking of __5__ 150 different countries in such a small space. The Queens restaurant industry was influenced by COVID-19, but now it's getting __6__.

Zihuatanejo, Mexico

This beach town—the neighbor of Ixtapa, the resort destination (度假胜地) on the Pacific Coast—and communities around it have developed environmental projects that travelers can __7__. The conservation nonprofit (非营利性保护组织) Whales of Guerrero has helped train fishermen as whale-watching __8__. Campamento Tortuguero Ayotlcalli __9__ opportunities to join turtle nest patrols (海龟巢巡逻) and let the little ones go. You can also check into Playa Viva, 50 miles south. The solar-powered (太阳能的) resort has helped save the nearby village of Juluchuca __10__ providing education and employment (就业) in conservation and tourism.

1. A. piece   B. group
   C. kind   D. cup
2. A. policemen   B. businessmen
   C. visitors   D. workers
3. A. terrible   B. unpleasant
   C. perfect   D. scary
4. A. hungry   B. thirsty
   C. sad   D. calm
5. A. more than   B. less than
   C. other than   D. rather than
6. A. crazy   B. difficult
   C. worse   D. better
7. A. come in   B. join in
   C. take in   D. break in
8. A. farmers   B. teachers
   C. actors   D. guides
9. A. offers   B. throws
   C. changes   D. develops
10. A. on   B. by
    C. at   D. before

词汇碎片

industry n. 产业   community n. 社区   opportunity n. 机会   provide v. 提供

重难句讲解

They are attracted both by the architectural beauties in the historic center and the family-friendly beaches of Sottomarina. 他们都被历史中心的建筑美景和索托马里纳适合家庭欢聚的海滩深深吸引着。

本句是被动句。be attracted by 意为"被……吸引";family-friendly 意为"适合家庭的"。

Tuesday B 阅读理解

According to the report, the number of winter leisure (休闲) tourists in China will reach 305 million in the 2021-2022 ice and snow season. Ice and snow tourism has changed from a new "fashionable lifestyle" to an important part of people's everyday lives in China.

Harbin	Zhangjiakou
1. Harbin International Ice and Snow Festival: snowfield football match; ice sculpture (冰雕) exhibitions. 2. The theme park "Harbin Ice and Snow World": large ice and snow sculptures.	1. Owning the largest natural ski (滑雪) areas in Northern China. 2. One of the main competition venues (竞赛场馆) for the Beijing 2022 Winter Olympics Games. 3. Chongli Ice Snow Resort (旅游胜地): a national level tourist resort.
Hulun Buir	Urumqi
1. Known as "the frozen city". 2. Lots of ice and snow sports facilities (设施): providing venues for speed skating and short track speed skating (短道速滑) training. 3. The Nadam Fair (那达慕大会): combining activities such as horse riding and archery (射箭) with winter-themed activities.	1. The Silk Road International Ski Resort: located in the Tianshan Mountains with a snow-making system (系统). 2. The winter sports scene: horse racing. 3. The Urumqi Silk Road Snow and Ice Festival: a New Year concert, snow-themed light show, folk song and dance performances.

1. Where could you do the horse riding?
   A. Harbin.
   B. Zhangjiakou.
   C. Hulun Buir.
   D. Hulun Buir and Urumqi.

2. If you want to enjoy large ice and snow sculptures, you can go to _____.
   A. Harbin Ice and Snow World
   B. Chongli Ice Snow Resort
   C. The Nadam Fair
   D. The Urumqi Silk Road Snow and Ice Festival

3. What will you see when you are in Zhangjiakou?
   A. Horse riding.
   B. Natural ski areas.
   C. Large ice sculptures.
   D. Folk song and dance performances.

according to 根据　　million num. 百万　　combine v. 组合；结合　　folk adj. 民俗的；传统民间的

Ice and snow tourism has changed from a new "fashionable lifestyle" to an important part of people's everyday lives in China. 冰雪旅游已经从一种新的"时尚生活方式"转变为中国人民日常生活的重要组成部分。

本句是简单句。change from... to... 意为"从……转变为……"；an important part of... 意为"……的重要组成部分"。

Wednesday C 阅读理解

"There are many places in the world that I love but Dalarna stole my heart completely," Mirka Mati told us.

Dalarna is a province in central Sweden. The word "Dalarna" means "valleys (山谷)". The area is a vacation destination (目的地) for Swedes from the south, who often travel there for summer vacations, attracted by its fishing lakes, campgrounds, and forests.

Cross-country skiing (越野滑雪) is a perfect way to discover Dalarna's mountains! Grövelsjön in the north of Dalarna offers some of Sweden's finest cross-country skiing. Stay in a comfortable cottage (小屋), a hostel (青年旅舍) or a four-star hotel, then get up for breakfast and set off once more.

Outdoor cooking is a typical Swedish experience. Do it fearlessly in winter to be even more like a local! You can grill (烧烤) some sausages (香肠) on a break from cross-country skiing. Or dig (挖掘) a snow pit, so you can relax and enjoy the crackling (噼啪声) of the fire as the food cooks. You can also try dog sledding (狗拉雪橇). Lots of places in the northern part of Dalarna offer those tours.

Meeting the reindeer (驯鹿) is another fascinating choice. Reindeer walk freely in the countryside around Idre in northern Dalarna. Idre is home to Sweden's southernmost Sami village and an ideal place to experience and learn about Sami culture.

Let's discover all that Dalarna has offered to make the most of this winter in Sweden.

1. Which country does Dalarna belong to?
   A. Italy. B. Canada.
   C. France. D. Sweden.
2. The activities that visitors can enjoy in winter in Dalarna are _____.
   ①skiing
   ②outdoor cooking
   ③meeting the reindeer
   ④surfing
   A. ①②③ B. ①②④
   C. ②③④ D. ①③④
3. Which of the following statement about Dalarna is TRUE?
   A. Dalarna only attracts Swedes from the south.
   B. Dalarna's mountains are perfect for skiing.
   C. You can't try dog sledding in Dalarna.
   D. Dalarna is a province in northern Idre.
4. What does the author most probably do?
   A. He is a designer.
   B. He is a tour guide.
   C. He is a teacher.
   D. He is a skiing instructor.

---

steal v. 偷窃   completely adv. 完全地   perfect adj. 完美的   fascinating adj. 极有吸引力的；迷人的

The area is a vacation destination for Swedes from the south, who often travel there for summer vacations, attracted by its fishing lakes, campgrounds, and forests. 这个地区是南方的瑞典人的度假胜地，他们夏天经常去那里度假，那里的钓鱼湖、露营地和森林吸引着他们。

本句是复合句。主句是 The area is a vacation destination for Swedes from the south；who 引导定语从句，修饰 Swedes from the south；attracted by 意为"被……吸引"。

Thursday D 阅读理解

The long, lonely Dempster Highway is considered to be one of Canada's toughest (艰难的) roads. The road is unpaved (未铺砌的). You can't make a phone call there. There's only one petrol station (加油站) around halfway (在中途) along. Anyone who drives on it needs to be prepared for bad things to happen, as I found out myself.

Small stones flew from beneath (在……下方) my wheels as I pressed on the south. It was not hunger or thirst that worried me. I was scared of wildfires, which have become increasingly common in the Canadian Arctic in summer, caused by lightning storms.

It began to rain. Then the spatter (溅；洒) of raindrops on my windows became a deluge (洪水). Before long, the car skidded sideways (侧滑) because of the mud (泥).

"It's happened a couple of times," the waitress at the motel's restaurant said, looking around the largely empty dining room. "The driver went too fast on mud and slid right off the side. It's like driving on ice."

Now, I'm on my way back to Dawson City. As I stood on the Klondike Highway some 40 km east of Dawson City, my car broke down. It was possible that rescuers (救援人员) would not drive by for hours. However, not for long, a good man picked me up. As he drove me to Dawson City, I realized that this had been part of the Dempster's <u>charm</u> all along: that whenever I'd come close to bad things, luck smiled on me.

Perhaps Canada's toughest road wasn't so tough after all.

1. What makes Dempster Highway one of the toughest roads in Canada?
   A. Unpaved road.
   B. Unable to make a call.
   C. Only one petrol station around halfway along.
   D. All of the above.

2. When the author was on the Dempster Highway, what worried him was _____.
   A. wildfires   B. hunger
   C. thirst   D. wild bears

3. Which of the following is the correct order to describe author's journey?
   a. The car skidded sideways.
   b. The author met with a waitress.
   c. A man drove the author to Dawson City.
   d. The car broke down.
   A. a-b-c-d   B. a-c-b-d
   C. a-b-d-c   D. b-a-c-d

4. The underlined word "charm" in Paragraph 5 is closest in meaning to _____.
   A. problem   B. beauty
   C. difficulty D. journey

---

consider v. 认为；考虑   common adj. 常见的；通常的

I was scared of wildfires, which have become increasingly common in the Canadian Arctic in summer, caused by lightning storms. 我害怕的是雷雨引起的野火，这种野火在加拿大北极地区的夏天越来越常见了。

本句是复合句。主句是 I was scared of wildfires；which 引导定语从句，修饰先行词 wildfires；caused by lightning storms 是过去分词短语作后置定语，修饰 wildfires。

Friday E 任务型阅读

体 裁	说明文	题 材	旅行交通	正确率	___/4	词 数	193
难 度	★★★★☆	建议用时	6分钟	实际用时		答案页码	115

The Tibet Autonomous Region (西藏自治区) received more than 41 million tourists last year, and tourism revenues (收入) were over 44 billion (十亿) yuan. Tibet has been a popular tourist attraction for tourists from home and abroad for years due to its rich heritage (遗产), natural sights and traditional cultures.

In recent years, the region has been busy with improving the quality of services for tourists. Cultural products and incentives (激励) have already been introduced (推行), which are good for both visitors and business operators (经营者). The region received more than 150 million tourists from 2016 to 2020. Tourism brought in nearly 213 billion yuan, more than double the amount from 2011 to 2015, according to *Xinhua News Agency* (新华社).

Wang Songping, the head of the region's Department of Tourism Development (旅游发展厅), said that tourism offers a window into the region's features. "Tourism departments should focus on Tibetan culture and natural resources (资源), particularly in rural areas, and allow more rural people to benefit (获益) from tourism," he said.

With its beautiful lakes, mountains, forests and lots of cultural activities, Nyingchi city is a major attraction in Tibet. It is home to 700 hotels owned by rural residents, and received 4 million visits last year.

阅读短文,回答下面1~4小题。

1. What makes Tibet a popular tourist attraction for years?
   _____
   _____

2. What has the region done to improve the quality of services?
   _____
   _____

3. Did tourism bring in more money for the region from 2016 to 2020 than that from 2011 to 2015?
   _____
   _____

4. In Wang's opinion, what should be the focus of tourism departments?
   _____
   _____

词汇碎片

sight *n.* 风景；名胜   product *n.* 产品   feature *n.* 特点；特征   rural *adj.* 农村的，乡村的

重难句讲解

Cultural products and incentives have already been introduced, which are good for both visitors and business operators. 现已推出游客和商户都能从中受益的各种文化产品和奖励措施。

本句是复合句。主句是 Cultural products and incentives have already been introduced；which 引导非限制性定语从句；be good for 意为"有益于；对……有好处"。

Shasta Lake

Shasta Lake is in Northern California and is a three-and-a-half-hour drive from San Francisco. (1) _____ 370 miles of shoreline (海岸线), it's no surprise that renting a houseboat is a popular activity. Visitors can also enjoy the view of Shasta Mountain, which has snow on its peak (山顶) year-round.

Castaic Lake

Castaic Lake is in the northeast of Los Angeles, (2) _____ it is the perfect outdoor area away from the smoggy (烟雾弥漫的) city. There are two main areas, the Upper and Lower lakes, and each one has (3) _____ own set of activities. The (4) _____ lake is reserved (保留) for canoeing (划独木舟), non-power boating and swimming from mid-May to mid-September. The Upper lake is where power boats are allowed, along with other activities (5) _____ as fishing and riding Jet Skis (摩托艇).

Big Bear Lake

Big Bear Lake is (6) _____ great choice for those wanting to take a day trip from Los Angeles. It (7) _____ only two hours to get there from downtown (市中心) Los Angeles. Animal lovers can stop by the Big Bear Alpine Zoo to get an up-close look at the (8) _____. The lake also has many hiking and biking trails along with plenty of fishing spots. Visitors can rent boats at six marinas (码头) around the lake's edge (边缘).

---

rent v. 租，租赁　　allow v. 允许，准许　　stop by 顺便探访

The lake also has many hiking and biking trails along with plenty of fishing spots. 湖附近还有许多登山步道、自行车道和很多钓鱼的地方。

本句是简单句。along with 意为"与……一起"；plenty of 意为"大量，许多"。

Week Twelve 异国风情

Monday A 完形填空

| 体 裁 | 说明文 | 题 材 | 异国风情 | 正确率 | ___/15 | 词 数 | 243 |
| 难 度 | ★★★☆☆ | 建议用时 | 15分钟 | 实际用时 | | 答案页码 | 117 |

On our recent trip to Europe, we spent over half our time in Spain. In my opinion, Spain is one of the world's __1__ countries for food. Having __2__ in the Philippines (菲律宾), Spanish food is very familiar to me. Many Filipino dishes were __3__ introduced (引入；介绍) by Spain or adapted (调整) from Spanish dishes.

Now I'm going to introduce some Spanish tapas. Tapas are appetizers (开胃菜) or __4__ popular in Spanish dishes. They're one of the most __5__ Spanish foods.

1. Tortilla Española

Tortilla española is a Spanish omelette (煎蛋饼) __6__ made with eggs, potatoes, and olive oil (橄榄油). It is often served as tapas or as a side dish. It can be made with __7__. __8__, the addition of onions is often met with controversy (争议). Some believe that onions have no __9__ in a real Spanish tortilla.

2. Calcot

A calcot is a kind of scallion (葱) __10__ in Spanish Catalan dishes. They're __11__ to leeks (韭菜) and are larger and milder (更温和的) in flavor (口感) than a typical green onion. In Spain, the best __12__ for having calcots is in its season, which happens around February and March. Calcots are typically grilled (烧烤) __13__ an open fire and wrapped (包裹) in newspaper to keep them softer.

More than Spanish food itself, what I found the most interesting was the people's eating __14__. Spanish people eat dinner late, around 9-10 pm, because they have long lunches that __15__ anywhere between 2-3 hours.

1. A. better   B. best
   C. worse   D. worst
2. A. put up   B. given up
   C. grown up   D. picked up
3. A. either   B. neither
   C. also   D. or
4. A. snacks   B. animals
   C. soaps   D. drinks
5. A. well-prepared B. well-educated
   C. well-dressed   D. well-known
6. A. carefully   B. quickly
   C. seriously   D. traditionally
7. A. potatoes   B. onions
   C. tomatos   D. eggs
8. A. Therefore   B. However
   C. So   D. And
9. A. place   B. season
   C. trouble   D. money
10. A. thick   B. honest
    C. popular   D. proper
11. A. ready   B. similar
    C. good   D. natural
12. A. thing   B. time
    C. project   D. weather
13. A. behind   B. before
    C. at   D. over
14. A. holidays   B. guides
    C. habits   D. journeys
15. A. take   B. spend
    C. pay   D. find

---

familiar adj. 熟悉的   typical adj. 平常的；典型的   interesting adj. 有趣的

词汇碎片

More than Spanish food itself, what I found the most interesting was the people's eating habits. 除了西班牙食物本身，我发现最有意思的是西班牙人的饮食习惯。

本句是复合句。主语是 what 引导的主语从句 what I found the most interesting。more than 放在名词之前，意为"不只是；不仅仅"；eating habits 意为"饮食习惯"。

重难句讲解

Tuesday B 阅读理解

Flamenco dance (弗拉明戈舞) is a highly-expressive (表现力强的) Spanish dance form. It is also a solo (单独的) dance with features of hand-clapping (拍手), beautiful footwork and body movements. The dance is usually <u>accompanied</u> by a singer and a guitar player.

Flamenco's greatest star—Lola Flores—made the art form internationally become a typical Spanish style.

Flamenco has four different elements (要素): voice, dance, guitar playing, and jaleo which refers to hand-clapping and foot-stomping (跺脚). But perhaps the most interesting flamenco word is *duende*, which in regular speech means elf (精灵) but in the context (语境) of flamenco refers to a mysterious and powerful (强大的) state of emotion and expression which only the most talented flamenco performers have.

Flamenco's fast-paced (快节奏的) Spanish guitar playing is what most outsiders are familiar with, but hand-clapping also plays an important role in the art form. Children who grow up in flamenco-loving families learn the art of hand-clapping and distinguish (区分) between hard and soft claps. In other words, if they can't sing, dance or play guitar, they'll be expected (指望；期待) to at least know how to clap.

1. What does the underlined word "accompanied" in the first paragraph mean in Chinese?
   A. 为……伴舞
   B. 为……而来
   C. 为……付款
   D. 为……伴奏

2. What do we know about flamenco dance from the passage?
   A. Lola Flores invented the dance.
   B. Flamenco dance only appears in Spain.
   C. Singing is one of the four elements of Flamenco.
   D. Duende means elf in the context of flamenco.

3. What's the last paragraph mainly about?
   A. People's favorite element about flamenco dance.
   B. The importance of guitar playing for flamenco dance.
   C. The importance of hand-clapping for flamenco dance.
   D. The life of children in flamenco-loving families.

---

mysterious *adj.* 神秘的   emotion *n.* 情感；情绪   important *adj.* 重要的

词汇碎片

In other words, if they can't sing, dance or play guitar, they'll be expected to at least know how to clap. 换句话说，如果他们不会唱歌、跳舞或弹吉他，他们至少应该知道如何拍手。

本句是复合句。if引导条件状语从句，主句用一般将来时，从句用一般现在时；how to clap 作 know 的逻辑宾语；in other words 意为"换句话说"；be expected to do sth. 意为"被期望做某事"；at least 意为"至少"。

重难句讲解

Wednesday C 阅读理解

| 体裁 | 应用文 | 题材 | 异国风情 | 正确率 | ___/4 | 词数 | 237 |
| 难度 | ★★★☆☆ | 建议用时 | 5分钟 | 实际用时 | ___ | 答案页码 | 118 |

Dear visitors,

  We are excited to announce that Venice's world-famous carnival (狂欢节) is back this year. With some pandemic restrictions (疫情防控) still in place, if you're planning to visit, here are some tips you need to know.

Time

  As is traditional, the 2022 Venice Carnival starts on February 12th (Saturday) and will run until March 1st. The main events (活动) take place over the weekend of February 19th-20th.

  This year's festivities (庆祝活动) will start with a music concert and a theatre program for children, and the Carnival officially opens on Sunday evening.

Events

  1. Venice Wonder Time

  It takes the form of a series (系列) of music, circus (马戏), puppets (木偶), clowns and theatrical displays held on weekends (February 12th-13th and 19th-20th) and from Thursday, February 24th to Tuesday, March 1st in all kinds of locations across the city.

  2. Nebula Solaris

  It is a light and circus show which will take place on the Venetian Arsenal.

COVID-19 Restrictions

  1. You're required to keep a distance of at least 1 meter.

  2. You're required to wear a mask (口罩) which must be of the FFP2 type.

  3. You're required to show a vaccination certificate (疫苗接种证明) or a recovery (康复) certificate showing the holder (持有者) has recovered from Covid in the past six months to watch the Nebula Solaris shows and to enter other events and exhibition spaces.

  Have a good time!

The 2022 Venice Carnival

1. When will the 2022 Venice Carnival officially open?
 A. On February 12th.
 B. On February 13th.
 C. On February 14th.
 D. On February 15th.

2. Which of the following displays can not be watched by visitors at the Venice Wonder Time?
 A. Circus.
 B. Puppets.
 C. The light show.
 D. Theatrical displays.

3. What are the requirements (要求) for taking part in the carnival?
 A. Wearing an FFP2 mask.
 B. Keeping a distance of at least 1 meter.
 C. Getting vaccinated.
 D. All of the above.

4. What type of writing is the passage?
 A. News.
 B. Fiction.
 C. Diary.
 D. Guide.

词汇碎片

announce v. 宣布　　clown n. 小丑　　display n. 表演；展示　　distance n. 距离

重难句讲解

You're required to wear a mask which must be of the FFP2 type. 须佩戴 FFP2 类别口罩。

本句是复合句。主句的主干是 You're required to wear a mask。which must be of the FFP2 type 是 which 引导的定语从句，修饰 mask。be required to do sth. 意为"被要求做某事"。

Thursday D 阅读理解

体裁	记叙文	题材	异国风情	正确率	___/4	词数	229
难度	★★★★☆	建议用时	6分钟	实际用时	___	答案页码	118

Fitting a small stone into a sling (吊索) made of yak wool (牦牛绒), Tsering Stobdan whipped (挥动) his wrist (手腕), sending the object flying across the dry land. This, he told me, was how he protected his sheep and asked them to return. It's just one of the skills he has learned in the last 60 years that allow him to raise his animals in such difficult conditions. Tsering Stobdan is a member of a nomadic group (游牧群体), who for centuries have raised yaks, sheep and goats in northern India, one of the most beautiful—if harsh (环境恶劣的) and wild—places on the earth.

Once <u>flourishing</u>, the nomadic group is now dwindling (衰退). Young people are being sent to nearby cities, where they can find better health care and educational opportunities. Their life is difficult all year. During the longer days of spring and summer, people milk and shear (剪毛) their animals in the early-morning hours before taking them out, often walking more than 12 miles a day at altitude (高地). Another round of milking and shearing takes place in the evening. But the work doesn't end there. Food must be cooked, sheds maintained (修缮棚屋), manure (粪肥) collected.

One of the greatest worries among the district is that their nomadic wisdom (智慧) will be lost in the coming years. Facing a generational exodus (离开), their rich culture collected over centuries, may be gone quickly.

1. How does Tsering Stobdan protect his sheep and ask them to return?
   A. Fitting a small stone into a sling.
   B. Whipping his wrist and letting the sling fly.
   C. Sending the object flying across the land.
   D. All of the above.

2. What can we learn about the nomadic group from this passage?
   A. Young people are leaving.
   B. Young people are coming back.
   C. Its culture will last forever.
   D. People there are living an easy life.

3. What does the underlined word "flourishing" in the second paragraph mean in Chinese?
   A. 荒凉的   B. 繁荣的
   C. 匆忙的   D. 战乱的

4. What is the main idea of this passage?
   A. Tsering Stobdan is skilled in protecting sheep.
   B. People in northern India have raised yaks for centuries.
   C. The life of nomadic people in northern India.
   D. How to raise yaks and sheep.

词汇碎片

century n. 世纪   opportunity n. 机会   take place 发生；举行

重难句讲解

Young people are being sent to nearby cities, where they can find better health care and educational opportunities. 年轻一代被送往附近的城市，在那里他们可以找到更好的医疗和教育机会。

本句是复合句。主句是 Young people are being sent to nearby cities，where 引导的非限制性定语从句修饰 cities。be sent to 意为"被送往"；health care 意为"医疗保健"；educational opportunity 意为"教育机会"。

Friday E 任务型阅读

1. _____

Back in the day, Irish (爱尔兰的) people would whack (重击) bread against doors and walls just before midnight to send any angry spirits (灵魂；精神) away. Whacking bread against the wall is also believed to make sure that your family won't get hungry for the next year.

2. _____

Some people believe that if you clean clothes on January 1st, you'll be "washing for the dead" and someone you love will die at some point in the coming year.

3. _____

According to this New Year's superstition (迷信), nothing should be removed (移开) from your house until after New Year's Day. If you throw something away on January 1st, everyone and everything around you will leave in the year to come.

4. _____

According to Philipine (菲律宾的) tradition, the more noise you make on December 31st, the better. It's also believed that noise helps to drive away evil spirits.

5. _____

In small villages around Japan, young men dress as demons (魔鬼) and go door to door to frighten (使惊恐) lazy people. These scary figures are believed to bring protection from illness and disasters (灾难), as well as a good harvest (丰收) and enough food all year round.

阅读短文，从下列选项中选出能填入文中空白处的最佳选项。选项中有一项为多余选项。

A. Don't even think about washing clothes on New Year's Day.

B. Dress up like a demon.

C. Burn effigies to be away from last year's bad luck.

D. Make lots of noise on New Year's Eve.

E. Don't take away anything until January 2nd.

F. Use bread to scare away spirits that mean you harm.

---

dead *adj.* 死亡的   die *v.* 死亡   throw *v.* 扔；投

Whacking bread against the wall is also believed to make sure that your family won't get hungry for the next year. 据说用面包敲打墙面还能保佑家人在新的一年不会挨饿。

本句是复合句。Whacking bread against the wall 是动名词短语作主语；that 引导一个宾语从句，作 make sure 的宾语。

Saturday F 短文填空

| 体裁 | 记叙文 | 题材 | 异国风情 | 正确率 | ___/10 | 词数 | 193 |
| 难度 | ★★★☆☆ | 建议用时 | 10分钟 | 实际用时 | | 答案页码 | 119 |

Diwali (排灯节), the five-day festival of lights, is one of the most popular (1)_____ (holiday) in India. People celebrate Diwali by (2)_____ (light) little oil lamps (灯) to mark the victory (胜利) of light (3)_____ darkness, and good over evil (邪恶).

Diwali gets its name from the Sanskrit (梵文) word *deepavali*, (4)_____ means "row of clay (黏土) lamps". Many people in India will light these lamps outside (5)_____ (they) homes to symbolize (象征) the inner (内在的) light that protects them (6)_____ spiritual darkness (精神黑暗).

The course of the five days includes cleaning the house, (7)_____ (buy) some new furniture and exchanging gifts (8)_____ loved ones. It also centers on traditions such as buying new kitchen utensils (厨房用具) to help bring good luck, as well (9)_____ other practices to attract the goodwill (善意) of spirits.

In the northern Indian town of Ayodhya, authorities lit about a million lamps along the banks of a river at the festival. Ayodhya is believed to be the birthplace of the Hindu god Lord Rama, and Diwali is (10)_____ (say) to be the day he returned home after destroying a demon. Across India, celebrations include fireworks and music. But amid the festivities, there are also concerns (担心) about air pollution caused by Diwali firecrackers.

阅读短文，在文中空白处填入适当的单词或用括号内单词的适当形式填空，使短文通顺，意思完整。

(1)_____
(2)_____
(3)_____
(4)_____
(5)_____
(6)_____
(7)_____
(8)_____
(9)_____
(10)_____

词汇碎片
row *n.* 一排　　include *v.* 包括，包含　　authority *n.* 当局，官方；权威机构

重难句讲解
Ayodhya is believed to be the birthplace of the Hindu god Lord Rama, and Diwali is said to be the day he returned home after destroying a demon. 阿约提亚被认为是印度神罗摩的诞生地，而排灯节据说是他摧毁恶魔后回家的那一天。

本句是 and 连接的并列句。he returned home after destroying a demon 是省略引导词 that 的定语从句，修饰先行词 the day；be believed to 意为"被认为"；be said to 意为"据说"。

Week Thirteen 自然生态

Monday A 完形填空

| 体 裁 | 记叙文 | 题 材 | 自然生态 | 正 确 率 | ___/10 | 词 数 | 194 |
| 难 度 | ★★★☆☆ | 建议用时 | 10 分钟 | 实际用时 | | 答案页码 | 120 |

In the ice-covered central Arctic Ocean (北冰洋), food on the ground is hard to find. Yet in 2011, when scientists were collecting samples (样本), they found something like a polar bear. __1__ Antje Boetius remembered, it was an almost __2__ piece of sea sponge (海绵). "In this area, you'd have maybe one sponge every square kilometer or so."

The sea sponges were feeding __3__ the fossilized (变成化石的) remains of what used to be an energetic tube worm colony (管状蠕虫群落). It's the first __4__ that scientists have found an animal that __5__ fossils. "The finding is very __6__ because sponges use food sources that other creatures cannot," says the scientist Jasper de Goeij.

They mostly move uphill, where it may be __7__ to catch local currents (水流) carrying little fossilized tube worms. Moving uphill may also make __8__ for the next generation (一代), allowing __9__ sponges to live in spots more protected from currents.

"These sponges have a very __10__ metabolism (新陈代谢)," a scientist says, "so I don't see how they could possibly finish their food here."

1. A. But   B. As   C. Though
2. A. relaxing B. interesting C. surprising
3. A. on   B. to   C. for
4. A. tear   B. team   C. time
5. A. hears   B. eats   C. looks
6. A. cold   B. calm   C. cool
7. A. easier   B. harder   C. longer
8. A. home   B. space   C. money
9. A. bigger   B. thinner C. smaller
10. A. low   B. high   C. fat

词汇碎片

collect v. 采集，收集　　remain n. 剩余（物）；遗迹　　energetic adj. 精力充沛的，充满活力的

重难句讲解

Yet in 2011, when scientists were collecting samples, they found something like a polar bear. 然而在 2011 年，当科学家们正在采集样本的时候，他们发现了类似北极熊的东西。

本句是复合句。句首的 Yet 表示转折；when 引导时间状语从句。

Tuesday B 阅读理解

| 体裁 | 说明文 | 题材 | 自然生态 | 正确率 | ___/5 | 词数 | 179 |
| 难度 | ★★★☆☆ | 建议用时 | 6分钟 | 实际用时 | | 答案页码 | 120 |

The air we breathe, the water we drink, the food we eat—all depend on biodiversity (生物多样性)—the variety (多样化) of all plant and animal life on Earth.

According to new data, biodiversity is reducing (减少) fast, with the UK in the bottom 10% of countries and last among the G7 Group of leading industrial nations.

The researchers say there's little room for nature in the UK because there is so much of the land that has long been built upon or used for intensive agriculture (集约型农业). And they warn that the world has lost so much biodiversity, and we have a risk of ecological meltdown (生态崩溃), a future in which we can't depend on nature to provide energy, food and timber (木材).

The study was published on the eve of the UN Biodiversity Conference, where world leaders will meet online to discuss plans for protecting nature over the next ten years.

None of the aims over the past ten years were achieved, and scientists say this is our last best chance for a sustainable (可持续的) future.

1. What is biodiversity?
   A. Biodiversity is the variety of all plant and animal life on Earth.
   B. Biodiversity is the variety of all plant life on Earth.
   C. Biodiversity is the variety of all animal life on Earth.

2. According to new data, biodiversity is _____.
   A. increasing
   B. reducing
   C. balanced

3. Why is there little room for nature in the UK?
   A. Because less trees are planted there.
   B. Because so many people live there.
   C. Because there are so much land for building.

4. Where will world leaders discuss plans for protecting nature?
   A. On the Internet.
   B. In an office.
   C. In the UK.

5. When is our last best chance for a sustainable future?
   A. The past ten years.
   B. Now.
   C. Ten years later.

词汇碎片

industrial *adj.* 工业的；产业的　　warn *v.* 警告　　publish *v.* 发表；出版，发行（书、杂志等）

重难句讲解

The researchers say there's little room for nature in the UK because there is so much of the land that has long been built upon or used for intensive agriculture. 研究人员指出，英国有如此多的土地长期以来用于建筑或集约型农业，留给大自然的空间所剩无几。

本句是复合句。say 后面是省略引导词 that 的宾语从句，作 say 的宾语；because 引导原因状语从句；原因状语从句中包含一个 that 引导的定语从句，修饰先行词 the land。

Wednesday C 阅读理解

In New Zealand, southern right whales (南露脊鲸) were hunted to near extinction (灭绝) about a century ago. But since then, the population has slowly risen.

Dr. Emma Carroll said, "I'm the lead scientist on a research project. We found there were around 2,000 whales in 2009." Emma's team is tracking (追踪) where the whales feed and whether climate (气候) change is influencing their behaviour.

"Historically (在历史上), we knew that the whales from New Zealand would travel north and east of New Zealand during the spring and summer months. However, none of our tracked whales show those migration (迁徙) models. Instead, most of them go west in fact," said Emma, "so these results are pretty important and give us hope—even with changing oceans, these whales have more than one method that they can use to find lots of food."

Scientists are using all of the modern tools to get a really complete picture of not just their recovery (恢复) but how they're using the oceans.

阅读短文，判断正（T）误（F）。

1. Southern right whales were hunted to extinction.

2. Around 2,000 whales could be seen in 2019.

3. In general, the whales from New Zealand would travel north and east during the spring and summer months.

4. The results about the whales are not important.

5. Scientists are using modern tools to get a really complete picture of whales.

词汇碎片

hunt v. 打猎，猎取　　population n. 种群；人口数量　　ocean n. 海洋　　complete adj. 完整的；彻底的

重难句讲解

Emma's team is tracking where the whales feed and whether climate change is influencing their behaviour. 艾玛的团队正在追踪这些鲸鱼的觅食地，并关注气候变化是否影响其行为。

本句是复合句。主句为 Emma's team is tracking...; where the whales feed 和 whether climate change is influencing their behaviour 是并列的两个宾语从句，作 is tracking 的宾语; climate change 意为"气候变化"。

Thursday D任务型阅读

Beloved sea cows are dying in amazing numbers again. __1__. Most deaths have come along in Indian River Lagoon (印第安河潟湖). Here, decades (十年) of pollution from farm fertilizers (肥料) and developments of houses have killed off huge seagrass—__2__.

Last November, Patrick Rose gave his warning. __3__: Sea cows are going to have to make an important choice about life or death—between dying sooner by having to go out for food in the cold or staying warm and hungry. In the past, __4__. But now, many sea cows have been weak for years of food shortages (短缺) and are reaching the breaking point.

To get through the cold time, __5__. Until pollution is solved and seagrass is restored (恢复), sea cows will continue to suffer (受苦) and die.

阅读短文，从下列选项中选出能填入文中空白处的最佳选项，其中有一项为多余选项。

A. Providing more seagrass is important
B. they are sea cows' main food source
C. sea cows will look for warm water to stay
D. Hunger and cold weather are the first reasons
E. This winter could be more difficult for sea cows
F. sea cows would easily have continued to live in the cold weather

Friday E 任务型阅读

Researchers recently found an unusual coral reef (珊瑚礁)—it was discovered near Tahiti in the South Pacific Ocean. The reef is thought to be one of the largest found at such depths (深度). And it seems untouched by climate change or human activities. It was deeper than others—between 35 meters to 70 meters.

Such depths are difficult to explore (探索). The dive team (潜水队) had special air tanks and did 200 hours of diving to study the reef. They took photos of the corals. Corals are tiny animals that grow and form reefs in oceans around the world.

Laetitia Hédouin said she first saw the corals months earlier. She was diving with a local diving group at that time. When she went there for the first time, Hédouin thought, "Wow—we need to study that reef. There's something special about it." She hopes scientists can better understand its role in the ocean. And more dives are planned in the coming months.

Around the world, coral reefs are damaged (破坏) due to overfishing and pollution. Climate change is also hurting corals.

根据短文内容，完成表格中所缺信息。

An unusual coral reef	Location: near (1) _____ in the South Pacific Ocean
	Depth: (2) _____
Laetitia Hédouin	She was (3) _____ with a local diving group when she first saw the corals.
	The coral reef is (4) _____.
Damage elements (因素)	Overfishing, (5) _____ and climate change

---

词汇碎片

unusual *adj.* 不同寻常的；独特的   tiny *adj.* 微小的；极小的   role *n.* 角色   pollution *n.* 污染

重难句讲解

Corals are tiny animals that grow and form reefs in oceans around the world. 珊瑚是一种微小的动物，在世界各地的海洋中生长并形成珊瑚礁。

本句是复合句。句中 that 引导定语从句，修饰先行词 tiny animals。

Saturday F 短文填空

It was a late afternoon in the heart of Masai Mara. During the time, the light was (1) _____ for photographing. On the horizon (地平线), the plains (平原) of the national park were (2) _____ of animals. I was sitting on a first-row seat (3) _____ the historic journey of thousands of wildebeests (角马) and zebras crossing in a (4) _____ group from Kenya's Masai Mara Natural Reserve to Serengeti National Park in Tanzania. This was just a moment of calm, peace and probably one of the (5) _____ experiences in my lifetime.

Over 2 million wildebeests always migrate (迁徙) in circles (6) _____ Kenya and Tanzania. With the only purpose of (7) _____ the rain, herds (兽群) of zebras, antelopes (羚羊) and wildebeests migrate all year round between Kenya and Tanzania. (8) _____ the rainfall (降雨) is decided by the seasons and changes in climate, there is no way to (9) _____ the exact (精确的) timing of the rainfall and the movement of these herds.

At the Serengeti National Park in Tanzania, the rainy season is in March, April and May. (10) _____ in Masai Mara, we will have our best chances to see wildebeests from August to early November.

阅读短文，从下列选项中选出能填入文中空缺处的单词，使短文通顺，意思完整。每空限填一词，必要时需适当改变单词形式，选项中有两项为多余选项。

perfect
see
large
protect
full
best
follow
and
between
because
predict
but

---

photograph v. 摄影；照相　　**historic** adj. 历史性的，有历史意义的　　**purpose** n. 目的

At the Serengeti National Park in Tanzania, the rainy season is in March, April and May. 在坦桑尼亚的塞伦盖蒂国家公园，雨季是在3月、4月和5月。

本句是简单句。At the Serengeti National Park in Tanzania 为地点状语；rainy season 意为"雨季"。

Week Fourteen 环境保护

Monday A 完形填空

| 体 裁 | 记叙文 | 题 材 | 环境保护 | 正确率 | ___/10 | 词 数 | 231 |
| 难 度 | ★★★★☆ | 建议用时 | 12分钟 | 实际用时 | ___ | 答案页码 | 123 |

Young people are taking the lead in addressing environmental challenges. Twenty-year-old Cheng Haosheng from Macao (澳门)—now studying at Tsinghua University—is one of them. He __1__ recalls (回想) his experience late last year at the Global Youth Summit (全球青年大会).

The summit is aimed at being a springboard (跳板) for the world's youth to take a more __2__ role in showing the collective spirit (集体精神) when facing pressing environmental __3__.

Cheng also played a positive role in writing media releases (媒体报道) about each activity during the __4__ and publishing them online. "I realized once again the __5__ of regional (区域的) and global teamwork for fighting climate change. Many scholars, students, young people and citizens from around the globe are already __6__ the problem," Cheng says.

"I could still __7__ the streets littered (使遍布) with fallen trees and the broken windows were about to break into pieces," Cheng says, adding that it was __8__ for Macao to suffer (遭受) five to six typhoons (台风) a year, but the loss caused by typhoon was __9__. "It was the first time that I came to know the influence of global climate change on our lives," he says.

At the same time, he works with other students to organize environmental activities, such as recycling and cleanup activities at Tsinghua University. "Through these activities, we __10__ to encourage behavioral changes," he says.

1. A. lazily   B. angrily
   C. easily   D. difficultly
2. A. interesting B. similar
   C. negative   D. active
3. A. examples   B. facts
   C. rules   D. problems
4. A. conversation B. communication
   C. meeting   D. promise
5. A. importance B. decision
   C. manner   D. instruction
6. A. coming on   B. working on
   C. turning on D. going on
7. A. reach   B. read
   C. remember   D. realize
8. A. impossible B. successful
   C. normal   D. clever
9. A. small   B. huge
   C. good   D. quick
10. A. invite   B. design
    C. hope   D. express

词汇碎片

be aimed at 目的在于；针对   pressing adj. 紧急的，急迫的   positive adj. 积极的；乐观的

重难句讲解

At the same time, he works with other students to organize environmental activities, such as recycling and cleanup activities at Tsinghua University. 与此同时，他还和其他同学一起组织多项环保活动，比如在清华大学举办的回收和清洁活动。

本句是简单句。At the same time 意为"与此同时"；such as recycling and cleanup activities at Tsinghua University 作状语；such as 意为"比如，诸如"。

Tuesday B 阅读理解

The holiday season is a time for celebrating (庆祝) with friends and family and during the holidays, people send gifts. Unluckily, this can lead to a lot of waste, for example, holiday cards, Christmas trees, entertaining (宴请), and gift wrap (包装). It is a great way to use things that can be recycled when celebrating the holidays.

Gift wrap	The concerns (担忧) about paper waste have made many people look at other choices for wrapping a gift. You can use reusable (可重复使用的) bags for gifts. Using old maps, pages from magazines, and art paper is advised. The person receiving the gift could use the wrapping for something else. You could also wrap a gift in a colorful scarf or tablecloth (桌布).
Holiday cards	For many people, sending holiday cards is a tradition. However, now many people use digital (数字的) or electronic cards. People are much more accepting of electronic holiday cards. Those who want to send traditional cards might choose ones printed on recyclable paper.
Christmas trees	The greener choice would be buying a real Christmas tree from a local farm. If you do buy a fake (假的) tree, you should consider the materials it is made from. Is it made with recycled materials? Or can it be recycled?
Entertaining	When having a celebration, avoid single-use plastics. Use things like regular plates and cups.

1. Which of the following materials is NOT mentioned to wrap a gift?
   A. Old maps.
   B. Reusable bags.
   C. Colorful scarves.
   D. Plastic boxes.

2. Which way is NOT advised while sending holiday cards to your friends or family?
   A. Using digital holiday cards.
   B. Sending electronic holiday cards.
   C. Sending traditional cards made of unrecyclable paper.
   D. Choosing holiday cards printed on recyclable paper.

3. The purpose of writing this passage is to tell us _____.
   A. how to celebrate holidays better
   B. how to buy a real Christmas tree
   C. how to cut down on holiday waste
   D. how to choose holiday gifts for friends

词汇碎片

waste n. 废弃物；浪费   recycle v. 回收利用；再循环   material n. 材料；物质   plastic n. 塑料

重难句讲解

It is a great way to use things that can be recycled when celebrating the holidays. 使用可以被回收的东西来庆祝节日是一种很好的方式。

本句是复合句。It是形式主语，真正的主语是后面的动词不定式 to use things; that can be recycled 是that引导的定语从句，修饰先行词things。

In their free time, most young people like to play on their smartphones. But Li Ruxue is different and he is often found in a forest. "Though the lifestyle is a little bit tiring, it's meaningful," the 27-year-old young man said in an interview.

After graduation, he joined a skywalker gibbon (天行长臂猿) protection organization, where one of his major tasks was picking up gibbon feces (粪便). The skywalker gibbon is a top-level state-protected animal whose population is smaller than that of wild giant pandas. By analyzing (分析) the DNA from their feces, researchers can know the inbreeding (近亲繁殖) among different groups and protect them better. So over the past four and a half years, Li has followed gibbons and collected their feces. But he has never regretted his choice or felt lonely, as he has found more young people taking part in nature protection.

Like Li, Chu Wenwen, has also worked to protect animals. As her father works on wildlife (野生动物) research, Chu has long been surrounded (包围) by wild animals, for example, beavers (河狸) and snow leopards. After graduation, she followed in her father's footsteps. The Mengxin beaver was listed as a first-class state-protected animal in China. And, to protect them, Chu initiated the "beaver canteen" program in 2018, which finally attracted over 1 million Internet users to donate money. A huge "canteen" of about 400,000 salix shrubs (柳灌丛) was built with the money from mostly young Internet users.

"Young people are the future of the world and the future of global biodiversity (生物多样性) protection," noted Xinhua Agency.

1. How does Li Ruxue feel about choosing this kind of lifestyle?
   A. Tired but meaningful.
   B. Disappointed and bored.
   C. Interested and proud.
   D. Lonely and tired.

2. What is Li Ruxue's main task in the skywalker gibbon protection organization?
   A. Protecting gibbons and wild giant pandas.
   B. Feeding the skywalker gibbons.
   C. Analyzing the DNA from gibbon feces.
   D. Following gibbons and picking up their feces.

3. Chu Wenwen, influenced by _____, works to protect animals.
   A. her friends
   B. her father
   C. a nature protection organization
   D. an animal protection program

4. What does the underlined word "initiated" in Paragraph 3 most probably mean in Chinese?
   A. 发起 B. 比较
   C. 忽略 D. 解决

5. What is the best title for the passage?
   A. Protecting the Forest
   B. Team Work Matters
   C. Young People Are Acting Now
   D. We Are the One

major adj. 主要的；重大的   regret v. 后悔；遗憾   donate v. 捐赠；赠送

And, to protect them, Chu initiated the "beaver canteen" program in 2018, which finally attracted over 1 million Internet users to donate money. 为了保护河狸，初雯雯在2018年发起了"河狸食堂"项目，最终吸引了一百多万名网友捐钱。

本句是复合句。主句的主干是 Chu initiated the "beaver canteen" program；to protect them 为动词不定式作目的状语；which 引导非限制性定语从句，修饰 the "beaver canteen" program；attract sb. to do sth. 意为"吸引某人做某事"；donate money 意为"捐钱"。

Thursday D 任务型阅读

The Chinese people have long been a major force in creating greener lands and bluer skies. From the forestation (造林) campaign that started years ago to the planting of "virtual (虚拟的) trees" on mobile phones today, thanks to the efforts of Chinese people, the country's forest coverage rate (森林覆盖率) has increased from 8.6 percent in the early years to 23.04 percent in 2020.

Behind these wonders, vivid stories and creative measures explain China's efforts to the improvement of air quality and the ecological (生态的) environment.

"Sandstorms come once a year and last for half a year" was once a common phrase to describe the ecology in northern China. In the past, due to overgrazing (过度放牧), the grass land would be eaten away by sheep before the rainy season, turning cropland (农田) into the sand.

At present, programs like "Ant Forest", which combined online and real tree-planting projects, are becoming increasingly popular in China. By 2020, the total number of people in the "Ant Forest" was over 500 million, and 39,000 hectares (公顷) of trees had been planted offline.

The Chinese government has also raised more than 10 billion yuan in forestry (林业) management subsidies (补贴).

During the 13th Five-Year Plan period (2016-2020), China forbade all commercial logging (商业砍伐) of natural forests nationwide. A national management and protection team including about 7 million people has been set up, using fully technical means to strengthen (加强) the protection of forestry resources (资源).

请认真阅读短文，并根据短文内容在表格中第1~10小题的空格里填入一个最恰当的单词。每个空格只填1个单词。

\multicolumn{2}{c}{Improvement of air quality and the ecological environment in China}	
Problems	Sandstorms in northern China would (1) _____ for a long time.
Measures	(2) _____ would eat up grass before the rainy season because of overgrazing, and this (3) _____ cropland into the sand in the past.
	"Ant Forest" is a program that combined (4) _____ and real tree-planting projects. And people had (5) _____ about 39,000 hectares of trees offline.
	Over 10 billion yuan in forestry management subsidies have been (6) _____ by the Chinese government.
	Cutting natural forests for commerce in the country was (7) _____ during the 13th Five-Year Plan period.
	A national management and protection team which (8) _____ around 7 million people has been established.
Result	With the (9) _____ of Chinese people, the country's forest coverage rate has increased (10) _____ 8.6 percent in the early years to 23.04 percent in 2020.

词汇碎片

thanks to 幸亏；由于　　measure n. 措施，办法　　forbid v. 禁止　　set up 建立；创建

重难句讲解

A national management and protection team including about 7 million people has been set up, using fully technical means to strengthen the protection of forestry resources.（中国）建立了一支约700万人的国家管理和保护队伍，充分利用技术手段加强对森林资源的保护。

本句是简单句。including about 7 million people 为介词短语作后置定语，修饰 A national management and protection team；using fully technical means to strengthen the protection of forestry resources 为现在分词短语作状语；technical means 意为"技术手段"。

Friday E 短文填空

体裁：说明文　题材：环境保护　正确率：___/5　词数：200
难度：★★★★☆　建议用时：7分钟　实际用时：___　答案页码：124

"If the world ends one day, these collections will bring (1) _____ of a new beginning to life on Earth," said Li Pei, a member of the Germplasm Bank of Wild Species (GBOWS) (中国西南野生生物种质资源库). Founded in 2007, GBOWS is a research and protection facility (设施) for rare and endangered plants and animals (珍稀濒危动植物).

With two in five plant species (物种) at (2) _____ of extinction (灭绝), it is a race against time to protect the nation's mysterious plant life. So how does the bank work? At first, scientists collect endangered and useful wild species and send them to the seed (种子) bank. And then, for future study, collectors have to record details of the plant, including where it was found, its size and the number of individual (单独的) plants in the surrounding area (周边地区).

The bank in Yunnan works with international partners on the collection of samples, communication and research. It holds 2,176 sets of seeds from 45 (3) _____ and districts, with each set covering (4) _____ individual seeds. "As China has rich biological (生物的) resources, we (5) _____ further protect our collections and go on deeper research, expecting to be good to biodiversity (生物多样性) protection, not only in China but the world," Li Pei said.

阅读短文，从方框中选择合适的单词或短语填空，使短文通顺，意思完整。

aim to

risk

countries

hope

thousands of

词汇碎片

protection n. 保护　　mysterious adj. 神秘的；不可思议的　　international adj. 国际的

重难句讲解

And then, for future study, collectors have to record details of the plant, including where it was found, its size and the number of individual plants in the surrounding area. 然后，为了将来的研究，采集人员必须记录这种植物的详细信息，包括采集地点、种子的体积、周边地区中单株植物的数量等。

本句是复合句。主句的主干是 collectors have to record details of the plant；including... in the surrounding area 作状语，其中包含 where 引导的宾语从句，作 including 的宾语。

Saturday F 短文填空

Eighteen-year-old Duncan Jurman (1) f_____ Florida, the United States, is now a student at Nova Southeastern University (诺瓦东南大学) in Davie, Florida. He is the founder (创始人) of an environmental (2) p_____ called "Bring Butterflies Back, Inspiring Youth to Protect Butterflies for Future Generations", which aims to bring back (3) b_____ populations.

He said, "I think one of the reasons that I really fell in (4) l_____ with butterflies, is that they're very accessible (可接近的). If you want to attract a butterfly, for example, you (5) p_____ a lot of flowers." Jurman started a butterfly garden at his home, where he has raised (饲养) and released (放生) over 5,000 butterflies over the years. To make it accessible to other students, he created a butterfly garden at his school. "Whenever a butterfly lands on them, or I put a caterpillar (毛毛虫) in their hands, the young students fall in love with them right away. (6) T_____ have a new interest in insects," he said.

"Butterflies are really (7) i_____ for the environment for two main reasons," he said. "No.1 is that they pollinate (给……授粉) the flowers like bees. They are one of (8) t_____ most important pollinators (传粉者) in the world. The other important (9) r_____ is that they are food for a lot of species like birds."

His environmental project, Bring Butterflies Back, (10) h_____ local schools with their gardens and helps further develop outreach (外展服务) efforts.

词汇碎片

attract v. 吸引   start v. 创办；开始；出发   land v. 降落；登陆   insect n. 昆虫

重难句讲解

Jurman started a butterfly garden at his home, where he has raised and released over 5,000 butterflies over the years. 尤尔曼在家里建立了一个蝴蝶花园，多年来他在那里饲养和放生了5 000多只蝴蝶。

本句是复合句。主句的主干是 Jurman started a butterfly garden；where 引导非限制性定语从句，修饰 a butterfly garden；start 在此处意为"创办，创立"。

答案解析

Week One

Monday【A 完形填空】

● 答案解析

1. B。考查动词辨析。A 项意为"等待"，B 项意为"展示"，C 项意为"拥有"，D 项意为"获得"。空格前的 It 指代上文提到的董书畅的获奖作品 The Golden Ring，根据空格后的内容"月球挡住了大部分的太阳圆面"可知，这是在描述照片的内容，所以 B 项符合语境，故选 B。

2. A。考查形容词辨析。A 项意为"薄的；瘦的"，B 项意为"长的"，C 项意为"胖的"，D 项意为"高的"。根据上文提到的月球挡住了大部分的太阳圆面可知，"薄的"符合语境，故选 A。

3. D。考查名词辨析。A 项意为"公园"，B 项意为"假期"，C 项意为"学校"，D 项意为"比赛"。根据上文可知摄影师董书畅于 9 月中旬荣膺年度天文摄影师总冠军，D 项代入后意为"该项比赛共收到来自 75 个国家和地区的 4 500 份参赛作品"，符合句意，故选 D。

4. B。考查动词短语辨析。A 项意为"起床"，B 项意为"为……准备"，C 项意为"跌倒"，D 项意为"经过"。根据下文 However, that didn't go as he expected. The COVID-19 pandemic made his plans stop in early 2020（然而，这并不像他预期的那样。2020 年年初的新冠肺炎疫情中止了他的计划）可知，2019 年年底时，他开始准备去拍照，所以 B 项符合语境，故选 B。

5. C。考查状语从句。A 项意为"直到……时"，后接时间状语从句；B 项意为"尽管"，后接让步状语从句；C 项意为"当……的时候"，后接时间状语从句；D 项意为"在……地方"，后接地点状语从句。根据下文可知，他使用长焦镜头拍照时，才可以细致入微地观察银河系，所以 C 项符合语境，故选 C。

6. A。考查动词短语辨析。A 项意为"把……转变为"，B 项意为"弥补；化妆"，C 项意为"确信"，D 项意为"由……制成"。空格前提到了银河系的红、绿、蓝三色，空格后提到了鲜明的轮廓，将 A 项代入后意为"通过摄影转化获得鲜明的轮廓"，符合句意，故选 A。

7. C。考查介词辨析。A 项意为"为了"，B 项意为"来自……"，C 项意为"在……之后"，D 项意为"在……之前"。空格前提到他的信心增加，空格后提到他获得最佳新人奖。由此可知他获得奖项在前，信心增加在后，所以 C 项符合语境，故选 C。

8. B。考查副词辨析。A 项意为"简单地"，B 项意为"最终，最后"，C 项意为"正常地"，D 项意为"快速地"。空格前提到他花了三年多的时间追逐星星，空格后提到他因这件事获得兴奋感和成就感，由此可知"最终，最后"符合语境，故选 B。

9. D。考查名词辨析。A 项意为"感觉"，B 项意为"改变"，C 项意为"微笑"，D 项意为"泪水"。上文提到摄影师董书畅花了三年多的时间追逐星星，最终有了一定的成就，可知整个过程是充满艰辛的。将 D 项代入后意为"汗水和泪水交织"，符合句意，故选 D。

10. A。考查形容词辨析。A 项意为"更好的"，B 项意为"更善良的"，C 项意为"更严肃的"，D 项意为"更便宜的"。空格前提到他将寻找新的摄影领域，将 A 项代入后意为"融合科学与艺术的更好的方式"，符合语境，故选 A。

Tuesday【B 阅读理解】

● 答案解析

1. C。细节理解题。根据 Although I did not get to serve as a volunteer, it's a great honor to be able to perform at the opening ceremony（虽然我没有成为一名志愿者，但能够在开幕式上表演是一种莫大的荣誉）可知，张衣笙一开始想担任志愿者，所以 C 项符合文意，故选 C。

2. C。推理判断题。A 项意为"懒散的"，B 项意为"聪明的"，C 项意为"努力的，勤奋的"，D 项意为"强壮的"。根据 Mayentao, the 24-year-old student from Mali, has visited the Bird's Nest for rehearsals no matter rain or shine 可知，无论是下雨还是天晴，张衣笙都会去鸟巢排练，所以"努力的，勤奋的"更能描述张衣笙，故选 C。

3. C。细节理解题。A 项和 B 项在文中没有提及，故排除；根据 I'm so excited. We've been working very hard to perform at the amazing opening ceremony（我太激动了。我们一直十分努力，就为了在令人惊叹的开幕式上表演）可知 C 项表述符合文意；根据 won a scholarship to study

in China when he was 18 years old（在18岁时获得了前往中国学习的奖学金）可知D项表述错误，故选C。

Wednesday【C 阅读理解】

● 答案解析

1. D。细节理解题。根据第一段第一句 Practicing a series of gentle tai chi moves, Khamisi Ally Abdi feels his body warm up in the cold morning（哈米西·阿利·阿卜迪练习了一系列轻柔缓慢的太极动作，在寒冷的早晨，他感到身体暖和起来了）可知阿卜迪身体暖和起来是因为练了太极，所以D项符合文意，故选D。

2. C。细节理解题。根据第二段第二句 Abdi has already developed the balance and deep rhythmic breathing that tai chi requires（阿卜迪已经掌握了太极所需的平衡和有节奏的深呼吸）可知练太极需要掌握的是平衡和有节奏的深呼吸，所以C项符合文意，故选C。

3. B。推理判断题。根据最后一段中的 When I return home, I will use my Chinese name to teach tai chi in my country（当我回家后，我将用我的中文名字在我的国家教授太极）可知阿卜迪回国后会教授太极，由此可推测阿卜迪所在的国家以后会有更多的人了解太极，所以B项符合文意，故选B。

4. B。主旨大意题。本文主要介绍了外国留学生阿卜迪喜欢太极，并且打算回国后教授太极，让更多的外国人可以受益于这种神奇的中国功夫，所以B项符合文意，故选B。

Thursday【D 阅读理解】

● 答案解析

1. B。细节理解题。根据第二段第三句中的 When users complete their daily exercise goals, their special electronic pets will also be full of energy（当用户完成日常锻炼目标时，他们独特的电子宠物也会充满活力）可知，要使得电子宠物充满活力，用户就要完成日常的锻炼目标，所以B项符合文意，故选B。

2. C。细节理解题。根据第二段第三句中的 when they go to bed too late at night, their pets will have black circles under their eyes（当他们晚上睡得太晚时，他们的宠物会有黑眼圈）可知，电子宠物有黑眼圈是因为其用户睡得太晚，用户的身体状况直接影响了电子宠物的状态，所以C项符合文意，故选C。

3. A。细节理解题。根据第二段倒数第二句中的 other digital pets that focused on the similarity with the user's appearance（其他数字宠物关注的是和用户外表的相似性）可知，以往的电子宠物与用户在外貌上极具相似性，所以A项符合文意，故选A。

4. B。细节理解题。根据第二段最后一句 The app is made to enable users to better know themselves and help them form good habits 可知，"谓尔"这款移动应用程序是为了帮助用户更好地了解他们自己，养成良好的习惯，所以B项符合文意，故选B。

5. A。推理判断题。文中提到用户的一些生活习惯或状态会影响到电子宠物的状态，电子宠物就像是用户在虚拟世界的另一个化身，由此可推测有了电子宠物后，用户可能会更关注自己的健康，所以A项符合文意，其他三项都无法根据文中的内容推测出来，故选A。

Friday【E 任务型阅读】

● 答案解析

1. Zhai's interest in painting started at an early age. 段落主旨句一般位于段首或段尾，第二段描述的都是翟进从小就开始画画的事情，所以第二段的主旨句就是第一句。

2. Because painting required him to stay still and avoid injury. 根据第二段第三句 It was an activity encouraged by his parents because it required him to stay still and avoid injury 可知，翟进的父母鼓励他画画是因为这样可以让他待着不动，避免受伤。

3. animated TV series and graphic novels。根据题干中的关键词 copying characters 可定位到第三段第一句，由 Influenced by animated TV series and graphic novels, he started copying characters 可知，翟进受到动画电视连续剧和漫画小说的影响开始模仿并创造自己的角色。

4. Painting for a customer。根据题干中的关键词 a sense of achievement 可定位到第四段最后一句，由 painting for a customer always gives him a sense of achievement 可知，翟进认为为顾客画画给他一种成就感。

Saturday【F 短文填空】

● 答案解析

（1）careful。空格后的 thought 为名词，所以应用 care 的形容词形式来修饰，故填 careful。

（2）serving。空格前面有 spend，spend 的习惯用法是 spend + 时间 / 金钱 (in) doing sth.，意为"花费时间或金钱做某事"，所以需将 serve 变成 -ing 形式，故填 serving。

（3）her。空格后面的 body 为名词，所以应用 she 的形容词性物主代词，故填 her。

（4）But。上文提到起初她没有太在意身体上的不适。下文又说她腰脊柱的刺痛感很快变得明显，由此可知前后为转折关系，however 和 but 都可以表示转折，但使用 however 时通常需用逗号将其与其他成分隔开，但空格后面没有逗号，故填 But。

（5）leave。空格前面有 suggested，suggest 的习惯用法是 suggest (that) sb. (should) do sth.，意为"建议某人应该做某事"，所以本空直接填动词原形，故填 leave。

（6）an/one。空格后面为可数名词 operation，且该词以元音音素开头，an 或 one 都符合此处语境，故填 an/one。

（7）second。上文提到周怡冰进行了一次手术后副作用比较大，由此可知这是第二次手术，所以应用序数词，故填 second。

（8）once。下文提到周怡冰抓住每一个机会赶上学习进度，可见她想要尽快恢复的心情是很急切的，at once 为固定搭配，意为"立刻，马上"，符合句意，故填 once。

（9）returned。文章的整体时态为一般过去时，所以应用 return 的过去式，故填 returned。

（10）preparations。空格前面有动词 making，所以空格处应用 prepare 的名词形式，且 make preparations for 为固定搭配，意为"为……做准备"，故填 preparations。

Week Two

Monday【A 完形填空】

● 答案解析

1. B。考查动词短语辨析。A项为"（飞机等）起飞；脱下"，B项意为"发生"，C项意为"拿走"，D项意为"承担；呈现"。根据下文 a learner can practice using their second language in a natural setting 可知，在任何地方都可以练习使用第二语言，也就是说沉浸式语言项目可以随地发生，故选B。

2. C。考查动词辨析。A项意为"得到"，B项意为"介绍"，C项意为"练习"，D项意为"意识到"。下文从英语技能"听、说、读、写"这四个方面展开说明，可知目的是练习这几项英语技能，故选C。

3. A。考查动词辨析。A项意为"表演；执行"，B项意为"讲话"，C项意为"阅读"，D项意为"发现"。音乐风格是由艺术家表演出来的，故选A。

4. B。考查形容词辨析。A项意为"传统的"，B项意为"优秀的"，C项意为"额外的"，D项意为"特殊的；特别的"。为了练习英语听力，选择的英语电影和电视节目应该是优秀的，故选B。

5. C。考查形容词辨析。A项意为"更容易的"，B项意为"更简单的"，C项意为"更困难的"，D项意为"更好的"。上文提到 Turn off the subtitles（关闭字幕），在不看字幕的情况下观看英语电影或电视节目，这对于英语初学者来说会更难，故选C。

6. B。考查代词辨析。A项意为"你；你们"，B项意为"你自己"，C项意为"我自己"，D项意为"他们自己"。本句是祈使句，全文使用的人称是 you，这里指用英语和自己交流，故选B。

7. C。考查上下文语义。A项意为"最近"，B项意为"因此"，C项意为"但是"，D项意为"和；而且"。空格上文提到用英语与自己交流很奇怪，下文又提到英语会变得更流利，由此可知，上下文句意发生转折，故选C。

8. A。考查定语从句。_____ is a big step towards becoming fluent 是一个非限制性定语从句，修饰前面整个句子，空格处的引导词在从句中作主语，故选A。

9. D。考查动词辨析。A项意为"选择"，B项意为"同意"，C项意为"移动"，D项意为"改变"。change... to... 为固定搭配，表示"把……改变成……"，这里指把社交媒体上使用的语言从自己的母语改成英语，故选D。

10. C。考查名词辨析。A项意为"陈述；说明"，B项意为"主题"，C项意为"评论"，D项意为"猜想"。make comments 为固定搭配，意为"做出评论"，根据上文 Follow English speakers（关注讲英语的人）可知，在社交媒体上关注讲英语的人并用英语发表评论，才能练习自己的英语能力，故选C。

11. A。考查名词辨析。A项意为"房子"，B项意为"公司"，C项意为"慈善团体；慈善事业"，D项意为"家乡"。根据下文 through your house 可知，是在家里放置小指示牌，故选A。

12. B。考查动词辨析。A项意为"打败"，B项意为"学会"，C项意为"使用"，D项意为"遇到"。将选项代入句中可知，"学会"符合句意，只有先学会才能使用，故选B。

13. C。考查固定搭配。act like 为固定搭配，意为"表现得像……，举止像……"，故选C。

14. A。考查动词辨析。A项意为"写"，B项意为"有"，C项意为"制作"，D项意为"给"。write a diary 意为"写日记"，符合句意，故选A。

15. C。考查名词辨析。A项意为"知识"，B项意为"娱乐；消遣"，C项意为"经历"，D项意为"预测"。根据上文 a diary or daily journal in English 可知，写英语日记记录的是生活中自己的经历，故选C。

Tuesday【B 阅读理解】

● 答案解析

1. C。细节理解题。根据 The video was praised by students and parents（这段视频受到了学生和家长的称赞）可知，家长对于小孩练习八段锦持赞成、积极的态度。positive 意为"积极的"，所以C项符合文意，故选C。

2. B。细节理解题。根据题干中的 topic 和 autumn 定位到对应的表格，由 foodstuffs like dishes and desserts（菜肴和甜点等类型的食物）可知，B项"与家人一起制作美味的月饼"符合学生在秋天可选的主题，故选B。

3. A。细节理解题。根据表格 The ways of participation 部分中的 Pupils in grade one or two can paint or draw 可知一、二年级的小学生可以通过画画的方式参与课程，所以A项符合文意，故选A。

4. D。推理判断题。根据表格 Time limit 部分中的 One or two months to finish the tasks 可知完成任务需要一到两个月。题干中提到布置任务的时间为 January 21st（1月21日），由此可知，你最晚应该在3月21日之前完成任务，符合要求的只有 D 项，故选 D。

5. A。细节理解题。根据表格 Importance 部分中的 deal with complex problems（处理复杂的问题）、work in groups and learn from their classmates by communicating（进行团队合作并通过交流互相学习）可知，B 项"团队合作"、C 项"交流技能"和 D 项"处理困难的问题"都是学生通过项目式学习可以学到的能力，A 项 writing skills（写作技能）在原文中没有明确提到，故选 A。

Wednesday【C 阅读理解】
答案解析

1. B。细节理解题。根据第二段第一句中的 classic opera scenes from Peking opera, Kun opera, Henan opera, Cantonese opera and Huangmei opera（京剧、昆曲、豫剧、粤剧、黄梅戏等曲种中的经典戏曲片段）可知这一活动主要展现了五种经典戏曲类型，故选 B。

2. C。细节理解题。根据第二段最后一句中的 students could get a deep understanding of operas and so develop a strong interest in traditional cultures of our nation（学生们可以深入地了解戏曲，从而培养对我国传统文化的浓厚兴趣）可知，这次活动举办的意义在于使学生对我国传统文化更加感兴趣，故选 C。

3. D。细节理解题。根据第二段中的 have invited famous opera actors and actresses to perform, educate and show classic opera scenes（邀请著名戏曲演员表演、教育和展示经典戏曲片段）和 the program includes lectures on opera history（该活动包括戏曲历史讲座），以及最后一段最后一句中的 Shenzhen Theater livestreamed all the performances in schools（深圳戏院直播了学校里的所有演出）可知，A、B、C 三项都是该项活动的几种方式，只有 D 项 Discussion with students who know well classic operas（与非常了解经典戏曲的同学进行讨论）在原文中没有提到，故选 D。

4. C。语篇理解题。画线单词上文提到 the modern Peking opera "A New Era" was popular at the Southern University of Science and Technology and Shenzhen Middle School（现代京剧《换人间》在南方科技大学和深圳中学大受欢迎），而说话者就是深圳中学的学生，所以 It 指代的是 the modern Peking opera "A New Era"，故选 C。

Thursday【D 任务型阅读】
答案解析

1. B。根据空格前的 When schools closed, countries' teaching and learning methods were greatly different around the world 可知，学校停课时，世界各国的教学方法大不相同。下文提到其他国家无法做出改变，but 表示前后语义发生转折，由此可知，空格处说明一些国家能很快做出改变，B 项"一些国家能够迅速转向在线学习"符合文意，且此处为 Some..., but others... 的句型结构，故选 B。

2. E。空格下文提到一些非洲国家的孩子没有笔记本电脑进行学习，可知此处为不同国家的孩子在学校停课期间是否有资源设备来进行线上学习的对比，结合 But 可知，E 项"在丹麦等欧洲国家，超过95%的学生使用笔记本电脑完成学业"符合文意，且 more than 与 fewer than 形成对比，故选 E。

3. D。空格上文提到没有数字资源的国家有其他方式让学生在课堂之外进行学习，由此可知，空格处说明学生在学校停课时进行在线学习的其他方式。D 项"在肯尼亚和俄罗斯等一些地方，教育电视和无线电广播有所增加"符合文意，其中 Educational television and radio broadcasts 是上文中 other ways 的具体所指，故选 D。

4. A。空格处位于段首，应是本段的主旨句。根据本段中的一些关键表述 teachers、mental health support、were afraid of being infected 可知本段主要讲述了疫情期间教师的心理状况，A 项"教师们也感受到了疫情带来的情绪影响"符合文意，故选 A。

5. C。空格上文有表示举例的标志词 for example，提到了印度教师在疫情期间的心理状况，下文提到了教师对于在疫情期间工作的担忧，由此可知空格处仍是对教师受到的情绪影响进行举例。C 项"在俄罗斯，64%的教师说在大部分时间都感到很疲惫"符合文意，故选 C。

Friday【E 短文填空】

答案解析

（1）down。空格所在的句子主干完整，空格处与 up 并列，结合选项可知 down 符合要求，up and down 为固定短语，意为"上上下下"，故填 down。

（2）song。空格前面有不定冠词 a，由此可知空格处为单数名词，空格前面的动词为 singing，故填 song。

（3）and。more and more 为固定短语，意为"越来越……"，故填 and。

（4）get。空格后面的 more outdoor knowledge 为名词短语，意为"更多的户外知识"，所以空格处应用动词，将所给的动词代入句中可知 get 符合要求，且 help 的习惯用法是 help sb. do sth.，故填 get。

（5）at。look at 为固定短语，意为"看"，故填 at。

（6）skills。空格前面为 develops their problem-solving，develops 缺少宾语，由此可知空格处需填入名词。将所给的名词代入句中，只有 skill 符合句意，因 skill 为可数名词，结合空格前的 their 可知此处填 skill 的复数形式，故填 skills。

（7）seeing。空格前面为介词 after，后面为名词短语 so much litter，由此可知空格处需填入动词，将所给的动词代入句中，只有 see 符合句意，因介词 after 后接名词或动名词，故填 seeing。

（8）them。空格前面是动词 gather，缺少宾语，由此可知空格处需填入一个名词。上文提到老师正看着孩子们用水桶装满海水或沙子，所以老师吹口哨是为了把分散的孩子们集合起来，them 符合句意及要求，此处 them 指代 children，故填 them。

（9）to plant。空格前面有动词 wanted，后面有名词 flowers，由此可知空格处为 to do 短语。在所给的动词中，只有 plant 与 flowers 可搭配，意为"种花"，符合句意，故填 to plant。

（10）what。空格前面有动词 decide，后面是一个成分完整的句子。分析句子结构可知，because 引导原因状语从句，在状语从句中，_____ they wish to learn each time 为宾语从句，作 decide 的宾语，宾语从句缺引导词，且该引导词在宾语从句中作 learn 的宾语，故填 what。

Saturday【F 短文填空】

答案解析

（1）to。thanks to 为固定搭配，意为"由于；幸亏"，故填 to。

（2）who/that。分析句子结构可知，as 引导原因状语从句，在状语从句中，_____ are too busy trying to make a living 是一个定语从句，修饰先行词 parents，设空处在从句中作主语，指人，故填 who/that。

（3）in。take part in 为固定搭配，意为"参加；参与"，故填 in。

（4）with。上文提到这个害羞的男生参加了竖笛俱乐部，这个奖项是和他的同学们一起获得的，with 在这里表示"和……一起"，故填 with。

（5）a。set a good example for 为固定搭配，意为"为……树立一个好榜样"，故填 a。

Week Three

Monday【A 完形填空】

● 答案解析

1. C。考查连词辨析。A项意为"尽管",B项意为"如果",C项意为"因为",D项意为"除非"。根据上文可知女儿都四岁了,还打扰我们睡觉,让我觉得不公平;下文提到弟弟睡得很好,没有打扰我们。弟弟睡得很好,而女儿常来打扰我们是让我觉得不公平的原因,故选C。

2. A。考查名词辨析。A项意为"习惯",B项意为"解答;解决办法",C项意为"问题",D项意为"策略"。上文提到因为女儿,我的睡眠模式发生变化,结合下文 increasing coffee consumption(日渐增加的咖啡消耗量)可知,这都是我个人生活习惯的改变,故选A。

3. B。考查动词辨析。A项意为"停止;阻止",B项意为"影响",C项意为"依靠;依赖",D项意为"推动"。根据第三段中的 Children begin influencing us even before they are born 可知,孩子不仅影响我的睡眠模式,从出生之前到成长的过程,都对我的生活产生影响,故选B。

4. B。考查固定搭配。plan for 为固定搭配,意为"为……做计划",故选B。

5. A。考查上下文语义。A项意为"穿衣服",B项意为"抓住",C项意为"毁坏",D项意为"清洁"。此处为"get+宾语+宾语补足语"的结构,动词的过去分词有形容词的特性,可作宾语补足语。根据下文的 the wrong socks or shoes(穿错袜子或鞋子)可知离开家之前在穿衣服,故选A。

6. B。考查形容词辨析。A项意为"幸运的",B项意为"恼怒的;生气的",C项意为"高兴的;满意的",D项意为"有创造力的"。根据本句的表述 unhappy children、one cries、get to work 可知,离家之前,父母要赶时间上班,还需要照顾孩子穿好衣服,若孩子哭泣,这会让父母很恼怒或者压力很大,故选B。

7. C。考查短语辨析。A项意为"特别,尤其",B项意为"首先",C项意为"按时",D项意为"通常;一般而言"。空格所在部分意为:试图_____上班。将选项代入文中可知"按时"符合句意,故选C。

8. A。考查名词辨析。A项意为"情况;形势",B项意为"项目;方案",C项意为"决定",D项意为"错误"。空格所在部分意为:在这种压力大的_____下。将选项代入文中可知"情况"符合句意,故选A。

9. D。考查副词辨析。A项意为"真诚地",B项意为"非正式地;随意地",C项意为"有礼貌地",D项意为"自由地"。下文提到 make their own choices(做出自己的选择),由此可知孩子们拥有自主性,想自由地、不受约束地行动,故选D。

10. D。考查动词辨析。A项意为"储存,储蓄",B项意为"建议",C项意为"开始",D项意为"意味着;打算"。将选项代入文中后可知"意味着"符合句意,故选D。

Tuesday【B 阅读理解】

● 答案解析

1. D。细节理解题。根据第二段第四、五句 Tao was so happy about his grandson's arrival, but he didn't have much time to spend with Guo that month. He was very busy with his volunteer work 可知,陶振国没时间和外孙待在一起是因为他在忙奥运会的志愿者工作,故选D。

2. C。推理判断题。根据第二段第三句 His daughter gave birth to a boy baby, Guo Xiaoyu, just days ahead of the opening ceremony in August(他的女儿在8月份奥运会开幕式前几天生下了男孩郭笑宇)可知,郭笑宇在2008年8月份出生,由此可推知,郭笑宇到2022年时是14岁,故选C。

3. C。细节理解题。根据第二段中陶振国所说的话 as an Olympics volunteer, I have to learn it to at least be able to communicate with foreign guests 可知,陶振国学习英语是因为作为一名奥运志愿者,他想要用英语与外国运动员和客人交流,故选C。

4. C。细节理解题。根据第三段第二句 He was helping with garbage sorting, traffic guidance and information inquiries in a community that was home to the Olympic Village 可知,郭笑宇在奥运村帮忙进行垃圾分类、交通引导和信息查询。C项中的 sort litter 和 direct traffic 分别对应原文中的 garbage sorting 和 traffic guidance,故选C。

5. B。细节理解题。根据第二段第二句可知,陶振国是2008年北京奥运会的志愿者。最后一段第一句提到 Both grandfather and grandson were volunteering at the Beijing 2022 Winter Olympics(祖孙两人都是2022年北京冬奥会的志愿者),由此可知陶振国总共做过两次奥运志愿者,故选B。

Wednesday【C 阅读理解】

● 答案解析

1. B。细节理解题。根据第一段中的 was inspired by her sister to develop an application to help deaf and hard-of-

hearing Mexicans（受到姐姐的启发，开发了一款应用程序，帮助失聪和有听力困难的墨西哥人）和第二段中对萨拉查的姐姐所患的疾病的描述可知，萨拉查开发这款应用程序受到了患有疾病的姐姐的启发，故选B。

2. B。细节理解题。根据第二段第三句中的 she would be unable to learn to sign because of her condition 可知佩拉由于身体状况无法学习手语，并结合第二段第一句可知 her condition 指代的就是 was born with a serious illness that influences mobility and hearing（生来就患有一种影响行动能力和听力的严重疾病）。由此可知，佩拉不能学习手语是因为她患有影响行动和听力的先天性疾病，故选B。

3. D。语篇理解题。根据第二段最后一句中的 After seeing the discrimination Perla faced（在看到姐姐佩拉面临的歧视后）可知，受到歧视的主体是佩拉，再结合上文 she was told by one sign language school that she would be unable to learn to sign because of her condition 可知佩拉被一所手语学校告知因身体状况而无法学习手语。由此可知，discrimination 指的是佩拉被一所手语学校拒绝，故选D。

4. C。细节理解题。根据第三段最后一句佩拉的话 I take pride in my sister（我为我的妹妹感到骄傲）可知，佩拉为妹妹开发应用程序一事感到骄傲。take pride in 为固定搭配，表示"为……感到骄傲"，所以 C 项符合文意，故选C。

5. D。细节理解题。萨拉查发明的应用程序可以实现手语与文本或语音之间的互相转换，而不是与图片的转换，所以 A 项错误；最后一段提到萨拉查正在寻找可以让她继续学习的美国大学，所以 B 项错误；佩拉的行动能力比以前有所提高，但原文并未提到她可以自由移动，所以 C 项错误；根据文中的一些表述 a 17-year-old science talent（17岁科学天才）、Salazar's study abilities allowed her to graduate three years early from high school（萨拉查的学习能力让她提前三年从高中毕业）以及 What am I doing to help my sister（我能做什么来帮助我的姐姐呢）可知，萨拉查本身很有天赋，而且对家人很关心，所以 D 项正确，故选D。

Thursday【D 任务型阅读】
● 答案解析

1. F。根据空格前罗珊妮的话可知她的两个孩子之间经常发生冲突，结合下文提到的孩子们互相惹对方生气可知，空格处还是在说两个孩子不好好相处。F 项"他们没办法在不吵架的情况下在餐桌旁坐十分钟"符合文意，且 F 项的主语为 They，可指代 a 16-year-old son and a 14-year-old daughter，与空格下文中的主语 They 一致，故选F。

2. C。根据空格前的 bickering among siblings is helpful 可知兄弟姐妹之间的争吵是有益的，空格处应承接上文，具体说明争吵带来的益处。C 项"它帮助孩子学会处理冲突，使他们更好地与他人沟通"符合文意，故选C。

3. A。根据本段的关键词 rivalry、compare 可知，本段主要讲兄弟姐妹之间存在竞争的一个因素是互相比较。设空处对段落进行总结，A 项"孩子的年龄越接近，竞争就越激烈"符合文意，且 A 项中有本段的关键词 rivalry，故选A。

4. B。本段主要讲兄弟姐妹之间出现竞争的另一个因素是公平，根据空格上文可知年幼的孩子比哥哥姐姐更早获得许可时，哥哥姐姐会觉得不公平。空格处对段落进行总结，B 项"这样就会造成冲突"符合文意，其中的 That 指代上文中提到的状况，故选B。

5. E。根据空格下文罗珊妮的话 But now, we're together at family parties 可知，长大后她和自己的兄弟姐妹相处融洽，结合转折连词 But 可推知，空格处描述的是罗珊妮与自己的兄弟姐妹相处不友好。E 项"在我成长的过程中，我和我的兄弟之间的矛盾很多"符合文意，故选E。

Friday【E 短文填空】
● 答案解析

（1）holiday。空格前面是名词短语 the 2022 Spring Festival，由此可知空格处需填入一个名词，在所给选项中 holiday 符合句意及要求，代入后意为"2022年春节假期"，故填 holiday。

（2）are supposed to。空格前面为主语 they，空格后面为动词原形。下文提到年轻人只要手边有手机或者平板电脑，就可以沉浸在游戏世界中，而 But 表示转折，由此可知，作者认为孩子们应该和朋友们出去玩，而不是沉迷于电子游戏。be supposed to do sth. 为固定搭配，表示"应该做某事"，主语是 they，时态为一般现在时，故填 are supposed to。

（3）all the time。空格所在句的主干完整，考虑空格处为状语，在所给选项中，all the time 符合要求，代入后表示年轻人一直沉迷于游戏世界，故填 all the time。

（4）worried about/worrying about。空格所在句子为问句，下文为问题的回答。根据下文关键词 violence 和 bad 可知，由于游戏中的暴力元素可能会对孩子产生不良影响，所以才会引起父母们对这一现状的担忧。选项中的 worry about 意为"担心，担忧"，符合句意。空格前是 be 动词 are，由此可知空格处可填入 worried about 与其构成固定搭配 be worried about sth./sb.，其中 worried 为形容词；也可填入 worrying about 与其构成现在进行时态，此时 worry 作动词。故填 worried about/worrying about。

（5）too much。空格所在句子为 There be 句型，空格后面为抽象名词 violence，所以空格处作定语修饰 violence。在所给选项中，too much 意为"太多"，符合句意，故填 too much。

（6）children。save sb. from 为固定搭配，表示"使……免于"。结合下文 What if children make full use of this one hour 可知，此处指让孩子们免于电子游戏的伤害，故填 children。

（7）playing。空格后面为名词短语 such games，可与之搭配的动词为 play，且 enjoy doing sth. 为 enjoy 的习惯用法，意为"喜欢做某事"，可知此处应用 play 的动名词形式，故填 playing。

（8）problems。空格前面为动词 cause，意为"导致；引起"，缺少宾语，由此可知空格处应为名词。电子游戏引起的问题不止一个，在所给选项中，problem 符合句意，且为可数名词，故填 problems。

（9）positive。空格前面为动词 offer，空格后面为名词 things，由此可知空格处需填入一个修饰 things 的形容词。在所给选项中，positive 意为"积极的；正面的"，符合句意，故填 positive。

（10）agreed。agree on 为固定搭配，表示"达成一致意见"。根据空格前的 have 可知，空格所在句子为现在完成时，所以空格处需填入 agree 的过去分词形式，故填 agreed。

Saturday【F 短文填空】
● 答案解析

（1）need。空格前为 are going to，空格后为名词 help，由此可知空格处需填动词原形，且根据下文 also need support 可知，空格处所在部分表示学生需要更多帮助，故填 need。

（2）speak。空格前面有 do not，空格后为名词 English，由此可知空格处需填动词原形。根据常识并结合句意可知，空格处应为表示"说英语"的动词，故填 speak。

（3）for。It is + adj.+ for sb. to do sth. 为固定句型，意为"对某人而言做某事……"，It 在句中作形式主语，后面的动词不定式为真正的主语，故填 for。

（4）example。for example 为固定短语，意为"例如，比如说"，故填 example。

（5）messages。空格前面为动词 send，缺少宾语，由此可知空格处需填入名词。根据下文 the message 可知，此处表示这款应用程序允许老师用英文发送信息给家长，message 为可数名词，结合空格前的 teachers 可知发送的信息不止一条，故填 messages。

（6）translated。根据上文可知，老师用英语发送的信息将被翻译成家长使用的语言，所以家长用自己的语言回复老师时，这些信息会被翻译回英语。空格处为被动语态，故填 translated。

（7）found。分析句子可知，空格处为空格所在句子的谓语动词，空格后面的 that 引导的是宾语从句。空格后是最近一项研究的发现和结论，结合所给的首字母可推知 find（发现）符合语境，时态应用一般过去时，故填 found。

（8）about。空格前面为 she did not know anything，主谓宾完整，空格后面的 special education 为 anything 的具体内容，所以考虑空格处需填入介词，about 意为"关于"，符合句意，且首字母为 a，故填 about。

（9）meeting。空格前面为不定冠词 a 和名词 school，由此可知空格处需填入一个名词。根据上文的 During a school meeting（在一次校会上）可知，meeting 符合句意，故填 meeting。

（10）parents。空格处与 families 并列，由此可知空格处需填入一个名词。第一段中提到 Parents need to feel like they can be actively involved in their children's schooling, regardless of any language difficulties（家长想要他们可以积极参与孩子的学校教育，即使有语言困难）。由此可知空格所在部分指的是为家长和家庭创造一个没有语言障碍的空间，故填 parents。

Week Four

Monday【A 完形填空】

答案解析

1. **D**。考查名词辨析。A项意为"市场",B项意为"机场",C项意为"车站",D项意为"家乡"。根据常识可知,江苏省淮安市是周恩来总理的故乡,故选D。

2. **A**。考查动词辨析。A项意为"选择",B项意为"决定",C项意为"跟随",D项意为"表扬"。根据下文 one of the new cities to be added to the UNESCO Creative Cities Network 可知,淮安被选为联合国教科文组织创意城市网络中的一员,故选A。

3. **C**。考查固定搭配。thanks to 为固定搭配,意为"由于;幸亏",代入原文后符合语境,故选C。

4. **B**。考查动词辨析。A项意为"庆祝",B项意为"给",C项意为"放",D项意为"拿走"。空格上文提到淮安的地理位置,下文提到淮安的美食兼具南北特色,由此可知,地理位置给淮安提供了兼具南北特色的中华美食,故选B。

5. **A**。考查名词辨析。A项意为"运输;公共交通",B项意为"成就",C项意为"交换",D项意为"经营;管理"。根据上文 The city lies alongside the Beijing-Hangzhou Grand Canal 可知淮安在京杭大运河旁,由此可知,这一位置有利于水利交通运输,故选A。

6. **C**。考查形容词辨析。A项意为"相似的",B项意为"单个的",C项意为"主要的",D项意为"可能的"。根据下文 Huaiyang cuisine—a term for dishes from Huai'an and Yangzhou 可知淮扬菜是淮安菜和扬州菜的统称,由此可知,淮安是淮扬美食的主要发源地之一,所以C项符合语境,故选C。

7. **D**。考查动词辨析。A项意为"组织",B项意为"储存",C项意为"想象",D项意为"影响"。上文提到淮安位于京杭大运河旁,结合下文清朝时期便利的水运将淮安美食传播到中国北方可推知,淮安美食的传播受到了京杭大运河 2 500 年历史的影响,所以D项符合语境,故选D。

8. **A**。考查动词辨析。A项意为"建立",B项意为"搬运;携带",C项意为"设置",D项意为"收集"。上文提到京杭大运河拥有两千多年的历史,所以"建立"代入原文后符合语境,故选A。

9. **C**。考查介词辨析。A项意为"在……之前",B项意为"在……之间",C项意为"包括",D项意为"从;从……起"。北京市属于中国北方地区,将选项代入原文可知"包括"符合语境,故选C。

10. **B**。考查动词短语辨析。A项意为"打开",B项意为"吸收;理解",C项意为"拿走",D项意为"关掉"。将选项代入原文可知"吸收"符合语境,故选B。

11. **D**。考查名词辨析。A项意为"城市",B项意为"世界",C项意为"乡村",D项意为"国家"。根据本段语境可知,淮安优越的地理位置和便利的水利交通使得淮安美食传播到全国各地,同样也可以吸收来自全国各地的美食烹饪方法,故选D。

12. **A**。考查定语从句。分析句子结构可知,_____ often has a sweet flavor... ingredient 是一个非限制性定语从句,修饰先行词 Huai'an cuisine,连接词在从句中作主语,指物,所以用 which,故选A。

13. **C**。考查形容词辨析。A项意为"对立的;相反的",B项意为"仔细的;谨慎的",C项意为"原来的;独创的",D项意为"沮丧的"。根据空格后的 taste of the ingredient 可知,这里是指淮安菜保留了鱼这一食材原本的味道,故选C。

14. **D**。考查名词辨析。A项意为"调味品;佐料",B项意为"调味汁;酱",C项意为"烹饪法,食谱",D项意为"佳肴;盘子"。根据下文 grand national banquet was completely based on Huaiyang cuisine(盛大的国宴完全以淮扬菜为基础)可知,国宴上也会有地方菜,所以D项符合语境,故选D。

15. **B**。考查名词辨析。A项意为"温度",B项意为"历史",C项意为"巡游;巡航",D项意为"优点"。将选项代入原文可知"历史"符合语境,故选B。

Tuesday【B 阅读理解】

答案解析

1. **C**。细节理解题。根据文章各段落的小标题可知,本文主要讲述了四种实现健康饮食的方法,故选C。

2. **B**。细节理解题。根据题干中的 planning your foods before eating 可以定位到 Log your intake 中的第一句,由此可知如果不擅长在吃之前规划饮食,可以采用的策略是 Log your intake(记录你的摄入),故选B。

3. **B**。细节理解题。根据题干中的 convenience foods 可

以定位到 Eat fewer ultra-processed foods 这一段，由最后一句 So instead, make your whole foods and meals by yourself 可知你应该自己做食物，故选 B。

4. B。细节理解题。A 项 Make your meal balanced 为第四个小标题 Balance your plate（平衡你的"餐盘"）的同义表达；C 项 Eat fewer convenience foods 对应第三个小标题 Eat fewer ultra-processed foods（少吃超加工食品）；D 项 Try a new vegetable each week 与原文中的 If you don't know everything about healthy eating, one way is to try a new vegetable each week（如果你不知道关于健康饮食的一切，一个方法是每周尝试一种新蔬菜）相符；只有 B 项 Drink much water if possible（尽可能多喝水）在原文中没有明确提到。故选 B。

5. C。推理判断题。本文主要讲述了实现健康饮食的四种方法，由此可推知，最可能在健康杂志上看到这篇文章，故选 C。

Wednesday【C 阅读理解】

● 答案解析

1. D。细节理解题。第一段第二句提到，The new research finds that people who take in 10 grams a day of olive oil have an up to 34% lower risk of dying（新研究发现，每天摄入 10 克橄榄油的人死亡风险最高可降低 34%）。结合第三句中的 People who consume more olive oil in their meals have lower risks of getting serious health conditions（在膳食中摄入更多橄榄油的人患严重疾病的风险较低）可知，D 项符合文意，故选 D。

2. D。细节理解题。根据第二段中的 people who had more olive oil on a regular basis were usually more physically active, less likely to smoke, and more likely to eat more fruits and vegetables... All of those reasons can lower your disease risk（那些经常食用较多橄榄油的人通常身体更有活力，不太可能吸烟，而且更可能吃较多的水果和蔬菜……所有这些因素都可以降低患病的风险）可知，吃橄榄油、保持身体的活力、少吸烟、多吃水果和蔬菜等因素可以降低患病的风险，D 项在文中没有明确提到，故选 D。

3. B。细节理解题。由题干中的 Dr. Tadwalkar 可定位至第三段第二句，该句提到 When fats are needed, plant oils from seeds, nuts, fruits, are the way to go（当需要烹调用

油时，从种子、坚果、水果中提取的植物油是正确的选择），由此可知，无法从 B 项提到的黄油中提取植物油，故选 B。

4. C。语篇理解题。第三段主要讲述了 Guasch-Ferré 与 Dr. Tadwalkar 对于食用橄榄油的态度和建议，所以 C 项符合文意，故选 C。

5. A。推理判断题。根据第三段 Dr. Tadwalkar 的观点 Olive oil, especially extra virgin olive oil, has been shown to be important when people are looking to improve their health（橄榄油，尤其是特级初榨橄榄油，已被证明在人们寻求改善健康方面发挥着重要作用）可知，他认为橄榄油对人们改善健康有重要作用；B 项与最后一段中作者的论述相符；C 项中 not healthy for your body 与 D 项中 shouldn't consume more olive oil 都和 Dr. Tadwalkar 的观点相反。故选 A。

Thursday【D 阅读理解】

● 答案解析

1. D。细节理解题。根据第一段中的 diets with fat from vegetables instead of from meat are connected with a lower risk of stroke 可知，从蔬菜中摄取脂肪的饮食与降低中风的风险有密切联系，故选 D。

2. B。细节理解题。根据第二段第三句 Dairy fat was not connected with increased risk of stroke（乳脂与中风风险的增加无关）可知 A 项不符合文意；根据第四段第二句中的 A TIA is a sign of a serious condition（短暂性脑缺血发作是一种严重疾病的征兆）可知 B 项符合文意；根据第二段第一句中的 people who ate the most vegetables and polyunsaturated fats were 12 percent less likely to have ischemic strokes（吃最多蔬菜和多不饱和脂肪的人患缺血性中风的可能性要低 12%）可知 C 项不符合文意；根据第四段第三句 Hemorrhagic strokes happen when an artery in the brain leaks blood, which could hurt brain cells（出血性中风发生在大脑动脉出血时，这会损伤脑细胞）可知 D 项不符合文意。故选 B。

3. C。语篇理解题。第三段主要描述了一些中风的症状，所以 C 项最能概括本段大意，故选 C。

4. B。细节理解题。最后一段最后一句提到 High blood pressure, smoking, diabetes and high cholesterol are the leading causes of stroke（高血压、吸烟、糖尿病和高胆固醇是中风的主要原因）。由此可知，A、C、D 三项符

合文意，B项（缺乏锻炼）在文中没有明确提到，故选B。
5. C。主旨大意题。本文第一段和第二段介绍了一项关于中风的新研究及其结论，第三段介绍了中风的症状，第四段介绍了两种中风以及中风的主要病因，由此可知本文主要介绍了一些关于中风的信息，故选C。

Friday【E 任务型阅读】
● 答案解析

1. E。空格后提到了年度最佳饮食竞赛中排名第三的饮食，结合上文提到的地中海饮食在年度最佳饮食竞赛中夺冠可知，空格处可能在介绍在饮食竞赛中名列第二的饮食法。E项"排名第二的是强调较少的盐摄入量的得舒饮食"符合文意，故选E。
2. G。空格上文主要介绍了年度最佳饮食竞赛中的前三名，即地中海饮食、得舒饮食和弹性素食饮食。空格位于段尾，由此可推测，空格处在对这三种饮食方式进行总结，说明其共同之处。G项"这三种饮食法都强调较少的加工食品的摄入，并在你的盘子里塞满水果、蔬菜、豆类和坚果"符合文意，故选G。
3. A。根据空格前的We want food we can enjoy（我们想要自己喜欢吃的食物）可知，空格处承接上文，说明我们真正想要的食物是什么样子的。A项"我们也想要能让我们保持健康的食物"符合文意，且与上文在结构和语义上保持一致，故选A。
4. F。空格上文主要讲述了地中海饮食的具体内涵及其主要包括哪些有利于保持健康的食物。F项"该饮食法也鼓励人们食用健康的鱼，而鸡蛋的摄入量要少得多"是对地中海饮食介绍的延续，符合文意，故选F。
5. C。空格处位于段首，可能是本段的主题句。根据空格下文的一些表述help reduce the risk for illnesses、stronger bones 和 a healthier heart and longer life 可知，本段主要介绍了地中海饮食的一些优点。C项"大量研究发现，地中海饮食有很多优点"符合文意，故选C。

Saturday【F 短文填空】
● 答案解析

（1）probably。空格后面为动词like，所以考虑空格处为副词作状语，修饰like。所给单词中只有probably为副词，且符合句意，故填probably。
（2）In。空格后面为the research，根据下文提到的科内利斯和她的团队研究的具体内容可知，空格所在部分表示"在研究中"，故填In。
（3）discovered。分析句子结构可知，空格前面的Cornelis and her team 为句子的主语，空格后面为that引导的宾语从句，所以空格处应填谓语动词。又因科内利斯和她的团队所做的研究发生在过去，所以这个动词应为一般过去时，所给单词中只有discovered符合要求及句意，故填discovered。
（4）enjoy。空格前面为why引导的宾语从句的主语some people，空格后为名词短语so many cups of coffee，所以空格处应填谓语动词。下文while others do not like it中的while表示对比，意为"然而"，所以空格处应填like的同义词或近义词，enjoy意为"享受，喜欢"，符合句意及要求，故填enjoy。
（5）drink。空格前面为need to，空格后面为名词more coffee，所以空格处为动词。根据下文drinking a lot of coffee并结合空格处句意可知，空格所在句子表示具有该基因的人代谢咖啡因的速度更快，因此需要喝更多的咖啡，故填drink。
（6）explain。空格前面为情态动词could，空格后面为why引导的宾语从句，所以空格处为动词。空格前的This指代上文的研究结论，由此可知，空格所在句子表示上述研究结论可以解释有些人喝很多咖啡都似乎没问题这一现象，explain意为"解释"，符合句意及要求，故填explain。
（7）anxious。根据空格前的or可知，空格所在的短语应为get nervous的同义表达，空格处为形容词。所给单词中，anxious与nervous语义相近，且符合句意，故填anxious。
（8）chocolate。空格前面为形容词dark，所以空格处为名词。根据第一段中的Prefer your coffee black? Then you probably like dark, bitter chocolate可知，此处表示人们想到咖啡时，就会想到苦苦的味道，也会喜欢黑巧克力，故填chocolate。
（9）foods。空格前面为形容词bitter，所以空格处为名词。根据最后一段中的for other bitter foods可知，foods符合句意，故填foods。
（10）with。deal with为固定搭配，意为"处理；解决；应付"，故填with。

Week Five
Monday【A 完形填空】
答案解析

1. A。考查名词辨析。A 项意为"机会"，B 项意为"邀请"，C 项意为"组织；机构"。根据下文 due to the COVID-19 可知，新冠肺炎疫情使得孩子们缺少广泛社交的机会，A 项代入后符合语境，故选 A。

2. C。考查动词短语辨析。A 项意为"提出；想出（主意、回答等）"，B 项意为"容忍, 忍受"，C 项意为"与……闲逛"。下文提到 Instead, they are the ones we believe completely（相反，他们是我们完全信任的人），这表示与朋友的亲密程度很深，由此可知，上文描述的是不那么亲密的朋友，C 项代入原文后意为"这些朋友不只是我们喜欢和他们一起出去玩的人"，符合句意，故选 C。

3. B。考查形容词辨析。A 项意为"坦率的"，B 项意为"重要的"，C 项意为"容易的"。根据下文 Close friendships in childhood help kids practice the skills they need（童年时期的亲密友谊有助于孩子练习他们所需要的技能）可推知，拥有健康的友谊是孩子拥有的一项重要技能，故选 B。

4. C。考查固定搭配。deal with 为固定搭配，意为"应对；处理"，故选 C。

5. B。考查名词辨析。A 项意为"采访；面试"，B 项意为"活动"，C 项意为"习惯"。分析句子结构可知，空格后的 that could be done with other children 是一个定语从句，修饰空格处的名词，根据下文中的 join in with games and activities（加入游戏和活动）可知"活动"符合句意，故选 B。

6. A。考查上下文语义。A 项意为"如何"，B 项意为"为什么"，C 项意为"什么"。空格所在部分为"teach sb. sth."的结构，A 项代入原文后意为"家长们也可以教孩子如何加入游戏和活动"，符合句意，故选 A。

7. C。考查副词辨析。A 项意为"简单地；仅仅"，B 项意为"不可能地"，C 项意为"极其；非常"。根据下文 who aren't used to relationships ending（他们还不习惯于结束一段友谊）可推知，孩子在童年时期，不知道如何处理一段人际关系的结束；对孩子而言，最好的朋友离开自己，这件事理解起来肯定非常困难，故选 C。

8. A。考查动词辨析。A 项意为"支持；支撑"，B 项意为"拯救；节约"，C 项意为"批评"。根据上文可知，孩子不知道要如何处理与好朋友分离的情况，所以家长在这时要适时地提供支持或帮助，故选 A。

Tuesday【B 阅读理解】
答案解析

1. C。细节理解题。根据第一段中彭霖倩童年时期的个人经历，以及结合第一段最后一句 When she grew up, she has been working to give a voice to the hearing-impaired because she knew the importance of self-expression（当她长大后，因为知道自我表达的重要性，她一直致力于为听力受损的人发声）可知，彭霖倩一直致力于帮助有听力障碍的孩子，因为她想帮助这些孩子们拥有自我表达的能力，故选 C。

2. B。细节理解题。根据第二段第二句中的 they designed many writing, storytelling and theater activities（他们设计许多写作、讲故事和戏剧活动）和最后一句中的 they also designed a few activities, for example, taking off their hearing aids or shouting（他们也设计了一些活动，如让大家摘下助听器或扯着嗓子大喊）可知，只有 B 项"经常锻炼"不是彭霖倩在项目中帮助听力受损的儿童使用的方法，故选 B。

3. C。词义猜测题。画线单词上文提到 The children were either too shy（孩子们要么过于害羞）。either... or... 用于连接两个性质相同的词或短语，意为"要么……要么……"，结合下文提到的一个女孩花一整天的时间折纸可推知，孩子们不愿意参加这些活动，unwilling 意为"不愿意的"，故选 C。

4. A。细节理解题。根据第三段最后两句 ...even the girl who liked paper folding left a message in the postcard shop she chose. She wrote: "Today, I had a wonderful time."（……甚至那个喜欢折纸的女孩还在她选择的明信片商店里留了言。她写道："今天，我过得很愉快。"）可知，喜欢折纸的女孩感觉很开心。Pleased 意为"开心的；愉快的"，Angry 意为"生气的"，Bored 意为"枯燥的"，Confident 意为"自信的"，A 项代入后符合文意，故选 A。

5. B。主旨大意题。通读全文可知，本文主要讲了彭霖倩童年时期的个人经历使她意识到表达自我的重要性，后来她参加表演讲习班项目，致力于帮助有听力障碍的儿童，让他们有机会去表达自己，B项"介绍彭霖倩为帮助有听力障碍的孩子所做的努力"最能概括文章主旨，故选B。

Wednesday【C 任务型阅读】

答案解析

（1）aimed/aiming。原短文中的表达是with the aim of bringing nature to children（其目标是把自然带给孩子们），对比两处可知空格处缺少表示"目标是；旨在"的单词。be aimed at doing sth. 和 aim at doing sth. 都是 aim 作动词时的习惯用法，空格前是be动词is，故空格处可填入 aimed 或 aiming。故填 aimed/aiming。

（2）lessons。空格所在句子为There be句型，且空格前有many，由此可知，空格处需填入可数名词的复数形式。根据空格所在句中的 City Blossoms、environmental science 等词定位到原文第二段第一句，可知 environmental science 等都是"城市之花"开设的课程，故填 lessons。

（3）teach。空格前有情态动词can，所以空格处需填入动词原形。原文中的表达是 teachers can also use the green space for reading lessons by reading a garden-related book or learning nature words（教师也可以通过阅读与园艺相关的书籍或学习与自然相关的词汇来利用绿色空间进行阅读教学），教师利用绿色空间的目的是教学生学会阅读，由此可知 teach 符合此处要求，故填 teach。

（4）organized。空格前有be动词，空格后有介词by，由此可知空格所在句使用了被动语态，空格处可填入一个动词的过去分词。原文中的表达是 students learn how to grow and harvest crops through the organization of City Blossoms' program（他们通过"城市之花"项目的组织来学习如何种植和收割作物）。原文中的 through 和空格后的 by 都可表示"方式"，但是空格所在部分缺少相应的表示"组织"的谓语动词，所以需将 organization 改成动词的过去分词形式，故填 organized。

（5）important。空格前有be动词 are 和副词 really，所以空格处可填入一个形容词。原文中的表达是 People have really woken up to the fact that green spaces are of great importance（人们已经意识到绿色空间是非常重要的），be of importance 等于 be important，表示"重要的"，故填 important。

Thursday【D 任务型阅读】

答案解析

1. E。空格前提到年轻一代如今更乐于接受国内产品，也就是说，年轻一代不再只迷恋国外品牌，E项"年轻人不会只为写着'意大利制造'的大牌买单"符合文意，且E项中的 Young people 与上文中的 the younger generation 为同义表达，故选E。

2. A。空格处位于段首，因此可能是本段的主旨句。本段主要介绍了一家国内公司为郑州市抗洪救灾工作提供支持一事，由此可推知，A项"鸿星尔克付出的巨大的努力给我留下了深刻的印象"符合文意，故选A。

3. D。根据空格前的 I used to be among the group that preferred foreign brands 可知作者之前喜欢国外品牌，空格处可能承接上文，且空格下文提到作者对国产商品的偏见，由此可推测空格处在进一步说明作者喜欢国外品牌的理由。D项"我一直认为使用外国货让我看起来很时尚"符合文意，故选D。

4. C。根据空格前的 I dropped my prejudice later when I tried some domestically made clothes by Chinese designers 可知，作者后来对国产品牌不再抱有偏见。由此可推知，空格处可能描述的是与进口产品相比，国内品牌的优势，C项"其质量与外国货一样好，但价格要实惠得多"符合文意，故选C。

5. F。空格上文提到人们对国家发展的信心和国内产品设计和质量的改进是国产品牌发展起来的主要原因。F项"这种态度的变化在年轻一代中更为明显，他们是在中国经济蓬勃发展的环境中成长的"进一步强调年轻人对国产品牌的态度变化，符合文意，故选F。

Friday【E 任务型阅读】

答案解析

1. Alice Jackson and her friend Rachel Chung. 根据题干中的关键词 came up with the idea of a telephone helpline 定位到第二段第一句，由 Alice Jackson, 22, and her friend Rachel Chung came up with the idea of a telephone helpline 可知是爱丽丝·杰克逊和她的朋友雷切尔·钟想出了求

助热线的主意。

2. asked; the number。根据题干中的关键词 bought a cheap phone 定位到第二段最后一句，对比原句可知句子中缺少的单词分别是 asked 和 the number。

3. 接听电话的志愿者们与来电者聊天并提供安慰，但有时来电者会担心自己的安全。

4. They can alert the police or call an ambulance if needs be. 根据题干中的关键词 the caller thinks she is not safe 定位到第四段，由 Volunteers like Alice are ready to alert the police or call an ambulance if needs be 可知志愿者们可以随时准备报警或者叫救护车。

5. safely。空格处修饰前面的短语 gets home，故空格处应填入副词，而所给的单词为形容词，所以需将形容词变成副词，safe 的副词形式为 safely。

6. I can call Strut Safe's free helpline from 7 pm—3 am on Fridays and Saturdays, and 7 pm—1 am on Sundays. 根据本文最后一段可知 Strut Safe 服务热线的在线时间。

Saturday【F 短文填空】

● 答案解析

（1）terrible。空格前面的 sounds 为系动词，由此可知空格处应填入形容词。空格后提到艾伦在办公楼被隔离以后仍然保持镇定，结合空格后的 But 可知空格所在句讲述的情况与下文存在转折关系。terrible 意为"可怕的"，代入原文后符合语境，故填 terrible。

（2）working。空格所在的部分 a director _____ at a company who was trapped in the company's building in Shanghai 作同位语修饰 Allen，解释说明其身份，由此可知艾伦是在一家公司工作的主管，work 意为"工作"，符合语境。根据句子结构可知，_____ at a company 作后置定语修饰 a director，且 work 与其逻辑主语 a director 之间为主动关系，所以填入 work 的现在分词形式，故填 working。

（3）peaceful。空格前面有 and，and 前后为并列成分，所以空格处应填入意思与 calm 相近的形容词，peace 为名词，其形容词形式 peaceful 意为"平静的"，符合语境，故填 peaceful。

（4）she。分析句子可知，空格处作句子主语。根据双引号可知这是艾伦对当时情况的回忆，结合空格下文中的 she said 可知，艾伦是一名女性员工，故填 she。

（5）to send。空格前面提到有人在网上订购了东西，再结合 others called family members 可推测，隔离员工打电话给家人的目的是让他们送物品来，此处为动词不定式作目的的状语，故填 to send。

（6）before。空格所在的句子主干完整，空格后面的 bedtime 为时间状语，所以空格处需填入一个介词。根据常识及语意可知，购买的床上用品应是在晚上就寝之前送到，故填 before。

（7）were given。空格所在句缺少谓语，由此可知空格处应填入谓语动词。将所给的动词一一代入句中，只有 give 符合句意，但此处主语为 Meal allowances，应是"餐补被给"，所以空格所在句子为被动语态。主语 Meal allowances 为复数名词，且文章整体时态为一般过去时，故填 were given。

（8）problem。空格前为形容词，且空格处所填单词在句中作主语，由此可知空格处应填入名词。将选项中的名词代入句中，只有 problem 符合句意，故填 problem。

（9）understanding。空格前为动词 showed，缺少宾语，所以空格处应填入一个名词。根据空格后面的 gave a thumbs-up 可知，被隔离的上班族们称赞政府的快速反应，所以空格处应同样是一个表示积极态度的名词。将所给的单词一一代入句中，可知 understand 符合句意，此处应用其动名词形式，故填 understanding。

（10）behaviors。and 前后为并列成分，且空格前有形容词 quick，所以空格处应填入一个名词。结合上文提到的政府和公司提供床上用品、给予餐补等行为可知，此处表示处于隔离状态的办公人员对其快速反应和行动称赞，behave 的名词形式为 behavior，且为可数名词，故填 behaviors。

Week Six

Monday【A 完形填空】

● 答案解析

1. A。考查形容词辨析。A项意为"受欢迎的；流行的"，B项意为"共同的；普遍的"，C项意为"自然的"。根据上文 has been selling like hotcakes 可知"冰墩墩"很畅销，由此可知本句是询问这个吉祥物受欢迎的原因，所以 A 项符合文意，故选 A。

2. B。考查介词辨析。A项意为"在……中间"，B项意为"……的"，C项意为"和；具有"。将三个选项代入原文，只有 B 项符合文意，意为"它的设计理念"，故选 B。

3. A。考查固定搭配。A项意为"告诉"，B项意为"讲话"，C项意为"说"。tell the story 为固定搭配，表示"讲故事"，故选 A。

4. C。考查副词辨析。A项意为"非正式地；随意地"，B项意为"虚弱地"，C项意为"清楚地"。根据下文 the exciting day of September 17th 以及曹雪对这一天的具体描述可知，曹雪对这一天印象深刻，记得很清楚，因此 C 项符合文意，故选 C。

5. B。考查动词辨析。A项意为"复习；评论"，B项意为"设计"，C项意为"接收"。根据上文可知最终入选的北京冬奥会吉祥物是曹雪团队设计的，故选 B。

6. B。考查名词辨析。A项意为"表现；表演"，B项意为"讨论"，C项意为"管理；经营"。将三个选项代入原文，只有 B 项符合文意，意为"经过许多专家的讨论，吉祥物有了一个新的名字"，故选 B。

7. C。考查形容词辨析。A项意为"干净的"，B项意为"现代的"，C项意为"传统的"。根据常识可知糖葫芦是中国的传统美食，所以 C 项符合文意，故选 C。

8. C。考查动词辨析。A项意为"失败"，B项意为"跳跃"，C项意为"乘飞机；飞行"。根据下文可知，曹雪和其设计团队到中国卧龙大熊猫博物馆进行实地观察，flew 是 fly 的过去式，fly to 意为"坐飞机去……"，符合文意，故选 C。

9. A。考查连词辨析。A项意为"但是"，B项意为"和；而且"，C项意为"或者"。上文提到"冰墩墩"的外壳是冷的，下文提到其形象看起来温暖又可爱，由此可知，空格前后内容在语义上发生转折，故选 A。

10. C。考查名词辨析。A项意为"文化"，B项意为"天赋"，

才能"，C项意为"温暖"。上文提到"冰墩墩"的外在形象给人温暖又可爱的感觉，下文的 this kind of 指代的应当是上文提到过的内容，只有 C 项 warmth 符合文意，warmth 是 warm 的名词形式，故选 C。

Tuesday【B 阅读理解】

● 答案解析

1. C。细节理解题。根据第一段中的 portraiture has told us elementary truths about human nature and identity（肖像画向我们讲述了关于人性和身份的基本事实）和 know more about social and cultural history（对社会和文化历史了解得更多）可知，我们可以通过肖像画了解到画中人物的身份以及社会和文化历史，文中没有提到从肖像画能看出画中人物的喜好，故选 C。

2. B。推理判断题。由题干中的 Self-portrait with Bandaged Ear 可定位至第二幅肖像画的介绍，根据 Van Gogh's Self-portrait with Bandaged Ear... shows his great determination to continue painting despite the hurt（梵高《割耳朵后的自画像》……展示了他不顾伤痛、继续作画的强大决心）可知，梵高即使受伤也要继续作画，由此可推测梵高十分热爱绘画，因此 B 项符合要求，故选 B。

3. D。推理判断题。本文第一段介绍了肖像画的功能，图表中介绍了三幅肖像画，都是与绘画艺术相关的话题，由此可推知可以在艺术类的报刊或网站上看到这篇文章，D 项 An art website 意为"一个艺术网站"，符合要求，故选 D。

Wednesday【C 阅读理解】

● 答案解析

1. B。细节理解题。根据第一段第一句 In Chinese culture, the tiger stands for energy and vitality（在中国文化中，老虎象征着力量和活力）和第二段中的 the traditional strong tiger（传统的猛虎）可知，中国文化中传统意义上的老虎形象是强大、有力量的。B 项中 Energetic（精力充沛的）为原文 energy 的形容词形式，故选 B。

2. C。细节理解题。根据第一段中的 His tigers are fat and lazy, often with interesting and foolish expressions（他创作的老虎又胖又懒，总是带着有趣又笨笨的表情）和 especially in this Year of the Tiger（尤其是在今年这个虎年）可知 A 项和 B 项都是胖虎受欢迎的原因，而 C 项

100

3. B。细节理解题。根据第二段中的 Cub Calling for Its Mother（《喊妈小老虎》）和 Fierce Tiger Descending the Mountain（《猛虎下山》）可知，本文主要提到了不二马的两幅作品，故选 B。

4. A。词义猜测题。根据画线词组前面的 the COVID-19 pandemic 可推测此处指新冠肺炎疫情在中国暴发，因此 A 项符合大意，其他两项均不符合文意和逻辑，故选 A。

5. A。细节理解题。根据最后一段第一句 My biggest trouble at present is that Panghu is so popular that I don't have enough time to learn new things and improve myself, which is a dangerous sign for me（我现在最大的问题是，胖虎太受欢迎了，我没有足够的时间学习新东西，提升自己，这对我来说是一个危险的信号）可知，不二马现在最烦恼的是没有时间学习新东西。题干中的 worried about 是原文中 trouble 的同义表达，因此 A 项正确。不二马的画受欢迎是一个现象，并不是他担忧的问题，故排除 B 项。C 项在原文中未提及。故选 A。

Thursday【D 任务型阅读】

答案解析

1. B。空格前的 The Dia Art Foundation invited the local artist Walter De Maria to create it in 1977 提到沃尔特·德·玛利亚于 1977 年创建了纽约地球屋。而 B 项意为"经过三年的建设，其于 1980 年向公众开放"，1980 年的三年之前就是 1977 年，因此 B 项可承接上文，故选 B。

2. A。空格前的 Art lovers can visit the unusual attraction, enjoy the mass of dirt and take in its earthy fragrance 提到了艺术爱好者在纽约地球屋可以做的事情。在所有选项中，A 项中的 dirt 与上文呼应，且 A 项意为"但是，他们被禁止踩踏泥土，甚至连触碰都不可以"，与上文在语义上构成转折关系，符合文意，故选 A。

3. D。空格后的 He spends his days sitting at a desk, counting visitors, answering questions, and looking mysterious（他每天坐在桌子旁，登记访客，答疑解惑，看起来很神秘）描写的是一个人的状态，由此可推测空格处应是对一个人物的描述。D 项为"地球屋的看护人比尔·迪尔沃思自 1989 年以来一直在回答访客的问题"，下文中的 He 正好可以指代 D 项中的 Bill Dilworth，并且下文中的 visitors 与 D 项中的 visitors 相呼应，因此 D 项符合文意，故选 D。

4. E。空格后提到 So I think what I really want people to know is that...（所以我认为，我真正想要人们知道的是……），由此可推测，空格处的内容应该是描述人们原本想知道的内容，因此 E 项"人们总是想知道这到底意味着什么，但艺术家从来没有赋予其任何意义"符合文意，故选 E。

5. C。根据空格前的 few people would happily go to see a large loft filled with dirt, but you would be wrong 可知，纽约地球屋的访客其实并没有想象中的那么少，因此可推测空格处应该是描述实际的参观人数，且参观人数比人们预想的要多。C 项"地球屋对外开放时，每天参观这一独特的艺术品的访客多达 100 人"符合文意，故选 C。

Friday【E 任务型阅读】

答案解析

1. Because Wang Ping found that there wasn't any headdress that fitted with the studio's costumes. 根据第二段中的 He found that there wasn't any headdress... So he decided to make them on his own 可知，王平决定自己动手制作头冠是因为没有能与工作室的衣服搭配的头冠。

2. The first step to make a headdress is to do a design drawing. 根据第二段第五句 To craft a headdress there are three steps 可知，制作头冠主要有三个步骤，下文提到了具体的三个步骤。由 Firstly, I do a design drawing 可知制作头冠的第一步是画设计图纸。

3. Because almost all of them are made from waste materials. 根据第二段中的 I decided to make the most out of these 'waste materials' 可知，王平制作的头冠非常环保，原因在于他大多使用的是废弃材料。

4. Wang Ping prefers to make traditional Chinese phoenix coronets. 根据第三段第一句 He prefers to make traditional Chinese phoenix coronets 可知，王平更热衷于制作中国传统的凤冠。

5. It takes about one year to complete. 根据第三段王平的话 It takes about one year to complete 可知，制作以龙为主题的服装大约需要一年的时间才能完成。

Saturday【F 短文填空】

● 答案解析

（1）at。be good at 为固定搭配，表示"擅长……"，故填 at。

（2）than。分析句子结构可知，空格所在句子为 that 引导的定语从句，修饰先行词 steampunk masks，根据句意可知此句是将机器和人类进行对比，结合带有"比较"意义的词 more 可知此处应用 than，故填 than。

（3）mainly。空格处修饰系动词 aren't，应用副词，作状语，故填 mainly。

（4）types。all types of 表示"各种各样的，各种类型的"，符合文意，故填 types。

（5）to change。in order to do sth. 为固定搭配，表示"为了做某事"，在句中作目的状语，故填 to change。

（6）his。根据下文的 basement 可知空格处修饰名词，应用形容词性物主代词，故填 his。

（7）looking。此处作介词 by 的逻辑宾语，应用动名词形式，故填 looking。

（8）honest。to be honest 为固定短语，表示"说实话；坦白来说"，因此此空 honest 不需要变形，故填 honest。

（9）gives。分析句子结构可知，that... heavy, vintage look 是 that 引导的定语从句，修饰先行词 The paint，that 在从句中作主语，指代 The paint，为单数，且结合上下文可知此处在陈述客观事实，应用一般现在时，故填 gives。

（10）who/that。分析句子结构可知，_____ are interested in this kind of design on social media platforms 是定语从句，修饰先行词 his fans。空格处为引导词，指代 his fans，在从句中作主语，指人，故填 who/that。

Week Seven
Monday【A 完形填空】

● 答案解析

1. C。考查名词辨析。A项意为"操场",B项意为"房子",C项意为"街道",D项意为"工厂"。根据下文North Sichuan Road(四川北路)可知,这里讲的是今潮8弄靠近的是一条街道,故选C。

2. D。考查动词辨析。A项意为"看见",B项意为"给予;给",C项意为"控制",D项意为"改变;转变"。将四个选项代入文中,D项符合文意和逻辑,表示这一地方是由百年建筑群改建而成的,故选D。

3. B。考查介词辨析。A项意为"除……之外",B项意为"包括",C项意为"在……之中",D项意为"穿过"。空格前面提到a century-old compound(百年建筑群),空格后面提到60 shikumen-Shanghai-style houses and eight stand-alone buildings(六十幢海派石库门房子和八幢独立建筑)。由此可知,这一百年建筑群有六十幢海派石库门房子和八幢独立建筑,所以"包括"符合句意,故选B。

4. A。考查名词辨析。A项意为"家;住所",B项意为"地方;场所",C项意为"地球;地面",D项意为"公司"。将四个选项代入文中,A项符合文意及逻辑,且be home to为固定搭配,意为"……的所在地",故选A。

5. A。考查副词辨析。A项意为"曾经;一次",B项意为"从不",C项意为"总是",D项意为"大概;或许"。将四个选项代入文中,A项符合文意和逻辑,意为"四川北路也曾经是中国第一家电影院和私立的上海美术学院的所在地",故选A。

6. C。考查名词辨析。A项意为"中间",B项意为"结束",C项意为"开始",D项意为"顶端"。from the beginning为固定搭配,表示"从一开始",代入句中符合句意,故选C。

7. A。考查介词辨析。A项意为"通过",B项意为"穿过",C项意为"在……之前",D项意为"在……下方"。空格上文提到to show Shanghai-style culture(展示海派文化),将四个选项代入文中可知,A项符合文意及逻辑,表示展示海派文化的方式,故选A。

8. A。考查形容词辨析。A项意为"现代的",B项意为"奇怪的;陌生的",C项意为"危险的",D项意为"乏味的"。将四个选项代入文中,A项符合文意及逻辑,意为"结合传统与现代设计",故选A。

9. C。考查动词辨析。A项意为"借来",B项意为"买",C项意为"用,使用",D项意为"比较"。根据下文restore the buildings(修复建筑物)以及keep the original look(保持其原来的样子)可知,C项符合文意及逻辑,表示为了使建筑具有历史感,在翻修中使用了古旧的砖块,故选C。

10. D。考查状语从句。A项意为"尽管",后接让步状语从句;B项意为"当……时",后接时间状语从句;C项意为"因此;所以",后接结果状语从句;D项意为"因为",后接原因状语从句。上文提到使用旧砖修复建筑物,下文提到developers want to keep the original look(开发商们想要保持其原来的样子)。由此可推知,使用旧砖是为了保持建筑物原有的风格,上下文形成因果关系,故选D。

11. B。考查形容词辨析。A项意为"懒惰的",B项意为"相似的",C项意为"疯狂的",D项意为"紧张的"。similar to为固定搭配,意为"和……相似",符合句意,故选B。

12. D。考查形容词辨析。A项意为"干净的",B项意为"有礼貌的",C项意为"勇敢的",D项意为"不同的"。根据下文列举的opera, jazz and modern dance(歌剧、爵士和现代舞)可知,这些艺术家来自不同的领域,所以D项符合句意,故选D。

13. C。考查动词辨析。A项意为"拒绝",B项意为"失败",C项意为"目的是,旨在",D项意为"表现"。将四个选项代入文中可知,C项符合文意和逻辑,且aim to do sth.为固定搭配,故选C。

14. A。考查动词辨析。A项意为"说",B项意为"讨论",C项意为"争辩",D项意为"哭泣"。下文提到崇邦集团的首席执行官对年轻人的期望,可知此处是他在表达观点,故选A。

15. B。考查动词短语辨析。A项意为"拿出",B项意为"参加,参与",C项意为"取走",D项意为"照顾"。将四个选项代入文中,可知B项符合句意,意为"参加当地的文化活动",故选B。

Tuesday【B 阅读理解】

● 答案解析

1. A。词义猜测题。根据画线单词后的 from a sleepy fishing port to an energetic and big city 可知五十多年的发展使得迪拜从一个沉睡的渔港变成了一个活力满满的大都市，由此可知 A 项符合文意，故选 A。

2. D。细节理解题。根据第二段第二句 It usually happens when natural resources such as water and soil are overburdened（它通常发生在水和土壤等自然资源负担过重的时候），第二段第三句中的 desertification is more and more serious... because of human activities such as overgrazing, modern farming and building development（由于过度放牧、现代农业和建筑开发等人类活动，……荒漠化都越来越严重），以及第二段最后一句中的 Desertification happens when rich land, usually at the borders of deserts, is overburdened [当肥沃的土地（通常是位于沙漠边缘的肥沃土地）负担过重时就会发生荒漠化] 可知，水和土地等资源负担过重、现代农业和建筑开发等人类活动以及干旱地区的土地负担过重都会造成荒漠化，D 项指极端炎热的天气，文中并未明确提到这是荒漠化出现的原因，故选 D。

3. D。细节理解题。根据第三段倒数第二句中的 Trees fix the soil, take in carbon, improve soil fertility（树木能固定土壤，吸收碳，提高土壤肥力）可知 A、B、C 三项都是干旱地区种树的优点，只有 D 项不是，故选 D。

4. A。语篇理解题。文章最后一段前两句表明要找到修复土地生产力的解决办法，然后提到一个古老的解决方案就是种树，再说明种树的好处，最后提到了一个种树项目，由此可知该段主要讲述的是种树是一项有效的解决方案，所以 A 项符合段意。B 项和 C 项都是该段的细节信息，并不能概括整段的意思，D 项并不是最后一段的内容，故选 A。

Wednesday【C 任务型阅读】

● 答案解析

1. China's first Emperor Qinshihuang. 根据第一段第一句中的 China's first Emperor Qinshihuang, the founder of China's Qin Dynasty 可知，中国第一个皇帝秦始皇是秦朝的建立者。

2. The museum is famous for the Terracotta Warriors. 根据第二段第一句中的 the Emperor Qinshihuang's Mausoleum Site Museum including the burial site of Qinshihuang, is famous for the Terracotta Warriors 可知，秦始皇帝陵博物院因兵马俑而闻名。

3. 25. 根据第二段第二句中的 The 25 pottery figurines were newly found 可知最新发现的陶俑有 25 件。

4. Pit No.1 of the well-known Emperor Qinshihuang's Mausoleum Site Museum. 根据第二段第二句 The 25 pottery figurines were newly found in Pit No.1 of the well-known museum 可知，陶俑是在著名的秦始皇帝陵博物院的一号坑被发现的。

5. To make the pottery figurines safe. 根据第二段倒数第二句中的 are being stored in the protection room in order to make them safe 可知，将这些陶俑存放在保护室是为了确保安全。

Thursday【D 任务型阅读】

● 答案解析

1. together with；well-known。(A) 处的 along with 为固定搭配，表示"和；和……一起"，与 together with 同义；(D) 处的 famous 意为"出名的；著名的"，与 well-known 同义。

2. was built。分析句子结构可知，空格处作谓语，结合时间状语 in 1844 可知本句应用一般过去时；主语为 It，指代上文的 The spire，谓语动词用单数形式，build 和 It 之间为被动关系，表示"塔尖被建"，被动语态的结构为"be 动词+过去分词"，故应填 was built。

3. Today, the cathedral is being built again."巴黎圣母院"可以写出完整译名 Notre Dame Cathedral，但由于上文已多次提到"巴黎圣母院"，所以此处也可以用 the cathedral 代替；翻译时需要注意时态的选择，结合"今天"和"正在"可知本句要用现在进行时。

4. Tomas van Houtryve。第三段中提到 I wanted to take a photo of the present architect and team of workers using the same technique（我想要使用相同的技术拍摄现代建筑师和工作团队）。这里的"I"是 Tomas van Houtryve。

5. spire；roof。只要是文中出现的与建筑相关的名词均可，如 spire、roof、church、cathedral、attic。

Friday【E 短文填空】

● 答案解析

（1）oldest。分析句子结构可知，此处为"one of +the+ 形容词最高级 + 名词复数"的结构，表示"最……的……之一"，形容词 old 的最高级形式为 oldest，故填 oldest。

（2）Arriving。分析句子结构可知，此句已经有谓语动词，因此 arrive 只能是非谓语动词形式，又因主语 visitors 和 arrive 为主动关系，所以此空填 arrive 的现在分词形式，故填 Arriving。

（3）shines。分析句子结构可知，空格处在句中作谓语，陈述客观事实应用一般现在时，主语 the Notre-Dame de La Garde 为第三人称单数，故填 shines。

（4）are。分析句子结构可知，此处为 there be 句型，结合空格前的 is 可知时态为一般现在时，yachts 为复数名词，所以应用复数形式 are，故填 are。

（5）walked。空格处在句中作谓语动词，本段的整体时态为一般过去时，所以空格处应填 walk 的过去式，故填 walked。

（6）feel。be easy to do 为固定用法，意为"容易做……"，所以此空填 feel 的动词原形，故填 feel。

（7）clearly。空格处修饰动词 noticed，应用副词，故填 clearly。

Saturday【F 短文填空】

● 答案解析

（1）date back。分析句子结构可知，空格所在的句子谓语部分不完整，can 后面需接动词原形，所给选项中只有 date back 符合语法要求，date back 可与介词 to 构成搭配，意为"追溯到"，符合句意，故填 date back。

（2）all types of。分析句子结构可知，空格所在的句子主干完整，空格后面是名词短语 stone tools，由此可知空格处作定语修饰 stone tools，在所给选项中，all types of 意为"各种各样的"，符合句意，故填 all types of。

（3）cultural communication。分析句子结构可知，空格所在的句子已有主语和谓语，缺少宾语，所以空格处应填名词或名词短语。在所给选项中，cultural communication 意为"文化交流"，符合句意，故填 cultural communication。

（4）such as。分析句子结构可知，空格所在的句子主干完整，空格后面的 fire pits, tombs and pottery（火坑、墓葬和陶器）是对人类活动的举例，故填 such as。

（5）are similar to。分析句子结构可知，空格所在的句子缺少谓语，主语是 the tombs。在所给的选项中，are similar to 意为"与……相似"，符合句意，故填 are similar to。

Week Eight

Monday【A 完形填空】

答案解析

1. B。考查动词辨析。A 项意为"出现；似乎"，B 项意为"预料；期望"，C 项意为"在意；关心"，D 项意为"分享"。根据下文他的作品竟让海内外观众感到惊讶可知，这里应该讲的是他没有"预料"到，故选 B。

2. A。考查形容词辨析。A 项意为"最小的"，B 项意为"最长的"，C 项意为"最大的"，D 项意为"最轻的"。空格所在句中有 biggest ceramic，由转折连词 but 可知，空格所在部分语义上发生了转折，所以空格处应该表示"最小的"，故选 A。

3. C。考查形容词辨析。A 项意为"成功的"，B 项意为"危险的"，C 项意为"不同的"，D 项意为"愚蠢的"。上文提到他没有见过微型陶瓷，下文提到制作微型陶瓷，所以空格处应该是想表示他想做的事情是与众不同的，故选 C。

4. D。考查动词辨析。A 项意为"相信"，B 项意为"爱"，C 项意为"理解"，D 项意为"怀疑"。由空格前面的 not easy 可知一开始事情进展得并不顺利，and 表示并列，由此可知空格处是在继续描述开端的艰难情况，所以人们应该是持"怀疑"的态度，故选 D。

5. D。考查动词短语辨析。A 项意为"仰望；查阅"，B 项意为"建立"，C 项意为"张贴；举起"，D 项意为"放弃"。根据下文王文化想出了好办法可知，虽然遭受质疑，但他并没有放弃，故选 D。

6. B。考查上下文语义。on one's own 为固定搭配，意为"独立地，独自地"。根据上下文可知此处的 one 指的是 Wang Wenhua 这个人，故选 B。

7. B。考查介词短语辨析。A 项意为"关于，至于"，B 项意为"根据"，C 项意为"为了"，D 项意为"万一"。这句话表示的是王文化在告诉大家制作微型陶瓷的关键，"根据"符合句意，故选 B。

8. C。考查形容词辨析。A 项意为"教育的"，B 项意为"不健康的"，C 项意为"有创造力的"，D 项意为"弱小的"。根据下文 We have a very good relationship 可知他和粉丝的关系很好，所以粉丝给他提供的应该都是正向的、好的想法，结合选项，只有 C 项符合句意，故选 C。

9. A。考查动词辨析。A 项意为"花费"，主语可以是 it 也可以是物；B 项意为"花费"，主语通常为人；C 项意为"支付"，主语通常为人；D 项意为"带来"。空格后面的宾语是 one or two days（一到两天的时间），"花费"符合句意，且空格所在句子的主语是 more creative works（更有创意的作品），为物，故选 A。

10. D。考查连词辨析。A 项意为"因为"，表因果关系；B 项意为"所以"，表因果关系；C 项意为"但是"，表转折关系；D 项意为"除非"，表条件关系。根据句意可知此处应该表示条件关系，故选 D。

Tuesday【B 阅读理解】

答案解析

1. D。细节理解题。根据首句 Major Cold, the last solar term in 24 solar terms 可知大寒是二十四节气中的最后一个节气，也就是第 24 个，故选 D。

2. C。细节理解题。根据第二段第二句 Although in some regions of China the weather during Major Cold is not colder than Minor Cold, the lowest temperatures of the whole year still occur in the Major Cold period in some coastal areas 可知，在我国，有些地区大寒气温不比小寒低，但在有些沿海地区大寒是一年中最冷的时候，A 项和 B 项以偏概全，故排除，D 项表述错误，故选 C。

3. C。细节理解题。根据第三段倒数第三句 The rolls can be salty or sweet 可知 rolls 是咸口的食物，然后结合上文可知 rolls 就是指 fried spring rolls，故选 C。

4. A。词义猜测题。colds 在这里作名词，表示"感冒；风寒"。根据 keep us warm 可知这里强调保暖的功效，所以 prevent colds 应该是"预防感冒（风寒）"的意思，故选 A。

5. B。细节理解题。根据第三段第二句中的 In Chinese, the word "rice cake" has the same pronunciation as the word "higher in a new year" 可知，rice cake 在汉语中的发音和 higher in a new year 一样。good luck 只是 rice cake 的象征意义，所以 B 项表述错误，故选 B。

Wednesday【C 阅读理解】

答案解析

1. D。词义猜测题。A 项意为"推迟"，B 项意为"占据"，C 项意为"来自"，D 项意为"远离"。根据第一段第三句 Tigers are seen as fearless creatures 可知，人们认为老虎是无所畏惧的动物,所以其形象应该是可以驱邪避灾,故"远离"符合句意,故选 D。

2. C。细节理解题。根据第三段第二句 For example, strong economies in the East—Singapore, Republic of Korea, China's Hong Kong and Taiwan—were called "The Four Asian Tigers" 可知,"亚洲四小龙"包括新加坡、韩国、中国香港和中国台湾,没有印度,故选 C。

3. D。细节理解题。根据第二段 Tigers have an important cultural meaning not just in China, but across Asia 可知不仅在中国,老虎在整个亚洲都有重要的文化意义,所以 A 项表述错误;根据第四段第一句和第二句 Instead of tigers, lions are considered as the king of all beasts in the West. Brave soldiers were given the name "the lion" 可知,狮子是西方人心目中的百兽之王,勇敢的战士被称为"狮子",所以 B 项和 C 项表述错误。根据第三段第一句中的 for many people in the West, tigers have become a cultural symbol of Eastern countries 可知对许多西方人来说,老虎已经成为东方国家的文化象征,所以 D 项表述正确,故选 D。

4. A。推理判断题。根据第四段最后一句中的 if you want someone to calm down, you can say "easy tiger" 可知,当有人情绪激动,需要让其冷静下来的时候可以说 easy tiger,故选 A。

5. B。观点态度题。A 项意为"兴奋的",B 项意为"难过的,遗憾的",C 项意为"感到无聊的",D 项意为"快乐的"。根据全文最后一句 I felt so sad that they were an endangered species and I wanted to help protect them 可知,作者对于老虎成为濒危物种感到很难过,故选 B。

Thursday【D 任务型阅读】
● 答案解析

1. B。第一段是对丽江的总体介绍。第一句强调了丽江拥有古建筑和丰富的民族文化,使用的短语是 is home to。在所给选项中,B 项中有 is also home to,且 B 项意为"它也是中国少数民族纳西族的家园",与空格前一句可以衔接,故选 B。

2. C。空格后一句在讲纳西族建立城镇的相关信息,里面提到了 settled(定居)。在所给选项中,C 项中的 live 与 settle 意思相近,且 C 项意为"纳西族的祖先决定在此地居住,并开展农业",与空格前后句语义衔接,故选 C。

3. A。空格前一句提到水井有三个出水口,下文讲述的是水井的三个出水口的不同用途,所以 A 项"它们有不同的用途,以此来节约水资源"承上启下,符合语境,故选 A。

4. F。空格和空格的前一句都在介绍第一个井口的用途。根据对第二个井口用途的介绍可知,文中先是说明井口水的特点,再介绍其用途。而空格前一句 Water in the first opening at the high level comes from the spring(高处第一个井口的水来自泉水)是在描述井水的特点,所以下一句应该是介绍其用途,因此 F 项"因此被指定为饮用水"符合语境,故选 F。

5. E。上文提到现代人已不再需要从井中取水了。下文提到你永远不会看到年轻或年长的纳西人在第一个井口洗菜,这说明虽然现代设施已经取缔了从井中取水的原始方式,但是纳西族人民内心深处仍然尊重传统。E 项意为"然而,古老的传统却仍然留存在每个当地人的记忆中",符合语境,故选 E。

Friday【E 任务型阅读】
● 答案解析

1. It is on the eighth day of the 12th lunar month./It is on the eighth day of *la yue*. 根据第一段第二句 The eighth day of this lunar month is *la yue chu ba*, or *laba* 可知腊八节是在农历十二月(腊月)初八。

2. The three major customs on Laba are ancestor worship, eating Laba rice porridge and making Laba garlic. 根据第二段 Three major customs on Laba are ancestor worship, eating Laba rice porridge and making Laba garlic 可知腊八节的三大习俗分别是祭祖、吃腊八粥、做腊八蒜。

3. *La* is the act of making sacrifices to ancestors. 根据第三段第一句中的 the Chinese called the act of making sacrifices to their ancestors *la* 可知"腊"在中国古代是一种祭祀祖先的行为。

4. The main ingredients of the Laba rice porridge are rice and sticky rice. 根据第五段第一句 The main ingredients of the Laba rice porridge are rice and sticky rice 可知熬制腊八粥的主要食材是白米和糯米。

5. They put the garlic into vinegar in a sealed glass bottle. 根据最后一段第二句 They put the garlic into vinegar in a

sealed glass bottle 可知制作腊八蒜需要将蒜浸泡在醋中，并密封在玻璃瓶中。

Saturday【F 短文填空】
● 答案解析

（1）order。分析句子可知，舞狮队表演是为了对唐人街进行宣传。in order to 是固定搭配，意为"为了……"，符合语境，故填 order。

（2）down。根据前一句可知，新冠肺炎疫情对唐人街造成了很大的影响，很多人都离开了，所以店铺应该是关门了。shut down 为固定搭配，意为"关闭，停工"，故填 down。

（3）of。空格后面的 last year 是名词词组。because 后不能直接跟名词，而是要引导句子。because of 意为"因为"，of 为介词，后面可接名词、代词、动名词等，故填 of。

（4）lift。空格所在的短语是 to do 不定式，所以空格处需填入一个动词原形。根据上下文可知，新冠肺炎疫情让唐人街变得萧条，大家精神不振，所以舞狮是为了提振大家的精神。lift one's spirit 表示"提振精神"，故填 lift。

（5）back。根据第一段最后一句中的 attract people to return（吸引人们回来）可知，舞狮的目的是吸引人们重新回到唐人街，所以这里应该是把人们"带回来"。bring sb. back 意为"把某人带回来"，故填 back。

（6）for。空格所在句子的时态为现在完成时，空格后面的 over 40 years 表示"40多年"，属于一段时间，表示持续一段时间时，介词用 for，故填 for。

（7）dance。根据语境可知，空格处应表示"舞狮"，上文提到过"舞狮"，即 lion dance，故填 dance。

（8）since。空格前面的 I've been training at the school 是现在完成进行时，空格后面的 2017 是具体的时间点。表示动作从某一时间点开始一直持续到现在时用 since，意为"自从"，故填 since。

（9）because。空格前一句说舞狮开始时很有挑战性，空格后面说身体不适应那样的移动，可知这两句是因果关系，故填 because。

（10）how。本句讲述的是学习舞狮时需要学着如何承受狮头的重量，说明空格处表示的是"如何去做"，故填 how。

Week Nine

Monday【A 完形填空】

答案解析

1. D。考查上下文语义。A项意为"商业",B项意为"道路",C项意为"表情;眼神",D项意为"步伐"。根据下文可知这项技术主要是用来监测奶牛的情况,尤其是其跛足的问题,所以此处应该是检测奶牛的"每一步",故选D。

2. A。考查动词辨析。A项意为"隐藏",B项意为"改变",C项意为"治疗;对待",D项意为"移动"。根据文章首句Cows have evolved to hide lameness可知奶牛常隐藏自己的跛足,故选A。

3. A。考查连词辨析。A项表示转折,B项表示因果,C表示假设,D项表示并列。根据句意可知,此处应该是人和机器的对比。人发现不了的事情,机器却可以精准地捕捉到,所以前后构成转折,故选A。

4. C。考查名词辨析。A项意为"奶牛",B项意为"动物",C项意为"人类",D项意为"机器"。根据上文可知,机器可以发现人类发现不了的事情,由此可知人工智能是替代人类对奶牛进行监测的,故选C。

5. B。考查形容词辨析。A项意为"晚期的",B项意为"早期的",C项意为"自然的",D项意为"流行的"。根据全文最后一句So technology that helps the farmer find the earliest signs of lameness可知,泰瑞·坎宁公司的技术可以对奶牛的早期跛足迹象进行检测,故选B。

6. C。考查动词辨析。A项意为"改善",B项意为"研究;学习",C项意为"产出",D项意为"尝试"。奶牛肯定是产出牛奶,故选C。

7. C。考查动词短语辨析。A项意为"扑灭",B项意为"取出;把……带出去",C项意为"淘汰;击倒",D项意为"发现"。空格上文If they cannot be treated in time意为"如果它们不能及时获得治疗",所以空格处讲的是奶牛不能及时获得治疗的后果,A、B、D三项都不符合语境,故选C。

8. B。考查上下文语义。A项意为"发明",B项意为"技术",C项意为"公司",D项意为"活动"。上文一直在介绍代替人类检测奶牛跛足的技术,故选B。

9. A。考查动词辨析。A项意为"经营;跑",B项意为"发展",C项意为"给予",D项意为"邀请"。将选项代入句中,可知"经营农场"符合句意,故选A。

10. D。考查上下文语义。A项意为"肉",B项意为"水",C项意为"(水果、蔬菜等的)汁",D项意为"牛奶"。莎拉·劳埃德博士一家经营的是奶牛农场,所以"牛奶"符合句意,故选D。

11. B。考查名词辨析。A项意为"金钱",B项意为"成本",C项意为"标志",D项意为"想法"。根据can't be covered by our milk price(我们的牛奶价格不够)可知,这里指的是技术成本,故选B。

12. B。考查短语辨析。A项意为"多于",B项意为"而不是",C项意为"除了",D项意为"少于"。prefer to do... rather than do...为固定搭配,意为"宁愿做……而不愿做……",故选B。

13. B。考查形容词辨析。A项意为"同样的",B项意为"不同的",C项意为"完美的",D项意为"糟糕的"。根据下文可知杰弗里·布雷博士的观点和莎拉·劳埃德博士的观点不同,且文中并未对两者的观点进行评价,故排除C项和D项,故选B。

14. D。考查连词辨析。A项表示转折关系,B项表示让步关系,C项表示选择关系,D项表示因果关系。空格前意为"奶牛天生就想要隐藏跛足",空格后意为"它们已经演变成了猎物",由此可知奶牛隐藏跛足的原因是它们是猎物,怕被猎手盯上,所以是因果关系,故选D。

15. C。考查形容词辨析。A项意为"有趣的",B项意为"严厉的",C项意为"有用的",D项意为"错误的"。根据上文可知杰弗里·布雷博士与莎拉·劳埃德博士的观点不同,而莎拉·劳埃德博士并不太认可这项技术,由此可以推测杰弗里·布雷博士认为这项技术是"有用的",故选C。

Tuesday【B 阅读理解】

答案解析

1. C。词义猜测题。根据表格中的介绍可知,Auto Redial是针对拨打电话的,而且上文已说明其中一种情况是"号码占线",所以picked up应该是另一种情况,也就是"未能接听",对照选项,故选C。

2. C。细节理解题。根据对应的表格可知,Auto Redial和Celebrations Passport这两款应用程序虽然都可免费下载,但是都有付费部分,只有Magic Photo Editor是完全免费的,故选C。

3. C。细节理解题。根据题干中的 Celebrations Passport 定位到对应的表格。由 45 Ratings 可知这款应用程序的使用者不多，所以不会很流行，排除 A 项。文中并未提及这款应用程序所占内存的大小，故排除 B 项。由 It lets you put together gift baskets or other things like that for different occasions like Mother's Day（它可以让您为母亲节等不同场合准备礼品篮或其他礼品）可知 Celebrations Passport 可用于节庆场合，所以 C 项正确。D 项中的"激进的广告策略"是对 Magic Photo Editor 的描述，故排除。故选 C。

4. D。细节理解题。根据第一段中的 We got you covered with the best new Android apps in February 可知，作者推荐的是 2 月最好的安卓新款应用程序，而不是 2022 年最好的应用程序，所以排除 A 项。根据 If we missed any great new Android apps, tell us about them in the comments area（如果我们遗漏了任何不错的安卓新应用，请在评论区告诉我们）可知作者并不一定遗漏了某些很好的应用程序，B 项属于过度推测，故排除。作者在介绍 Magic Photo Editor 时讲述了推荐理由，也讲述了其不被用户喜欢的方面，所以无法得知作者最喜欢这款应用程序，C 项属于无中生有。作者从名称、价格、评分、用途等方面详细介绍了这三款应用程序，所以 D 项符合文意，故选 D。

5. A。推理判断题。根据 tell us about them in the comments area 中的 comments area（评论区）可知，这篇文章是发布在网络上的，最有可能是官网，对照选项，故选 A。

Wednesday【C 阅读理解】
● 答案解析

1. C。语篇理解题。wear 作动词时可表示"穿戴"，wearer 表示"穿戴……的人"。根据上文可知，人们佩戴的这种物品在紫外线的照射下会发光，还能显示病毒的踪迹。结合文章首句可知，该物品是一款新型口罩，所以 C 项符合语境，故选 C。

2. D。细节理解题。根据第一段最后一句可知，只有当佩戴者感染了新型冠状病毒时，口罩才会在紫外线的照射下发光，故 A 项错误。根据第三段第一句可知，研究团队注射的是灭活的新型冠状病毒，而不是活性的，故 B 项错误。根据第三段第二句中的 get antibodies from the eggs of these ostriches 可知，抗体是从鸵鸟蛋中提取的，并非鸵鸟体内，

故 C 项表述错误。故选 D。

3. A。词义猜测题。根据画线单词所在句可知，这里需判断 glow、the patients、viral load 的关系，病人病情好转，口罩发出的光减弱，也就意味着病毒载量减少，故选 A。

4. D。语篇理解题。A 项意为"被毁灭"，B 项意为"被暂停"，C 项意为"受伤"，D 项意为"得到许可"。get the green light 可直译为"开绿灯"，表示"得到许可"。根据文章最后一句中的 to sell the masks 也可以推测出，该研究人员是希望得到政府许可，从而合法售卖这种口罩，故选 D。

5. D。主旨大意题。本文对日本科学家们研发出的新型口罩进行了介绍。A 项以偏概全，无法概括主旨。B 项和 C 项无中生有。故选 D。

Thursday【D 阅读理解】
● 答案解析

1. B。细节理解题。根据第一段第一句 Small rocks impact all the time 和第二句中的 Something the size of a small car hits Earth's atmosphere about once a year 可知，小岩石无时无刻不在撞击地球，且一辆小型汽车大小的东西大约每年会撞击地球大气层一次，"小岩石"和"一辆小型汽车大小的东西"指的都是小行星，所以 B 项符合要求，故选 B。

2. A。词义猜测题。根据画线单词所在句子可知，用航天器撞小行星是为了避免其对地球的撞击。而要避免小行星对地球的撞击，就应该改变小行星运行的轨道，所以 A 项最符合逻辑，故选 A。

3. A。细节理解题。根据第二段中的 NASA is testing a new technique called Double Asteroid Redirection Test, or DART（美国国家航空航天局正在测试一项名为"双小行星重定向测试"的新技术，又称 DART）可知，DART 技术仍在测试中，文中并没有表明其已经投入使用，故 A 项与原文不符。B、C、D 三项均与原文相符，故选 A。

4. D。细节理解题。根据第三段可知，美国人死于飞机失事的概率是三万分之一，死于龙卷风的概率是六万分之一，死于小行星撞击的概率是七万五千分之一。对比三个概率，可知死于飞机失事的概率最高，死于小行星撞击的概率最低，所以 D 项符合文意。A、C 两项在文中并未提及，B 项与文章所述不符，故选 D。

5. D。主旨大意题。A 项和 C 项在文中有体现，但都是文中的细节信息，属于以偏概全。B 项中的 always 夸大事实，

Friday【E 短文填空】

● 答案解析

（1）A。分析句子结构可知，空格处修饰名词短语 global climate，故空格处可填形容词。选项中只有 changeable 和 able 是形容词，而 able 意为"有能力的"，放在此处不符合语境，故选 A。

（2）G。空格前面为形容词 small，后面为介词 of，所以空格处可填入名词。根据 small 前面的不定冠词 a 可以排除复数名词，由此可知只有 amount 符合要求。a small amount of 意为"少量的"，符合语境，故选 G。

（3）B。be able to do sth. 是固定搭配，意为"能够做某事"，代入原文后意为"能够更好地抵御洪水"，符合语境，故选 B。

（4）E。空格所在部分为"one of the+ 名词复数"的结构，表示"……之一"，所以空格处可填入一个复数名词。根据空格后提到的 they are easily destroyed by high temperatures（它们容易被高温损毁）可知，这应该是道路可能出现的问题之一，problems 符合语境，故选 E。

（5）F。空格前提到 Extreme heat can soften roads（极端高温会软化路面），空格后提到 more cracks or surface depressions（更多裂缝或表面凹陷），前后构成因果关系，且"裂缝"和"凹陷"应该是高温导致的。leading to 意为"导致"，符合语境，故选 F。

Saturday【F 短文填空】

● 答案解析

（1）number。a number of 为固定搭配，意为"许多；若干"，符合语境，故填 number。

（2）won。空格所在从句缺少谓语，空格后面是名词短语 the BBC's MasterChef TV competition（BBC《厨艺大师》电视比赛），所以空格处需填入一个动词。根据空格后面的名词短语和首字母 w 可知，安德森应该是赢得了比赛，win 意为"获胜"，符合语境。根据空格前的 back in 2011 可知时态为一般过去时，故填 won。

（3）dishes。空格前面为 would make，所在从句缺少宾语，所以空格处需填入一个名词。由上文可知蒂姆·安德森是一个专业厨师，且下文在解释机器人厨师是如何运作的，再结合首字母 d 可知 dish 符合句意。因 dish 意为"菜肴"时为可数名词，故填 dishes。

（4）cook。空格前面为 would，所以空格处需填入一个动词原形。根据语境可知安德森是被雇来做菜的，且下文出现 through the recipe（按照食谱），故填 cook。

（5）movements。空格所在句子缺少主语，所以空格处需填入一个名词。上文提到人类厨师做出动作展示，进而让机器人模仿。根据空格前的 Those 可知，空格所填词在上文应该出现过，上一段中的 movements 代入后符合上下文语境，故填 movements。

（6）same。空格前面有定冠词 the，后面为名词 dish，所以空格处需填入一个形容词。根据上文提到的 a consistent program（一致的程序）可知，通过一致的程序，肯定是做出一样的菜。same 意为"同样的"，符合语境，故填 same。

（7）improve。分析句子结构可知，空格所在的短语与 reduce viruses in food 并列，空格所在的部分已有名词，所以空格处需填入一个动词原形。上文提到食物中的病毒减少了，也就意味着清洁和卫生状况得到了改善，improve 意为"改善"，符合语境，故填 improve。

（8）result。空格前面有情态动词 could，所以空格处需填入一个动词原形。根据 warns 可知，这里讲述的是机器人厨师的弊端。job loss 意为"失业"，由此可知此处讲的是机器人厨师会与人类争夺工作岗位，导致人类失业。result in 为固定搭配，意为"导致"，符合语境，故填 result。

（9）while。分析句子结构可知，空格所在的部分为 that 引导的宾语从句，作 says 的宾语，宾语从句中有两个完整的句子，缺少连词。空格所在部分提到 kitchen robots offer convenience（厨房机器人提供了便利），下文提到 they won't be of interest to the higher end of the market（高端市场不会对它们感兴趣），由此可知前后构成转折关系，需填入表示转折的连词。while 引导让步状语从句时，常位于句首，意为"尽管；虽然"，符合语境，故填 while。

（10）wouldn't。根据空格后面 like to do 和首字母 w 可知，这里空格处应该填的是 would 或者 wouldn't，表示是否情愿。根据 kitchen robots are a good thought 可知，让厨房机器人做饭，应该是对于"不愿意在家做饭的人"来说是一个好的想法，故填 wouldn't。

Week Ten

Monday【A 完形填空】

答案解析

1. A。考查上下文语义。A 项意为"皮划艇运动员"，B 项意为"游泳运动员"，C 项意为"赛跑运动员"，D 项意为"跳高运动员"。根据下文 potential paddlers 可知徐诗晓是一位皮划艇运动员，故选 A。

2. C。考查名词辨析。A 项意为"河流"，B 项意为"湖泊"，C 项意为"山"，D 项意为"云"。根据上文 in a mountainous area 可知徐诗晓的家乡在山区，四周环山，故选 C。

3. C。考查动词短语辨析。A 项意为"游览；到处看"，B 项意为"向上看；查阅"，C 项意为"寻找"，D 项意为"回头看"。根据句意可知教练是来寻找有潜力的皮划艇运动员，故选 C。

4. A。考查固定搭配。A 项意为"注意"，B 项意为"讨论"，C 项意为"兴趣"，D 项意为"对话"。attract one's attention 意为"引起某人的注意"，属于固定搭配，故选 A。

5. D。考查动词短语辨析。A 项意为"克服；恢复"，B 项意为"过来"，C 项意为"接管"，D 项意为"翻转；翻身"。根据下文 drank lots of water in rivers 可知徐诗晓喝了很多河水，由此可推测她的皮划艇翻了许多次，故选 D。

6. A。考查名词辨析。A 项意为"打击；猛击"，B 项意为"叹气"，C 项意为"手"，D 项意为"项目"。give a heavy blow 意为"给……重击"，代入文中后意为"女子皮划艇仍未列入奥运会比赛项目，这个消息给了徐诗晓重重一击"，符合句意，故选 A。

7. B。考查动词辨析。A 项意为"继续"，B 项意为"退役"，C 项意为"决定"，D 项意为"庆祝"。根据下文徐诗晓放弃皮划艇回家工作可知，教练给她提供了两个建议，一个是换项目，另一个就是放弃，即退役，故选 B。

8. B。考查形容词辨析。A 项意为"可能的"，B 项意为"不可能的"，C 项意为"有乐趣的"，D 项意为"可相信的"。根据下文可知徐诗晓放弃了皮划艇并找了份别的工作，可知她没有换项目，因此可推测对于 21 岁的她来说换项目是不可能的，故选 B。

9. A。考查上下文语义。A 项意为"电话"，B 项意为"礼物"，C 项意为"秘密"，D 项意为"看"。根据 asking about 可知教练应该是打电话来询问她，故选 A。

10. C。考查上下文语义。A 项意为"姐妹"，B 项意为"兄弟"，C 项意为"搭档"，D 项意为"母亲"。根据下文 women's canoe double 500m event 可知徐诗晓参加的是女子 500 米双人划艇赛事，她应该是和搭档一起赢得了比赛，所以"搭档"符合语境，故选 C。

Tuesday【B 阅读理解】

答案解析

1. B。细节理解题。根据 English writing test will be on June 22nd, 8:30 am-10:00 am 可知英语写作测试将在 6 月 22 日举行，故选 B。

2. D。词义猜测题。画线单词后面有 bone cancer（骨癌），这是一种病症，所以"诊断"符合句意，故选 D。

3. D。细节理解题。根据 The sport was then in its infancy. There was little infrastructure, no common rules, and no global competitions 可知 A、B、C 三项所述的困难他们都曾遇到过，故选 D。

Wednesday【C 阅读理解】

答案解析

1. D。语篇理解题。第二段主要介绍了托尼是如何训练拉斐尔的，故选 D。

2. A。词义猜测题。根据下文 Toni used to knock balls towards him 可知，拉斐尔一定是哪里做得不好，他的叔叔托尼才会用球敲打他。再根据画线单词前面的 mind 可推测，这里应该是指拉斐尔的注意力不集中，所以 A 项符合句意，故选 A。

3. B。观点态度题。A 项意为"勇敢的"，B 项意为"严厉的"，C 项意为"聪明的"，D 项意为"可怕的"。本文主要讲述了托尼叔叔对拉斐尔的严格训练促成了拉斐尔的成功，文中也有托尼叔叔严格训练拉斐尔的多个事例，由此可知，托尼叔叔是严厉的，故选 B。

Thursday【D 阅读理解】

答案解析

1. C。细节理解题。根据第二段第二句 As he was always into the arts, he decided to go to Ho Chi Minh City to study makeup and hairdressing 可知，他是因为非常喜欢艺术才去学习化妆和美发的，故选 C。

2. D。词义猜测题。A 项意为"寻求帮助",B 项意为"一事无成",C 项意为"捐赠很多钱",D 项意为"出名"。根据下文 Nguyen Phat Tri's designs have millions of views on social media 可知阮发知的设计在网上有很高的观看量,所以这个短语应该是表示他在越南发型界很有名,故选 D。

3. D。细节理解题。根据第三段第一句中的 Nguyen Phat Tri's designs have millions of views on social media 可知阮发知的设计在网上有很高的观看量,所以 A 项错误;根据第三段第一句中的 few people can realize just how much work goes into each one of them 可知很少有人能意识到每一个造型需要付出多少努力,所以 B 项错误;根据第三段第二句中的 The simplest design takes 1 to 2 days to complete 可知完成最简单的造型需要耗时一到两天,而不是几个小时,所以 C 项错误;根据第三段第二句中的 the most complex of them can take 2 to 3 months to complete 可知最复杂的造型可能需要两到三个月才能完成,所以 D 项正确,故选 D。

4. D。细节理解题。根据题干中的关键词 turn down a lot of requests 定位到第四段,由 Nguyen Phat Tri usually turns down more requests than he accepts, because he prefers to spend his time researching new designs and techniques 可知通常他拒绝的请求比他接受的要多,是因为他更愿意把时间花在研究新的设计和技术上,故选 D。

Friday【E 阅读理解】
● 答案解析

1. D。细节理解题。第一句提到拉塔·曼吉茜卡于 2022 年 2 月 6 日去世,第二段首句提到她出生于 1929 年,所以可以计算出她享年 93 岁,故选 D。

2. D。细节理解题。根据第二段中的 she has been making her living acting in films, but she wasn't happy 可知曼吉茜卡并不喜欢演戏,所以 A 项错误。根据第二段中的 She was never formally educated 可知曼吉茜卡没有接受过正规教育,所以 B 项错误。根据第一段可知曼吉茜卡是印度的文化标志和国家宝藏,是印度最受欢迎的歌手,对印度来说十分重要,所以 C 项错误,D 项正确,故选 D。

3. B。语篇理解题。第二段主要按照时间顺序讲述了拉塔·曼吉茜卡成为知名歌手的过程,故选 B。

4. D。推理判断题。题干中短语所在句的句意为"她永恒的音乐无疑给数以百万计的印度人带来了快乐,并成为他们生活的配乐",由此可知本句在总结拉塔·曼吉茜卡的音乐在印度的影响力,所以 D 项正确,故选 D。

Saturday【F 任务型阅读】
● 答案解析

1. "Fear" has three different feelings: excitement, uncertainty, and pressure. 根据第二段第二句 "Fear" is really a term for three different feelings: excitement, uncertainty, and pressure 可知"恐惧"在作者看来可以算是三种不同感觉的总称,即兴奋、不确定和压力。

2. Fearless or capricious. 根据题干中的关键词 extreme sports athletes 定位到第三段第一句,由 It's easy to think of extreme sports athletes as fearless or capricious 可知大家通常认为极限运动员无畏且任性。

3. She deals with the pressure by boosting her self-esteem and making her need for expectations weaker. 根据题干中的关键词 deal with the pressure 可以定位到倒数第二段第一句,由 deal with the pressure of "prove yourself" by boosting my self-esteem and making my need for expectations weaker 可知作者是通过增强自尊,并减弱自己对于外界的期待的需求来应对压力的。

Week Eleven

Monday【A 完形填空】

答案解析

1. B。考查短语辨析。A项意为"一片；一块"，B项意为"一群"，C项意为"一种"，D项意为"一杯"，因为短语修饰的对象是islands（岛屿），所以"一群"符合句意，故选B。

2. C。考查名词辨析。A项意为"警察"，B项意为"商人"，C项意为"游客"，D项意为"工人"。根据空格后的They are attracted both by the architectural beauties in the historic center and the family-friendly beaches of Sottomarina（他们都被历史中心的建筑美景和索托马里纳适合家庭欢聚的海滩深深吸引着）可知，空格处所指的"人"应该是游客，故选C。

3. C。考查形容词辨析。A项意为"糟糕的"，B项意为"使人不愉快的"，C项意为"完美的"，D项意为"可怕的"。根据空格上文所介绍的the architectural beauties in the historic center and the family-friendly beaches of Sottomarina（历史中心的建筑美景和索托马里纳适合家庭欢聚的海滩）可知，这座城市会是一个自行车旅行的"好"地方，所以空格处应该选择有正面意义的词汇，故选C。

4. A。考查形容词辨析。A项意为"饥饿的"，B项意为"渴的"，C项意为"悲伤的"，D项意为"冷静的"。下文对皇后区的介绍主要集中在该地区的各种各样的食物上，所以"饥饿的"符合语境，故选A。

5. A。考查短语辨析。A项意为"多于"，B项意为"少于"，C项意为"除了"，D项意为"而不是"。这里主要强调皇后区内的食物种类有很多，故选A。

6. D。考查形容词辨析。A项意为"疯狂的"，B项意为"困难的"，C项意为"更糟糕的"，D项意为"更好的"。本句前半部分提到了皇后区的餐饮业受到了新冠肺炎疫情的影响，空格前的but表示前后构成转折关系，所以空格处应该表示的是情况变好，故选D。

7. B。考查动词短语辨析。A项意为"进来"，B项意为"参加"，C项意为"吸收"，D项意为"闯入"。将选项一一代入句中可知"参加"符合句意，意为"游客可以参与其中的环保项目"，故选B。

8. D。考查名词辨析。A项意为"农民"，B项意为"教师"，C项意为"演员"，D项意为"导游"。将选项一一代入文中，只有D项符合文意和逻辑，意为"非营利性保护组织'格雷罗鲸鱼'帮助培训渔民成为观鲸向导"，故选D。

9. A。考查动词辨析。A项意为"提供"，B项意为"扔掉"，C项意为"改变"，D项意为"发展"。将选项一一代入文中，可知"提供"符合句意，故选A。

10. B。考查介词辨析。A项意为"在……上面"，B项意为"通过"，C项意为"在（某地或某时刻）"，D项意为"在……之前"。空格前面提到这个采用太阳能的度假村帮助拯救了附近的村子，空格后面讲的是拯救的方式和手段，所以空格处的介词应该是"通过"，故选B。

Tuesday【B 阅读理解】

答案解析

1. D。细节理解题。根据图表可知，对呼伦贝尔和乌鲁木齐的介绍中分别提到了horse riding（骑马）和horse racing（赛马），故选D。

2. A。细节理解题。根据图表可知，在4个冬季旅游胜地中，哈尔滨的哈尔滨国际冰雪节和主题公园"哈尔滨冰雪大世界"提供冰雪雕塑展览，故选A。

3. B。细节理解题。根据图表可知，张家口有中国北方地区最大的天然滑雪场，故选B。

Wednesday【C 阅读理解】

答案解析

1. D。细节理解题。根据第二段第一句Dalarna is a province in central Sweden可知达拉纳是瑞典中部的一个省，故选D。

2. A。细节理解题。题干问游客冬季在达拉纳可以参加的活动，其中①②③都有在文中出现，④"冲浪"是无中生有，故选A。

3. B。细节理解题。文中提到达拉纳是南方的瑞典人的度假胜地，并不是说达拉纳只吸引南方的瑞典人，故排除A项。根据第四段中的You can also try dog sledding可知在达拉纳是可以尝试狗拉雪橇的，故排除C项。根据第二段第一句Dalarna is a province in central Sweden可知达拉纳是瑞典的一个省，而不是伊德勒的，故排除D项。故选B。

4. B。推理判断题。题干问文章作者的职业最有可能是什么。

全文介绍了瑞典达拉纳的旅游资源，所以作者最有可能是导游，故选B。

Thursday【D 阅读理解】
答案解析

1. D。细节理解题。根据题干中的 one of the toughest roads 定位到第一段，由 The road is unpaved. You can't make a phone call there. There's only one petrol station around halfway along（道路未铺砌，不能打电话，中途还只有一个加油站）可知 A、B、C 三项都是登普斯特高速公路成为加拿大最难驾驶的道路之一的原因，故选 D。

2. A。细节理解题。根据题干中的 worried 定位到第二段，由第二句 It was not hunger or thirst that worried me（让我担心的不是饥饿或口渴）可排除 B、C 两项。根据第二段第三句中的 I was scared of wildfires 可知作者真正害怕的是野火，故选 A。

3. C。文章排序题。根据文章内容可知，作者先是车发生侧滑（the car skidded sideways），然后遇见一位女服务员（the waitress at the motel's restaurant said），后来在返回道森市的路上车抛锚（my car broke down），最后有好心人载他一程（a good man picked me up），故选 C。

4. B。词义猜测题。A 项意为"问题"，B 项意为"魅力；美丽"，C 项意为"困难"，D 项意为"旅程"。冒号后的内容对画线单词所在部分的意思进行了解释，由 that whenever I'd come close to bad things, luck smiled on me（每当我接近灾难时，幸运会向我微笑）可知，在登普斯特高速公路上行驶虽然很艰难，但也有其美好的一面，故选 B。

Friday【E 任务型阅读】
答案解析

1. Rich heritage, natural sights and traditional cultures make Tibet a popular tourist attraction for years. 根据第一段最后一句 Tibet has been a popular tourist attraction for tourists from home and abroad for years due to its rich heritage, natural sights and traditional cultures 可知使西藏成为深受游客欢迎的旅游胜地的是其历史遗产、自然风光和传统文化。

2. It has already introduced cultural products and incentives. 根据第二段第二句中的 Cultural products and incentives

have already been introduced 可知西藏自治区推出了各种各样的文化产品和奖励措施来改善服务质量。

3. Yes, it did. 根据第二段中的 Tourism brought in nearly 213 billion yuan, more than double the amount from 2011 to 2015（旅游业带来了近 2 130 亿元的收入，是 2011 年至 2015 年的两倍多）可知 2016 年至 2020 年的旅游收入比 2011 年至 2015 年的旅游收入高，故答案是肯定的。

4. Tibetan culture and natural resources. 根据第三段中王松平的发言 Tourism departments should focus on Tibetan culture and natural resources 可知，旅游部门的关注点应当是西藏的文化和自然资源。

Saturday【F 短文填空】
答案解析

（1）With。空格后的 it's no surprise that renting a houseboat is a popular activity 是主句，由此可知空格所在部分应该是状语，表伴随，with 意为"具有，带有"，符合句意，故填 With。

（2）so。空格前后是两个完整的句子，由此可知空格处是一个连词。空格前一句意为"卡斯泰克湖位于洛杉矶的东北部"，空格后一句意为"这里是远离雾霾城市的完美户外场所"。后一句中的"雾霾城市"就是指洛杉矶，而卡斯泰克湖正好可以成为人们逃离雾霾的世外桃源，所以空格前后两句应该是因果关系，故填 so。

（3）its。空格前的 each one 意为"每个"，这里强调每个区域都有自己的活动，所以应该用第三人称的形容词性物主代词，故填 its。

（4）Lower。上文提到湖区分为上湖和下湖两个区域，下文介绍了 The Upper lake（上湖），所以此处介绍的肯定是下湖，故填 Lower。

（5）such。根据空格后的 fishing and riding Jet Skis（钓鱼和骑摩托艇）可知此处罗列的是可以在上湖进行的活动，such as 意为"例如"，代入原文后符合语义，故填 such。

（6）a。空格后面是名词短语 great choice，且 choice 是可数名词，由此可知空格处缺少冠词。great 为辅音音素开头的单词，故填 a。

（7）takes。空格前面为主语 It，后面为 two hours（两个小时），是一个时间段，作宾语，由此可知空格处缺少表示"花

115

费时间"的动词。It takes (sb.) + 时间段 +to do sth. 是固定搭配，表示"（某人）花费时间做某事"，全文时态为一般现在时，故填 takes。

（8）bears。空格前面是动词短语 get an up-close look at，由此可知空格处需填入一个名词。根据上文提到的 Animal lovers、the Big Bear Alpine Zoo 和 Big Bear Lake 可知，来到这个公园，对于动物爱好者来说可以近距离观察的应该是熊，故填 bears。

Week Twelve

Monday【A 完形填空】

答案解析

1. B。考查形容词辨析。A 项意为"更好的",B 项意为"最好的",C 项意为"更差的",D 项意为"最差的"。本文主要介绍西班牙美食,所以此空应该是褒义词,因此可排除 C 项和 D 项。"one of +the+ 形容词最高级 + 名词复数"为固定搭配,因此该空应当填形容词的最高级形式,故选 B。

2. C。考查动词短语辨析。A 项意为"张贴;举起",B 项意为"放弃",C 项意为"成长",D 项意为"捡起"。下文提到菲律宾的食物多从西班牙引入,而西班牙食物对"我"来说又很熟悉,所以"我"应该是在菲律宾长大的,故选 C。

3. A。考查词义辨析。A 项意为"要么;(两者之中)任意一个",B 项意为"两者都不",C 项意为"也",D 项意为"或者"。either... or... 为固定搭配,意为"要么……要么……",代入原文意为"许多菲律宾菜看要么是由西班牙引进的,要么是西班牙菜改良的",符合文意,故选 A。

4. A。考查名词辨析。A 项意为"小吃;零食",B 项意为"动物",C 项意为"肥皂",D 项意为"饮料"。根据上文"Tapas 是开胃菜"可知 Tapas 是在饭前吃的,应该是小吃或零食一类的东西,故选 A。

5. D。考查形容词辨析。A 项意为"准备完全的",B 项意为"受过良好教育的",C 项意为"衣着讲究的",D 项意为"著名的"。在各选项中,只有 D 项代入原文符合文意及逻辑,意为"它们是最著名的西班牙美食之一",故选 D。

6. D。考查副词辨析。A 项意为"小心地",B 项意为"快速地",C 项意为"严肃地",D 项意为"传统地"。这里是在介绍 Tortilla Española 的做法,在各选项中,只有 D 项代入原文符合文意和逻辑,意为"Tortilla Española 指的是传统上用鸡蛋、土豆和橄榄油制成的西班牙煎蛋饼",故选 D。

7. B。考查上下文语义。A 项意为"土豆",B 项意为"洋葱",C 项意为"西红柿",D 项意为"鸡蛋"。根据下文 the addition of onions is often met with controversy 可知放洋葱是会引起争议的,而该句又是承接空格所在句,所以空格处指的就是"洋葱",故选 B。

8. B。考查上下文语义。A 项意为"因此",B 项意为"然而",C 项意为"所以",D 项意为"和"。上文提到这道西班牙美食可以添加洋葱,空格所在句说放洋葱会引起争议,所以这两句是转折关系,故选 B。

9. A。考查名词辨析。A 项意为"地方;地点",B 项意为"季节",C 项意为"麻烦",D 项意为"金钱"。have no place in 表示"在……没有立足之处",符合文意,因此 A 项正确,故选 A。

10. C。考查形容词辨析。A 项意为"厚的;浓密的",B 项意为"诚实的",C 项意为"流行的;受欢迎的",D 项意为"合适的"。这四个选项中只有 C 项代入原文符合逻辑,同时根据文意可知作者要向读者介绍西班牙受欢迎的小吃,故选 C。

11. B。考查形容词辨析。A 项意为"准备好的",B 项意为"相似的",C 项意为"好的",D 项意为"天然的"。本段是介绍西班牙的一种大葱,只有 B 项代入原文符合文意及逻辑,be similar to 为固定搭配,意为"与……相似",故选 B。

12. B。考查名词辨析。A 项意为"东西;物",B 项意为"时间",C 项意为"项目",D 项意为"天气"。根据下文 which happens around February and March 可知这里讨论的是吃西班牙大葱的最佳时间,故选 B。

13. D。考查介词辨析。A 项意为"在……后面",B 项意为"在……之前",C 项意为"在(某地点、场所、时刻)",D 项意为"在……上"。只有 D 项代入原文符合文意,意为"大葱通常放在明火上烤",故选 D。

14. C。考查名词辨析。A 项意为"节日",B 项意为"指南",C 项意为"习惯",D 项意为"旅程"。下文介绍的是西班牙人的吃饭时间,可知这里指的是"饮食习惯",故选 C。

15. A。考查动词辨析。A 项意为"花费",主语为物或事;B 项意为"花费",主语为人;C 项意为"付款",主语为人;D 项意为"寻找"。根据句意可知这里指"午餐要花两到三个小时",故排除 C 项和 D 项。此处主语是物,所以排除 B 项,故选 A。

Tuesday【B 阅读理解】

答案解析

1. D。词义猜测题。画线单词下文是 a singer and a guitar

player（歌手和吉他手），由吉他手和歌手的身份可知二者应该都是为舞蹈伴奏的，其他三个选项均不符合逻辑，故选 D。

2. C。细节理解题。根据第二段可知 Lola Flores 对于弗拉明戈舞起到的是国际推广作用，并不能说明弗拉明戈舞就是她发明的，所以 A 项错误；文中提到弗拉明戈舞已在国际舞台推广开来，所以肯定不会只在西班牙出现，所以 B 项错误；根据第三段第一句以及第一段最后一句可知弗拉明戈舞的四元素中有 voice，且该舞蹈有歌手伴唱，所以 C 项正确。根据第三段最后一句可知 Duende 在普通语言中的意思才是"精灵"，所以 D 项错误。故选 C。

3. C。语篇理解题。最后一段第一句为该段的主旨句：Flamenco's fast-paced Spanish guitar playing is what most outsiders are familiar with, but hand-clapping also plays an important role in the art form. 这句话表明大多数门外汉熟悉的是弗拉明戈舞那种快节奏的吉他演奏，但同时拍手也非常重要，接着下文对拍手的重要性进行了举例。由此可知这段主要是描述拍手在弗拉明戈舞蹈中的重要性，故选 C。

Wednesday【C 阅读理解】

● 答案解析

1. B。细节理解题。根据 Time 板块的最后一句 the Carnival officially opens on Sunday evening 可知狂欢节于周日晚上正式开幕，又从该板块第一句得知威尼斯狂欢节于 2 月 12 日（周六）开始，由此可知狂欢节的正式开幕时间是在 2 月 13 日，故选 B。

2. C。细节理解题。根据 Events 板块 Nebula Solaris 中的 It is a light and circus show which will take place on the Venetian Arsenal 可知，灯光秀只出现在 Nebula Solaris 中，故选 C。

3. D。细节理解题。根据 COVID-19 Restrictions 板块可知，需要遵守 A、B、C 三项才可以参加狂欢节，故选 D。

4. D。推理判断题。A 项意为"新闻"，B 项意为"小说"，C 项意为"日记"，D 项意为"指南"。本文是 2022 威尼斯狂欢节主办方给参观者的一些介绍和注意事项，所以这篇文章应该是一篇指南，故选 D。

Thursday【D 阅读理解】

● 答案解析

1. D。细节理解题。根据第一段第一句 Fitting a small stone into a sling made of yak wool, Tsering Stobdan whipped his wrist, sending the object flying across the dry land 可知，A 项、B 项和 C 项都是他保护羊群以及唤回羊群的步骤，故选 D。

2. A。细节理解题。根据第二段第二句中的 Young people are being sent to nearby cities 可知该游牧群体的年轻人都去了附近的城市，年轻人口越来越少了，所以年轻人不是正在回来，而是正在离开，故选 A。

3. B。词义猜测题。根据下文 the nomadic group is now dwindling 和 Young people are being sent to nearby cities 可知该游牧群体正在衰退，年轻人正离开那里。而 flourishing 所在短语描述的是该游牧群体曾经的情况，和现在的情况相反，所以 flourishing 应该是"繁荣的"的意思，故选 B。

4. C。主旨大意题。通读全文可知，文章主要介绍了印度北部一个游牧群体的游牧生活，该族群日益衰败的现状，以及该地区的担忧，这些都属于他们生活的方方面面，因此 C 项正确。A 项、B 项和 D 项都是文章的细节信息，不足以概括文章大意，故均错误。故选 C。

Friday【E 任务型阅读】

● 答案解析

1. F。根据空格下文可知，爱尔兰的新年传统是用面包敲打门和墙面，目的是 send any angry spirits away，即驱赶怨灵。F 项为"用面包吓跑对你有害的恶灵"，符合下文语义，故选 F。

2. A。根据空格下文可知，该段提到的新年传统是不能在 1 月 1 日洗衣服，只有 A 项中提到了 washing clothes，故选 A。

3. E。根据空格下文可知，此段提到在新年这天不能扔东西，E 项 take away 意为"拿走；带走"，take away anything 和该段中的 throw something away 同义，因此 E 项正确。C 项虽然提到了 be away from，但是其内容为 be away from last year's bad luck，与空格下文语义不符，故 C 项错误。故选 E。

4. D。根据空格下文可知，菲律宾的新年传统中提到了 the

more noise you make... the better（……越吵闹越好），体现了在菲律宾新年中"制造噪声或吵闹"的重要性，因此 D 项符合空格下文语义，故选 D。
5. B。根据空格下文可知，日本的新年传统中提到了 young men dress as demons，B 项与之相符，故选 B。

Saturday【F 短文填空】

● 答案解析

（1）holidays。"one of +the+ 形容词最高级 + 可数名词复数"为常见用法，故填 holidays。

（2）lighting。空格前面的 by 是介词，介词后面的动词需为动名词，故填 lighting。

（3）over。(win) the victory over sth./sb. 为固定搭配，表示"战胜；赢过"，且分析句子可知 light _____ darkness 和后面的 good over evil 为并列结构，所以 over 符合要求，在这里表示"优于"，故填 over。

（4）which。分析句子可知，本句是一个非限制性定语从句。空格处是引导词，且作从句的主语。先行词是 word，为物，故填 which。

（5）their。空格后面为名词，所以空格处应为形容词性物主代词，修饰后面的名词 homes，故填 their。

（6）from/against。protect sb. from/against sth. 表示"保护某人不受……的伤害"，这里意为"保护他们远离精神黑暗"，故填 from/against。

（7）buying。分析句子可知，本句中有 3 个并列的动宾短语，cleaning 和 exchanging 都是动名词形式，所以此处 buy 也应该是动名词形式，故填 buying。

（8）with。exchange sth. with sb. 为固定搭配，表示"和某人交换某物"，故填 with。

（9）as。as well as 为固定搭配，表示"也；和……一样"，故填 as。

（10）said。be said to 为固定搭配，表示"据说"，因此该空填 say 的过去分词形式，故填 said。

Week Thirteen

Monday【A 完形填空】

答案解析

1. B。考查连词辨析。A项意为"但是",B项意为"正如",C项意为"虽然,尽管"。根据语境可知,这里是波提乌斯的回忆,只有B项代入原文中符合句意,故选B。

2. C。考查形容词辨析。A项意为"令人放松的",B项意为"有趣的",C项意为"令人惊讶的"。空格上文提到在北冰洋中部的海底很难找到食物,由此可知在此处发现类似北极熊的海绵是令人惊讶的,故选C。

3. A。考查固定搭配。feed on 为固定搭配,意为"以……为食",故选A。

4. C。考查固定搭配。It's the first time that... 是固定句型,意为"这是第一次……",故选C。

5. B。考查动词辨析。A项意为"听",B项意为"吃",C项意为"看"。上文提到这种动物以化石为食,所以"吃"符合句意,故选B。

6. C。考查形容词辨析。A项意为"寒冷的",B项意为"镇静的;沉着的",C项意为"酷的;凉爽的"。下文提到海绵能利用其他生物不能利用的食物来源,所以 cool 符合句意,故选C。

7. A。考查形容词辨析。A项意为"更容易的",B项意为"更难的;更努力的",C项意为"更长的"。空格后面的动词不定式短语 to catch local currents carrying little fossilized tube worms 表示"赶上携带小型管状蠕虫化石的局部水流",将选项代入句中后可知 easier 符合句意,故选A。

8. B。考查名词辨析。A项意为"家",B项意为"空间",C项意为"金钱"。make space for 意为"为……腾出空间",符合语境,故选B。

9. C。考查形容词辨析。A项意为"更大的",B项意为"更瘦的",C项意为"更小的"。上文提到海绵向山上移动是为下一代腾出空间,所以"更小的"符合句意,故选C。

10. A。考查形容词辨析。A项意为"低的",B项意为"高的",C项意为"胖的"。空格下文提到科学家不明白海绵是怎么能够吃完食物的,由此可推测海绵的新陈代谢比较低,故选A。

Tuesday【B 阅读理解】

答案解析

1. A。细节理解题。根据第一段 The air we breathe, the water we drink, the food we eat—all depend on biodiversity—the variety of all plant and animal life on Earth 可知,生物多样性指的是地球上所有动植物的多样性,故选A。

2. B。细节理解题。根据第二段中的 biodiversity is reducing fast 可知,生物多样性正在迅速缩减,故选B。

3. C。细节理解题。根据第三段第一句 The researchers say there's little room for nature in the UK because there is so much of the land that has long been built upon or used for intensive agriculture 可知,英国留给大自然的空间少是因为有很多的土地长期以来用于建筑或集约型农业,故选C。

4. A。细节理解题。根据第四段中的 world leaders will meet online to discuss plans for protecting nature 可知,世界各国领导人将在线上讨论自然保护计划,故选A。

5. B。细节理解题。根据最后一段科学家说的话 this is our last best chance for a sustainable future 可知,现在是实现可持续未来的最后良机,故选B。

Wednesday【C 阅读理解】

答案解析

1. F。根据第一段中的 southern right whales were hunted to near extinction about a century ago 可知,南露脊鲸在一个世纪前并没有灭绝,而是濒临灭绝,所以本句错误,故填F。

2. F。根据第二段中的 We found there were around 2,000 whales in 2009 可知,2009 年大约有 2 000 头鲸鱼,而非 2019 年,所以本句错误,故填F。

3. T。根据第三段第一句 Historically, we knew that the whales from New Zealand would travel north and east of New Zealand during the spring and summer months 可知,新西兰南露脊鲸向来会在春夏月份迁徙到新西兰的北部和东部,所以本句正确,故填T。

4. F。根据第三段中的 these results are pretty important and give us hope 可知,研究结果是非常重要的,所以本句错误,故填F。

5. T。根据最后一段中的 Scientists are using all of the

modern tools to get a really complete picture of not just their recovery but how they're using the oceans 可知，科学家们正在使用所有的现代工具来获得鲸鱼真正的全貌，不仅了解它们数量上的回升，还了解它们利用海洋的方式，所以本句正确，故填 T。

Thursday【D 任务型阅读】

● 答案解析

1. D。空格前面提到海牛再次以惊人的数量死亡，空格后面提到海牛死亡事件的主要发生地点，由此可知空格处仍在介绍与海牛死亡有关的信息。在所给选项中，D 项 Hunger and cold weather are the first reasons（饥饿和寒冷的天气是首要原因）交代了海牛死亡的主要原因，符合要求，故选 D。

2. B。空格前面有破折号，破折号后面的内容一般是对破折号前面内容的补充或解释。在所给选项中，B 项 they are sea cows' main food source（它们是海牛的主要食物来源）符合语境，且与海牛的死因有关，故选 B。

3. E。空格后面有冒号，冒号后面的内容一般是对冒号前面内容的补充或解释。冒号后面提到海牛在寒冷中将不得不做出重要的关于生与死的选择，在所给选项中，E 项 This winter could be more difficult for sea cows（今年冬天对于海牛来说可能更加艰难）代入文中后符合上下文语境，故选 E。

4. F。空格前后有表示时间的短语 In the past 和 But now，结合下文可知，空格处在介绍海牛过去应对寒冷的状况。在所给选项中，F 项 sea cows would easily have continued to live in the cold weather（海牛很容易在严寒中生存下来）代入文中后符合上下文语境，故选 F。

5. C。空格前面的动词不定式短语 To get through the cold time（为了度过寒冷的时刻）表目的，由此可知空格处在介绍海牛度过寒冷时刻的方法。在所给选项中，C 项 sea cows will look for warm water to stay（海牛将寻找可停留的温暖水域）代入文中后符合上下文语境，故选 C。

Friday【E 任务型阅读】

● 答案解析

（1）Tahiti。根据第一段第一句 Researchers recently found an unusual coral reef—it was discovered near Tahiti in the South Pacific Ocean 可知，新发现的不同寻常的珊瑚礁靠近南太平洋塔希提岛，故填 Tahiti。

（2）between 35 meters to 70 meters。根据第一段最后一句 It was deeper than others—between 35 meters to 70 meters 可知这处珊瑚礁比其他的更深，深度在 35 米到 70 米之间，故填 between 35 meters to 70 meters。

（3）diving。根据第三段第二句 She was diving with a local diving group at that time 可知，海都因第一次见到这些珊瑚的时候，正和当地的一个潜水小组在潜水，故填 diving。

（4）special。根据第三段中的 we need to study that reef. There's something special about it 可知，海都因认为此处的珊瑚礁是特别的，故填 special。

（5）pollution。根据最后一段中的 coral reefs are damaged due to overfishing and pollution. Climate change is also hurting corals 可知，珊瑚礁会因过度捕捞、污染和气候变化而受到损害，故填 pollution。

Saturday【F 短文填空】

● 答案解析

（1）perfect。空格前面有 be 动词 was，后面是介词短语 for photographing，所以空格处可填入一个形容词。在所给选项中，perfect 意为"完美的"，符合句意及语境，故填 perfect。

（2）full。空格前面有 be 动词 were，后面有介词 of，所以空格处可填入一个形容词。在所给选项中，full 意为"满的"，且 be full of 为固定搭配，意为"充满"，符合句意及语境，故填 full。

（3）seeing。分析句子可知，空格所在的句子主谓完整，由此可知空格部分在句中作状语。空格后面为名词短语 the historic journey（历史性的旅程），所以空格处需填入一个动词。在所给选项中，see 意为"看见，看到"，符合句意及语境，又因 see 在句中作状语，且和其逻辑主语 I（我）之间为主动的关系，所以应改为其现在分词形式，故填 seeing。

（4）large。空格前面有不定冠词 a，后面是名词 group，所以空格处可填入一个形容词。在所给选项中，large 意为"大的"，符合句意及语境，故填 large。

（5）best。空格前面有定冠词 the，后面是名词 experiences，所以空格处需填入一个形容词。且空格所在的部分为固定短语"one of the+ 形容词最高级 + 名词复数"，表示"……中最……的一个"。在所给选项中，best 意为"最好的"，符合句意及语境，故填 best。

（6）between。分析句子可知，空格所在的句子主谓完整，由此可知空格所在的部分在句中作状语。根据上文可知角马在肯尼亚和坦桑尼亚之间迁徙，且 between... and... 为固定用法，意为"在……和……之间"，故填 between。

（7）following。空格所在的部分在句中作状语，空格前面为介词 of，后面为名词 the rain，所以空格处需填入一个动词。根据下文可知动物的迁徙受到降雨的影响。在所给选项中，follow 意为"跟随；沿着"，符合句意及语境，因空格前面有介词 of，所以需改为其动名词形式，故填 following。

（8）Because。分析句子可知，逗号将前后两句隔开，所以空格处需填入一个连词。空格所在句子提到降雨量是由季节和气候变化决定的，逗号后面提到无法知道降雨的准确时间和兽群的活动，由此可知，逗号前后两个句子为因果关系，且前为因，后为果，所以 because 符合句意及语境。空格处位于句首，首字母要大写，故填 Because。

（9）predict。空格所在的部分为 to do 不定式短语，所以空格处需填入一个动词。在所给选项中，predict 意为"预测"，代入文中后意为"没有办法预测降雨的准确时间和这些兽群的活动"，符合句意，故填 predict。

（10）But。空格上文提到坦桑尼亚塞伦盖蒂国家公园的雨季是在3月、4月和5月，下文提到马赛马拉的雨季是8月到11月月初，由此可知这两地的雨季时间是不一样的，所以用 but 表示转折。空格处位于句首，首字母要大写，故填 But。

Week Fourteen
Monday【A 完形填空】
● 答案解析

1. C。考查副词辨析。A项意为"懒散地",B项意为"生气地",C项意为"容易地",D项意为"困难地"。根据下文程浩生对这次大会的描述和参加的活动可知,他对这次大会印象深刻,由此可推知,他轻而易举地就能回忆起大会上的事情,故选C。

2. D。考查形容词辨析。A项意为"有趣的",B项意为"相似的",C项意为"消极的",D项意为"积极的"。根据上文中的Young people are taking the lead in addressing environmental challenges(年轻人在应对环境挑战中发挥着带头作用)可知,年轻人发挥的作用是积极的,故选D。

3. D。考查名词辨析。A项意为"例子",B项意为"事实",C项意为"规则",D项意为"问题"。上文提到Young people are taking the lead in addressing environ-mental challenges(年轻人在应对环境挑战中发挥着带头作用),由此可知"问题"符合句意,故选D。

4. C。考查名词辨析。A项意为"对话",B项意为"交流",C项意为"会议",D项意为"承诺"。上文提到程浩生参加了全球青年大会,由此可知程浩生是为这次大会期间的活动撰写新闻稿件并发表到网上,故选C。

5. A。考查名词辨析。A项意为"重要性",B项意为"决定",C项意为"礼貌;礼仪",D项意为"指示;说明"。将选项代入句中,可知"重要性"符合句意,故选A。

6. B。考查动词短语辨析。A项意为"加油;快来",B项意为"忙于;从事",C项意为"打开",D项意为"进行;继续"。将选项代入句中,可知"忙于;从事"符合句意,故选B。

7. C。考查动词辨析。A项意为"到达",B项意为"阅读",C项意为"记得",D项意为"意识到"。根据上下文内容可知,空格所在句子是程浩生在回忆台风来临时的景象,因此C项符合句意,故选C。

8. C。考查形容词辨析。A项意为"不可能的",B项意为"成功的",C项意为"正常的",D项意为"聪明的"。根据常识可知,澳门在沿海地区,每年遭受五到六次台风是正常的,故选C。

9. B。考查形容词辨析。A项意为"小的",B项意为"极大的",C项意为"好的;优质的",D项意为"快速的"。根据常识和上下文语境可知,台风造成的损失是巨大的,故选B。

10. C。考查动词辨析。A项意为"邀请",B项意为"设计",C项意为"希望",D项意为"表达"。将选项代入句中,可知"希望"符合句意和语境,故选C。

Tuesday【B 阅读理解】
● 答案解析

1. D。细节理解题。根据Gift wrap部分中的表述可知可重复使用的袋子、旧地图、颜色鲜艳的围巾都可用来包装礼物,只有D项Plastic boxes(塑料盒)在文中没有提到,故选D。

2. C。细节理解题。根据Holiday cards部分中的第二句However, now many people use digital or electronic cards(然而,现在许多人使用数字贺卡或电子贺卡)和第四句Those who want to send traditional cards might choose ones printed on recyclable paper(那些想送传统贺卡的人可以选择用可回收纸张印制的贺卡)可知A项、B项和D项都属于环保的赠卡方式,而C项Sending traditional cards made of unrecyclable paper(送由不可回收纸张制作的传统贺卡)会造成纸张浪费,故选C。

3. C。主旨大意题。本文主要从礼物包装、节日贺卡、圣诞树和宴请(用具)四个方面介绍了减少节假日垃圾的方法,故选C。

Wednesday【C 阅读理解】
● 答案解析

1. A。细节理解题。根据第一段中李如雪在采访中说的话Though the lifestyle is a little bit tiring, it's meaningful可知,李如雪觉得这种生活方式虽然有点累,但很有意义,A项Tired but meaningful(疲劳但有意义的)符合文意。B项Disappointed and bored(失望且枯燥的)、C项Interested and proud(感兴趣且自豪的)、D项Lonely and tired(孤独且疲劳的)均不符合文意,故选A。

2. D。细节理解题。根据第二段第一句After graduation, he joined a skywalker gibbon protection organization, where one of his major tasks was picking up gibbon feces(大学毕业后,李如雪加入了一个保护天行长臂猿的组织,其主要工作内容之一就是捡猿粪)可知D项符合文意,故

选 D。

3. B。细节理解题。根据第三段中的 As her father works on wildlife research（由于其父亲从事野生动物研究工作）和 she followed in her father's footsteps（初雯雯追随了她父亲的脚步）可知，初雯雯是受到她父亲的影响而从事动物保护工作的，故选 B。

4. A。词义猜测题。画线单词 initiated 的宾语为 the "beaver canteen" program（"河狸食堂"项目），将选项代入句中后，只有 A 项符合句意及逻辑，意为"发起了'河狸食堂'项目"，故选 A。

5. C。主旨大意题。通读全文可知，本文主要讲述了以环保工作者李如雪和初雯雯为代表的年轻人致力于野生动物的保护，投入到保护全球生物多样性工作中的故事，由此可推知，C 项 Young People Are Acting Now（年轻人在行动）最符合文意，因此 C 项正确。A 项提到的保护的对象与文章不符，B 项和 D 项与文章内容无关，故选 C。

Thursday【D 任务型阅读】
● 答案解析

（1）last。分析句子结构可知，设空处在句中作谓语。根据第三段第一句中的 Sandstorms come once a year and last for half a year（沙尘暴一年刮一次，一次刮半年）可知沙尘暴持续的时间很长，故填 last。

（2）Sheep。分析句子结构可知，设空处在句中作主语。结合第三段第二句中的 the grass land would be eaten away by sheep before the rainy season 可知，在雨季到来之前，羊就把草吃完了，故填 Sheep。

（3）turned。根据时间状语 in the past 可知句子时态为一般过去时。结合第三段第二句中的 turning cropland into the sand 可知，这里应填 turn 的过去式，故填 turned。

（4）online。分析句子结构可知，连词 and 连接两个并列的形容词作定语，修饰名词词组 tree-planting projects。结合第四段第一句中的 programs like "Ant Forest"，which combined online and real tree-planting projects 可知，"蚂蚁森林"项目结合了网络和现实植树，故填 online。

（5）planted。分析句子结构可知，设空处在句中作谓语。结合第四段最后一句中的 39,000 hectares of trees had been planted offline 可知，线下植树面积达 3.9 万公顷，

故填 planted。

（6）raised。分析句子结构可知，设空处在句中作谓语。根据倒数第二段 The Chinese government has also raised more than 10 billion yuan in forestry management subsidies 可知，中国政府筹集了 100 多亿元的林业经营补贴。此处为被动语态，应用 raise 的过去分词形式，故填 raised。

（7）forbidden。分析句子结构可知，设空处所在句的谓语不完整。根据最后一段第一句中的 China forbade all commercial logging of natural forests nationwide 可知，天然林商业性采伐已经在中国被全面禁止。此处为被动语态，应用 forbid 的过去分词形式，故填 forbidden。

（8）includes/has。分析句子结构可知，设空处所在部分为 which 引导的定语从句，修饰 A national management and protection team。根据最后一段最后一句中的 A national management and protection team including about 7 million people has been set up 可知，一支约 700 万人的国家管理和保护队伍被建立了，所以可以填表示"包括"或"有"的单词。因 which 在从句中作主语，修饰的先行词为单数，所以此处应用第三人称单数形式，故填 includes/has。

（9）efforts。分析句子结构可知，设空处需填入名词。根据第一段最后一句中的 thanks to the efforts of Chinese people 可知是中国人民的努力使森林覆盖率上升，故填 efforts。

（10）from。分析句子结构可知，设空处需填入介词。根据第一段最后一句中的 the country's forest coverage rate has increased from 8.6 percent in the early years to 23.04 percent in 2020 可知，森林覆盖率从早期的 8.6% 增加到 2020 年的 23.04%，这里有固定搭配 increase from... to...，意为"从……增加到……"，故填 from。

Friday【E 短文填空】
● 答案解析

（1）hope。空格前面为动词 bring，缺少宾语，所以设空处需填入一个名词。空格后的 of a new beginning 作后置定语修饰设空处的单词。在所给单词或短语中，hope 符合句意，且 bring hope to 为固定搭配，意为"为……带来希望"，故填 hope。

（2）risk。at risk of 为固定搭配，意为"有……风险"，符合句意，故填 risk。

（3）countries。设空处后面的连词 and 连接两个并列名词，且 and 前后的名词在数上应保持一致，所以设空处的单词为复数形式。在所给选项中，只有 countries 符合语法条件及句意，故填 countries。

（4）thousands of。分析句子结构可知，设空处作定语，修饰名词短语 individual seeds。在所给选项中，thousands of 为固定短语，意为"数以千计的"，符合句意，故填 thousands of。

（5）aim to。分析句子结构可知，设空处在句中作谓语，且空格后面的 protect 为动词原形，在所给选项中，aim to 后可接动词原形，意为"打算/旨在做某事"，符合语法条件及句意，故填 aim to。

Saturday【F 短文填空】

● 答案解析

（1）from。根据下文的美国佛罗里达州可知，此处表示尤尔曼来自这一地方，故填 from。

（2）project。空格前面有不定冠词 an 和形容词 environmental，所以空格处需填入一个名词。根据文章最后一段中的 His environmental project, Bring Butterflies Back（尤尔曼的环境项目"让蝴蝶回归"）可知这是一个环境项目，故填 project。

（3）butterfly。空格前面有动词短语 bring back，所以空格处需填入一个名词。根据上文尤尔曼创建的环境项目的名称 Bring Butterflies Back, Inspiring Youth to Protect Butterflies for Future Generations 可知，这一项目旨在让蝴蝶回归，使蝴蝶的数量回升，故填 butterfly。

（4）love。fall in love with 为固定短语，表示"爱上；喜欢"，符合句意，故填 love。

（5）plant。分析句子结构可知，空格处需填入一个动词。根据下文 a lot of flowers 和 a butterfly garden 可知，为了吸引蝴蝶，需要种植很多花，故填 plant。

（6）They。空格所在的句子缺少主语。结合上文年轻学生们对蝴蝶和毛毛虫的反应可推知，空格处的主语是 the young students，结合所给首字母可知，可用 they 来代替 the young students 作主语。句首单词首字母要大写，故填 They。

（7）important。空格前面有 be 动词 are，后面有介词 for，所以空格处需填入一个形容词。根据下文对蝴蝶作用的具体阐释和 The other important 可知，蝴蝶对于环境来说很重要，故填 important。

（8）the。空格所在的部分为固定结构"one of the + 形容词最高级 + 名词复数"，意为"……中最……的之一"，故填 the。

（9）reason。空格前面为形容词 important，所以空格处需填入一个名词。根据上文 for two main reasons 可知，此处表示蝴蝶对环境重要的另外一个原因，故填 reason。

（10）helps。分析句子结构可知，空格处在句中作谓语，且 and 连接两个并列结构，所以空格处所填单词的词义应与下文的 helps 相同或者相近。根据所给的首字母 h 可知，空格处的动词可为 help，并与 with 构成搭配，表示"帮助做……"，符合句意，又因该句主语为单数，故填 helps。

云图英语

时文速递

参考译文

云图分级阅读研究院·编著

强化篇

北京理工大学出版社
BEIJING INSTITUTE OF TECHNOLOGY PRESS

Contents 目录

Week One

Monday	【A 完形填空】	001
Tuesday	【B 阅读理解】	001
Wednesday	【C 阅读理解】	001
Thursday	【D 阅读理解】	002
Friday	【E 任务型阅读】	002
Saturday	【F 短文填空】	002

Week Two

Monday	【A 完形填空】	004
Tuesday	【B 阅读理解】	004
Wednesday	【C 阅读理解】	005
Thursday	【D 任务型阅读】	005
Friday	【E 短文填空】	005
Saturday	【F 短文填空】	006

Week Three

Monday	【A 完形填空】	007
Tuesday	【B 阅读理解】	007
Wednesday	【C 阅读理解】	007
Thursday	【D 任务型阅读】	008
Friday	【E 短文填空】	008
Saturday	【F 短文填空】	008

Week Four

Monday	【A 完形填空】	010
Tuesday	【B 阅读理解】	010
Wednesday	【C 阅读理解】	010
Thursday	【D 阅读理解】	011
Friday	【E 任务型阅读】	011
Saturday	【F 短文填空】	011

Week Five

Monday	【A 完形填空】	013
Tuesday	【B 阅读理解】	013
Wednesday	【C 任务型阅读】	013
Thursday	【D 任务型阅读】	014
Friday	【E 任务型阅读】	014
Saturday	【F 短文填空】	015

Week Six

Monday	【A 完形填空】	016
Tuesday	【B 阅读理解】	016
Wednesday	【C 阅读理解】	016
Thursday	【D 任务型阅读】	017
Friday	【E 任务型阅读】	017
Saturday	【F 短文填空】	018

Week Seven

Monday	【A 完形填空】	……………019
Tuesday	【B 阅读理解】	……………019
Wednesday	【C 任务型阅读】	……………019
Thursday	【D 任务型阅读】	……………020
Friday	【E 短文填空】	……………020
Saturday	【F 短文填空】	……………020

Week Eight

Monday	【A 完形填空】	……………021
Tuesday	【B 阅读理解】	……………021
Wednesday	【C 阅读理解】	……………021
Thursday	【D 任务型阅读】	……………022
Friday	【E 任务型阅读】	……………022
Saturday	【F 短文填空】	……………022

Week Nine

Monday	【A 完形填空】	……………023
Tuesday	【B 阅读理解】	……………023
Wednesday	【C 阅读理解】	……………024
Thursday	【D 阅读理解】	……………024
Friday	【E 短文填空】	……………024
Saturday	【F 短文填空】	……………025

Week Ten

Monday	【A 完形填空】	……………026
Tuesday	【B 阅读理解】	……………026
Wednesday	【C 阅读理解】	……………026
Thursday	【D 阅读理解】	……………027
Friday	【E 阅读理解】	……………027
Saturday	【F 任务型阅读】	……………028

Week Eleven

Monday	【A 完形填空】	……………029
Tuesday	【B 阅读理解】	……………029
Wednesday	【C 阅读理解】	……………029
Thursday	【D 阅读理解】	……………030
Friday	【E 任务型阅读】	……………030
Saturday	【F 短文填空】	……………030

Week Twelve

Monday	【A 完形填空】	……………032
Tuesday	【B 阅读理解】	……………032
Wednesday	【C 阅读理解】	……………032
Thursday	【D 阅读理解】	……………033
Friday	【E 任务型阅读】	……………033
Saturday	【F 短文填空】	……………034

Week Thirteen

Monday 　　【A 完形填空】…………035

Tuesday 　　【B 阅读理解】…………035

Wednesday【C 阅读理解】…………035

Thursday 　【D 任务型阅读】………035

Friday 　　 【E 任务型阅读】………036

Saturday 　【F 短文填空】…………036

Week Fourteen

Monday 　　【A 完形填空】…………037

Tuesday 　　【B 阅读理解】…………037

Wednesday【C 阅读理解】…………037

Thursday 　【D 任务型阅读】………038

Friday 　　 【E 短文填空】…………038

Saturday 　【F 短文填空】…………038

Week One

Monday【A 完形填空】
● 参考译文

23 岁的摄影师董书畅因其拍摄的《金环》,于 9 月中旬荣膺年度天文摄影师总冠军。这幅杰作是去年在中国西南部西藏自治区的阿里地区拍摄的。它显示的是月球挡住了大部分的太阳圆面,只留下一个薄薄的闪耀的光环。

该项比赛共收到来自 75 个国家和地区的 4 500 份参赛作品。2019 年年底,董书畅开始为此行拍照做准备。然而,这并不像他预期的那样。2020 年年初的新冠肺炎疫情中止了他的计划。突然之间,一切都变得不确定了。多亏中国成功地控制了疫情,董书畅在 2020 年年中推进了他的计划。

他说当他使用长焦镜头拍照时,他可以细致入微地观察银河,以及它的红、绿、蓝三色,这些颜色可以通过摄影转化获得鲜明的轮廓。董书畅凭借他的作品《天地共舞》获得最佳新人奖后信心增加。董书畅说,尽管三年多的追星经历经常汗水和泪水交织,但最终给他带来了兴奋和成就。

在谈到自己未来的计划时,董书畅说他将寻找新的摄影领域和融合科学与艺术的更好的方式。

Tuesday【B 阅读理解】
● 参考译文

当 2022 年冬奥会于周五晚上在北京开幕时,北京第二外国语学院的国际学生张衣笙(Komani Mayentao)与其他外国学生和教授一起自豪地走上了国家体育场(又被称为鸟巢)闪闪发光的舞台。

张衣笙从小就对中国文化和中国功夫感兴趣,他参加了面向外国学生的世界性汉语水平竞赛"汉语桥",并在 18 岁时获得了前往中国学习的奖学金。

中文说得不错的张衣笙被选为开幕式的表演者。"虽然我没有成为一名志愿者,但能够在开幕式上表演是一种莫大的荣誉。我在北京实现了我的冬奥梦想。"他说。

自从去年被选为冬奥会开幕式上的表演者以来,无论是下雨还是天晴,这位 24 岁的马里学生张衣笙都会去鸟巢排练。在国家体育场排练时,他结交了很多来自其他国家的表演者。

张衣笙认为,说不同语言和有不同文化背景的人在一起工作,正好展现了北京的文化多样性,这将是他未来生活和工作的一段宝贵经历。奥运圣火在鸟巢点燃后,张衣笙说:"我太激动了。我们一直十分努力,就为了在令人惊叹的开幕式上表演。"

Wednesday【C 阅读理解】
● 参考译文

哈米西·阿利·阿卜迪(Khamisi Ally Abdi)练习了一系列轻柔缓慢的太极动作,在寒冷的早晨中,他感到身体暖和起来了。这位 25 岁的学生在中国北方的河北省沧州职业技术学院练习这一动作缓慢的中国传统武术已经两年了,现在是(太极)超级粉丝。

该学院为所有外国学生开设太极课程。阿卜迪已经掌握了太极所需的平衡和有节奏的深呼吸。这让他能够充分体验到这一训练方法,在锻炼和强健肌肉的同时,还能让头脑平静下来。在学习太极时,阿卜迪遇到了许多来自非洲和亚洲的功夫迷。沧州因其武术历史悠久,在 1992 年被体育部门命名为"武术之乡"。

通过练习太极,阿卜迪对中国文化有了全面的了解,现在他更喜欢人们叫他的中文名字。他说:"当我回家后,我将用我的中文名字在我的国家教授太极,这样就有更多的人可以受益于这种神奇的功夫。"

Thursday【D 阅读理解】
● 参考译文

中国学生正在展示他们对移动应用软件的热情和创新思维，方法是推出一系列创新应用软件来解决社会问题，帮助改善生活质量。浙江大学学生李想与两位同学一起开发了一款移动应用软件，这款软件可以通过创建和喂养虚拟电子宠物来帮助用户养成良好的习惯。

这一独特的数字宠物创建于应用程序"谓尔"（发音与英语单词"well"相似）中。用户的日常行为被用来帮助宠物成长。当用户完成日常锻炼目标时，他们独特的电子宠物也会充满活力；当他们晚上睡得太晚时，他们的宠物会有黑眼圈。数字宠物就像是用户在虚拟世界中的一个化身。但不同于其他数字宠物关注的是和用户外表的相似性，该应用程序更多的是反映用户的内在性格和行为。该应用程序旨在让用户更好地了解自己，帮助他们养成良好的习惯。

该应用程序是超过 500 所大学的学生开发的 1 400 个项目中的一个，这些项目都提交给了由浙江大学和美国科技公司苹果联合举办的 2021 移动应用创新赛。比赛于 12 月中旬结束。

在大赛中，学生们还设计了应用程序，以帮助解决保护传统文化和照顾家庭成员等社会难题。

Friday【E 任务型阅读】
● 参考译文

漫画艺术家翟进正在寻找有新意的方式来充分享受生活，激发他的创造力。从 18 岁到 32 岁，漫画家翟进几乎没有离开过自己在安徽省的家。他被诊断患有成骨不全症，这种疾病使他容易骨折。

翟进对绘画的兴趣很早就开始了。在大约 3 岁的时候，他喜欢在纸上乱涂乱画。这是受他父母鼓励的一项活动，因为这要求他待着不动，避免受伤。

受动画电视连续剧和漫画小说的影响，他开始模仿角色，设计自己的角色，并在脑海中为这些角色构思新的故事。为了提高自己的角色设计能力，他练习创作基于真人的漫画角色，他后来了解到这种风格与日本漫画艺术非常相似。

他了解到对此类漫画的需求，并对自己的能力充满信心，于是 2019 年推出了自己的品牌"阿进似颜绘"，在现场或网上提供个性化的漫画创作。他经常在市集摆摊，坐在顾客面前，询问并了解他们想要被创作成什么样的。他说，为顾客画画总是给他一种成就感。

他还在哔哩哔哩上开设了一个账户，该账户目前拥有约 7 000 名粉丝。他会发布自己创作漫画和日常生活的视频。

Saturday【F 短文填空】
● 参考译文

周怡冰是北京市清华大学的一名学生。她在 2021 年 6 月实现了自身的学术梦想，激励了全国人民。

尽管因为两次脊柱手术而无法参加 2020 年高考，但她还是实现了自己的梦想。经过仔细考虑，周怡冰选择了测控技术与仪器专业。她想用自己的一生为国家的发展和创新服务。

2020 年 4 月，周怡冰突然觉得自己的身体麻木了，那时离高考只有不到两个月的时间。起初，她没有太在意。但她腰脊柱的刺痛感很快变得明显。周怡冰被诊断为先天性峡部裂。医生建议周怡冰离开学校做手术。

2020 年 5 月，周怡冰接受了手术，认为一次手术足以解决她的脊柱问题。然而，术后并发症使她经历了各种副作用。一个月后,周怡冰回到手术室。第二次手术很成功,两周后,她不再卧床。她立即全身心投入康复,抓住每一个机会赶上学习进度。三个月后,周怡冰回到了上海交通大学附属中学的高中课堂。

在老师和同学的支持下,她重拾信心,开始为2021年高考做准备。周怡冰说:"只要还没有失去生活的勇气,所有的事情都能从头再来。"

Week Two

Monday【A 完形填空】

● 参考译文

你听说过沉浸式语言项目吗？这些项目可以发生在学校或其他地方，学习者可以在自然环境中练习使用他们的第二语言。以下是可以帮助你练习四种英语技能的一些方法。

听

• 聆听讲英语的艺术家表演你最喜欢的音乐风格。如果你喜欢听自己唱歌，请跟着一起唱吧。

• 在线观看优秀的英语电影和电视节目。关闭字幕来加大难度。

说

• 用英语与自己交谈。起初，这可能会让人感到奇怪。但是，你练习得越多，就越会用英语进行思考，这是向（说出）流利的英语迈出的一大步。

• 在线玩英语游戏。在学习的同时获得乐趣可以让你更轻松地记住所学的内容。

读

• 将你的社交媒体语言更改为英语。关注讲英语的人并用英语发表评论。

• 在你的房子里放置小指示牌，用英语标明常见物品的名称。在你学会了这些单词之后，你可以像一个节目主持人一样，讲述你在家中的动向。

写

• 用英语写下你的待办事项清单或营销清单。

• 用英语写日记或做记录。写下你自己的经历将帮助你学习对你的生活很重要的词汇。

让我们一起想办法让沉浸式项目变得有趣吧！

Tuesday【B 阅读理解】

● 参考译文

一段小朋友练八段锦的视频在网上非常受欢迎，这是由一群三年级学生制作的，是他们项目式学习的成果。这段视频受到了学生和家长的称赞，他们在自己的社交网站账户上进行了分享。以下就是该项目式学习的一些相关信息。

目标	让学生参加一些特殊的课程，鼓励他们根据特定的主题去自主地探索世界
主题	春天	植物和花展
	夏天	高温环境下的工作
	秋天	菜肴和甜点等类型的食物或者医疗保健
	冬天	冬季奥林匹克运动会
参与方式	不同年龄段的学生接收的任务不同： 一、二年级的小学生可以画画； 三到六年级的小学生可以用更复杂的方式展示自己的研究
时间限制	完成任务需要一到两个月
要求	深入思考； 做研究； 与他人交流； 运用跨学科技能展示研究结论
意义	帮助学生： 适应新型高中入学考试； 收获独立学习的技能； 结合所学知识来处理复杂的问题； 激发学习的好奇心和动力； 进行团队合作并通过交流互相学习； 寻求基础教育与关键能力之间的平衡

Wednesday【C 阅读理解】
● 参考译文

由深圳戏院承办的戏曲活动2021"戏曲进校园"再一次取得了成功。不同类型的传统戏曲受到了大学生、小学生和中学生的关注。

承办单位邀请著名戏曲演员表演、教育和展示京剧、昆曲、豫剧、粤剧、黄梅戏等曲种中的经典戏曲片段,为学生营造一个学习古老表演艺术的环境。据承办单位介绍,该活动包括戏曲历史讲座、服饰展览、戏曲化妆体验、戏曲表演和戏曲剧场课堂,通过这些,学生们可以深入地了解戏曲,从而培养对我国传统文化的浓厚兴趣。

在深圳市第三职业技术学校,国家一级演员蒋文瑞做了关于粤剧的讲座。近2 600名学生听了讲座。除此以外,现代京剧《换人间》在南方科技大学和深圳中学大受欢迎。深圳中学的一名学生表示:"这让我们感到十分惊喜。我很高兴看到戏曲演员能来到我们学校,和我们分享戏曲背后的故事和文化。我认为这非常棒。"

深圳正在积极探索利用新媒体技术推广中国传统文化的新途径。例如,据一份报告称,深圳戏院直播了学校里的所有演出,观看量达42万次。

Thursday【D 任务型阅读】
● 参考译文

如何在学校停课期间让学生继续学习,一直是疫情中最困难的问题之一。

但是,家庭、学校和国家之间的不平等意味着一些学生比其他人更容易在疫情期间取得成功。当学校停课时,世界各国的教学方法大不相同。一些国家能够迅速转向在线学习,但其他国家根本无法做出这种改变。

在丹麦等欧洲国家,超过95%的学生使用笔记本电脑完成学业。但在布基纳法索和肯尼亚等非洲国家,只有不到10%的学生拥有笔记本电脑。没有数字资源的国家有其他方式让学生在课堂之外进行学习。在肯尼亚和俄罗斯等一些地方,教育电视和无线电广播有所增加。但当学校停课时,许多学生无法接受任何学校教育。布基纳法索的大多数学生以及肯尼亚约五分之一的学生至少有四个月没有做过任何作业。

教师们也感受到了疫情带来的情绪影响。例如,在印度,85%的教师表示,他们需要额外的心理健康支持。在俄罗斯,64%的教师说在大部分时间都感到很疲惫。一些国家的很多教师害怕在工作时感染新型冠状病毒。很多校领导说,在疫情期间心理健康资源的使用有所增加。

Friday【E 短文填空】
● 参考译文

在香港的一个城区——西贡区,一群学生在一个树木覆盖的斜坡上跑上跑下,用英语唱着一首歌:"我爱山,我爱阳光如此灿烂。"

在这里的枫树下,孩子们和他们的老师正在尝试一种越来越受欢迎的新型学习方式——森林学校。这是一种将孩子与自然联系起来、培养孩子主导学习的方式。"这可以帮助我的儿子获得更多的户外知识,并保持好奇心。这有利于培养他们不同的能力。"一位母亲一边说,一边看着她四岁的儿子在树下将泥和水混在一起。森林学校让孩子们变得自信,培养他们解决问题的能力。比如,有一次他们看到海滩上有很多垃圾后都想做点什么。

在西贡的海滩上,看着孩子们用水桶装满海水或沙子，老师吹起哨子，把孩子们集合起来开始下一项活动。当被问及下一项活动是什么的时候，孩子们说他们想种花。那就确定下来了，因为每次都是孩子们决定他们想学什么。

Saturday【F 短文填空】

● 参考译文

草埔小学由于其成功的竖笛演奏教学，最近被评为艺术教育特色学校，是深圳市十所上榜学校中的一所。

该校校长许春生表示，音乐能激发能量。他还认为，艺术教育可以温暖孩子们的心，因为这些孩子有时会受到忙于生计的父母的忽视。学校之所以选择教竖笛，是因为竖笛比较容易学，而且价格便宜。这所学校的所有学生都可以演奏竖笛，一、二年级的学生每周参加一次竖笛训练，三至六年级的学生在每节音乐课上演奏15分钟竖笛。

更重要的是，音乐丰富了学生的生活，培养了他们的自信。在这些学生中，有个害羞的男孩，他一直独来独往，不知为什么就是不开心。自从参加了竖笛演奏俱乐部并和同学们一起获奖后，他变得更加自信了。

这种努力也得到了家长们的认可。一位妈妈说："我儿子每天写完作业后都会演奏竖笛。现在这就像在家里开音乐会一样，他的行为也为他的妹妹树立了一个很好的榜样，她也开始对音乐感兴趣。"

Week Three
Monday【A 完形填空】
● 参考译文

我从没想过四岁的女儿还会打扰我们睡觉,这感觉特别不公平,因为她的弟弟就睡得很好。我曾经试着告诉她不要叫醒我们,解释说这会让我们第二天感到疲倦。她想了想,然后回答道:"不过你累了也没关系,因为你明天可以喝咖啡。"

看吧,她已经改变了我的习惯,包括我日渐增加的咖啡消耗量。事实上,她可能在更深层次上影响了我,不只是影响了我的睡眠模式。

孩子们甚至在他们出生之前就开始影响我们:我们为孩子的到来做好计划,改变我们的生活来欢迎他们。他们在婴儿时期控制我们的睡眠和情绪。然而,保持冷静并不总是那么容易。要让两个不开心的孩子穿好衣服、准备离开家门,而当一个孩子为穿错袜子或鞋子而哭泣时,这会让父母很生气,尤其是在试图按时上班的时候。在这种压力大的情况下,认识到孩子有他们自己的能动性,想要自由地行动,做出自己的选择会有所帮助。

最后,我们都在互相学习。接受这一点,并回应孩子们的需求,让生活变得更顺利——即使这意味着在又一夜断断续续的睡眠之后多喝一杯咖啡。

Tuesday【B 阅读理解】
● 参考译文

亲爱的朋友们:

在国际奥委会主席托马斯·巴赫(Thomas Bach)宣布闭幕后,2022年冬季奥运会以令人难忘的方式落下帷幕。今天我想谈谈志愿者在奥运会中的关键作用。

陶振国就是一个很好的例子。当陶振国准备为2008年北京奥运会做志愿者时,他当上了外公。他的女儿在8月份奥运会开幕式前几天生下了男孩郭笑宇。陶振国对于外孙的到来感到很高兴,但那个月他没有太多时间和郭笑宇在一起,因为他在忙着志愿者工作。陶振国不会说英语,但他明确表示"作为一名奥运志愿者,我必须学会英语,至少要能够与外国客人交流"。陶振国说:"我希望当我遇到外国运动员和客人时,我能说'北京欢迎你'。"

后来,郭笑宇也成了一名奥运志愿者。他在奥运村所在的社区帮忙进行垃圾分类、交通引导和信息查询。郭笑宇说他从外公那里学到了很多。他听过陶振国做志愿者的经历,并开始做社区工作。

祖孙两人都是2022年北京冬奥会的志愿者。他们给予了很大的帮助,也很可爱。我为我的祖国而骄傲,也为有这么多优秀的志愿者而骄傲。谢谢!

Wednesday【C 阅读理解】
● 参考译文

来自墨西哥城附近一个小镇的17岁科学天才埃斯特拉·萨拉查(Estrella Salazar)受到姐姐的启发,开发了一款应用程序,帮助失聪和有听力困难的墨西哥人更易交流。

萨拉查的姐姐佩拉(Perla)生来就患有一种影响行动能力和听力的严重疾病,被称为MERRF综合征。25岁的她做了多次手术,接受了多年的治疗。一所手语学校告知她,由于她的身体状况,她将无法学习手语。萨拉查的学习能力让她提前三年从高中毕业。在看到姐姐佩拉面临的歧视后,她问自己:"我能做什么来帮助我的姐姐呢?"

后来,她开始开发一款连接墨西哥手语(MSL)使用者和听力正常的用户的应用程序——允许人们将手语转换为文本或语音，反之亦然。萨拉查建立了一个由近90名参与者组成的组织——包括母语人士和口译员——来开发这款名为Hands with Voice的应用程序，她希望这款应用程序能在今年投入市场。最近几个月，随着佩拉行动能力的提高，这家人开始学习手语。"我为我的妹妹感到骄傲，"佩拉说，"我喜欢在这个过程中找到一个群体。"

现在，萨拉查正在寻找一所能让她继续学习的美国大学。

Thursday【D 任务型阅读】
● 参考译文

46岁的罗珊妮（Roseanne）是一位住在美国新泽西州的母亲，她有一个16岁的儿子和一个14岁的女儿，这两个孩子从小时候起就没有好好相处过。"他们之间有很多冲突。他们没办法在不吵架的情况下在餐桌旁坐十分钟。他们总是不断地担心对方、评论对方、惹对方生气。"罗珊妮说。

几乎所有有兄弟姐妹的人都知道，竞争是很常见的。在许多家庭中，兄弟姐妹之间的争吵是有益的。它帮助孩子学会处理冲突，使他们更好地与他人沟通。作为人类，我们喜欢比较。例如，因为兄弟姐妹们通常有相似的经历，他们容易就学业或者体育上的成功进行比较，又或者争论谁是爸妈"最喜欢的"孩子。孩子的年龄越接近，竞争就越激烈。

兄弟姐妹间竞争的另一个主要驱动力是公平。父母更有可能给年龄较小的孩子特权，而不是给年龄较大的孩子。当年幼的孩子比哥哥姐姐更早获得许可时，哥哥姐姐会觉得不公平，这样就会造成冲突。

专家建议父母要鼓励兄弟姐妹在成年后发展亲密的关系。罗珊妮说："在我成长的过程中，我和我的兄弟之间的矛盾很多。但现在，我们会一起出席家庭聚会，聊聊我妈妈的事——尽管这是很久以后才发生的事。"

Friday【E 短文填空】
● 参考译文

在2022年14天的春节假期里，腾讯公司总共只允许孩子们玩14个小时的电子游戏。有小孩能抵制住玩电子游戏的诱惑吗？据我所知，一个也没有。事实上，他们应该和他们的朋友和同学一起在户外玩。但我看到的是，只要手边有手机或平板电脑，年轻人就可以一直沉浸在游戏世界中，对任何人的呼唤置若罔闻。

为什么父母会担心这种情况呢？在我看来，一些流行游戏中有太多的暴力元素。无论是对儿童还是对成年人来说，这些游戏都没有好处。此类内容不仅存在于游戏中，还存在于书籍和电影中。但是，限制电子游戏时间，以期儿童免受伤害的想法不是那么明智。如果孩子们充分利用这一个小时玩这样的游戏呢？每天一小时足以引起问题。

我们应该提供积极的内容，让孩子们随心所欲地玩耍，同时要确保他们的健康。对于我13岁的儿子，我们约定好在玩完游戏后休息20分钟，留出时间来学习、锻炼和睡觉。

Saturday【F 短文填空】
● 参考译文

随着美国学校的英语学习者人数不断增加，需要更多帮助的不仅仅是学生，不会说英语的家长和家庭也需要支持。家长想要他们可以积极参与孩子的学校教育，即使有语言困难。

家长和家庭能够用他们自己的语言进行交流非常

重要。珍妮特·休格-约翰逊（Janet Huger-Johnson）是东纽约卓越小学的校长。她说，例如，她的学校使用手机应用程序，允许教师用英语发送信息，而这些信息将被翻译成家长使用的语言。当家长回复时，信息会被翻译回英文。有时学校需要雇用社区中的人来帮助翻译。

最近的一项研究发现，费城的学校通常很少为移民父母提供支持。一些家长表示，学校提供的翻译服务很差。曼迪（Mandy）是费城一位说普通话的家长。她的孩子有特殊需要。在一次校会上，一位电话译员说她对特殊教育一无所知，拒绝翻译。最近，在一次校会上，她不得不带一个朋友来学校翻译。

为家长和家庭创造一个没有语言障碍的参与空间很重要。

Week Four

Monday【A 完形填空】
● 参考译文

淮安位于中国东部江苏省。作为已故总理周恩来的家乡，淮安因其丰富的美食历史，被选为联合国教科文组织创意城市网络的新增城市之一。

淮安坐落在中国南北分界线上，地理位置为这座城市提供了兼具南北特色的中华美食。

淮安位于京杭大运河旁，是重要的水运口岸。它也是淮扬菜（淮安菜和扬州菜的统称）的主要发源地之一。淮安美食深受运河2 500年历史的影响。早在春秋时期，京杭大运河便围绕淮安修建。清朝时期，随着水运的发展，淮安菜肴传播到了包括北京在内的中国北方地区。淮安美食也开始吸收全国各地的烹饪方法。

鱼是淮安菜的另一种重要食材，它通常带有一种甜甜的味道，保留了食材的原汁原味。地方菜往往是国宴的重头戏。根据1949年中华人民共和国成立后首次举行国宴的北京饭店的历史记载，"盛大的国宴完全以淮扬菜为基础"。

Tuesday【B 阅读理解】
● 参考译文

保持健康最重要的事情之一是饮食均衡且营养。什么是"健康饮食"呢？怎样才能开始健康饮食，并坚持很长时间呢？以下是实现健康饮食的最佳策略。

缓慢开始

如果你不知道关于健康饮食的一切，一个方法是每周尝试一种新蔬菜。挑一种你以前从未尝试过的蔬菜，研究一个新食谱把它做成一顿饭。这是一种健康饮食的方式，而不会让你不堪重负。

记录你的摄入

如果你在吃东西之前没有计划好你的饮食，那么也许你会发现你的饮食没有你计划的那么健康。写下你想要健康饮食的原因（减肥、增加能量，等等），每天读读你的清单。当你真正记录下你吃的东西时，你可能会感到很惊讶。

少吃超加工食品

事先做好的食物是非常方便的，尤其是当你忙于工作的时候。有些食品，如在商店买的饼干、冷冻玉米热狗和类似的方便食品，其中添加的糖类和卡路里含量通常很高。所以，不如你自己制作食物和饭菜。

平衡你的"餐盘"

想想你的餐盘上有什么。水果和蔬菜应该是你一餐的基础。你应该在每次就餐时吃点水果，以及鸡蛋、鸡胸肉或鱼等富含精益蛋白质的食物。

Wednesday【C 阅读理解】
● 参考译文

多年来，营养学家一直建议在饮食中使用橄榄油，而不是黄油和其他乳脂。新研究发现，每天摄入10克橄榄油的人死亡风险最高可降低34%。在膳食中摄入更多橄榄油的人患阿尔茨海默病、心血管病和癌症等严重疾病的风险较低。

是不是研究中食用更多橄榄油的人更健康呢？研究人员指出，与那些食用橄榄油较少的人相比，那些经常食用较多橄榄油的人通常身体更有活力，不太可能吸烟，而且更可能吃较多的水果和蔬菜。所有这些因素都可以降低患病的风险。

"医生应该建议患者不要食用某些烹调用油，如人造黄油和黄油，可以换成橄榄油，以改善他们的健康状况。"专家瓜施·费雷（Guasch-Ferré）说。泰德沃卡（Tadwalkar）博士对此表示赞同："当需要烹调用油时，从种子、坚果、水果中提取的植物油是正确的选择。橄榄油，尤其是特级初榨橄榄油，已被证明在人们寻求改善健康方面发挥着重要作用。"

你是否应该考虑将饮食中的某些烹调用油换成橄榄油呢？即使橄榄油有助于降低某些健康风险，但仍然存在许多问题。例如，尚不清楚人们应该摄入多少才能起到保护作用。

Thursday【D 阅读理解】
● 参考译文

据报道，新研究发现，从蔬菜而不是从肉类中摄取脂肪的饮食与较低的中风的风险有关。

在研究中，与吃最少蔬菜和多不饱和脂肪的人相比，吃这些最多的人患缺血性中风的可能性要低12%。摄入最多动物脂肪（不包括乳脂）的人比摄入最少动物脂肪的人患中风的可能性高16%。乳脂与中风风险的增加无关。大约87%的中风是血流受阻引发的缺血性中风。

中风的症状包括突然神志不清、剧烈头痛、行走困难、视觉障碍，以及面部、手臂或腿部无力或麻木。如果迅速开展紧急治疗，存活的概率更大。

短暂性脑缺血发作（TIA）和出血性中风是其他类型的中风。一名医学教授指出："短暂性脑缺血发作是一种严重疾病的征兆，如果没有医疗帮助，这种疾病是不会消失的。"出血性中风发生在大脑动脉出血时，这会损伤脑细胞。虽然中风的风险随着年龄的增长而增加，但中风可能发生在各个年龄阶段。高血压、吸烟、糖尿病和高胆固醇是中风的主要原因。

Friday【E 任务型阅读】
● 参考译文

根据《美国新闻与世界报道》的报道，地中海饮食连续第五年在年度最佳饮食竞赛中夺冠。排名第二的是强调较少的盐摄入量的得舒饮食。排名第三的是弹性素食饮食，鼓励在大多数时间当一个素食主义者，但偶尔可以吃个汉堡。这三种饮食法都强调较少的加工食品的摄入，并在你的盘子里塞满水果、蔬菜、豆类和坚果。

一般来说，排名靠前的饮食法是由你能吃什么决定的，而不是你不能吃什么。而现在，在疫情肆虐的艰难时期，这对人们尤其有帮助。我们想要自己喜欢吃的食物。我们也想要能让我们保持健康的食物。排名靠前的饮食法就提供了这些。地中海饮食是简单的、以植物为基础的烹饪，每一餐都含有水果和蔬菜、全谷物、少量坚果和橄榄油。该饮食法也鼓励人们食用健康的鱼，而鸡蛋的摄入量要少得多。

大量研究发现，地中海饮食有很多优点。地中海饮食有助于降低患记忆衰退、抑郁症和癌症等疾病的风险。这种饮食还与骨骼强健、心脏健康和长寿有关。

Saturday【F 短文填空】
● 参考译文

你更喜欢黑咖啡？那么，根据一项新的研究，你可能会喜欢黑而苦的巧克力。

研究发现，适量的黑咖啡——每天3到5杯——已被证明可以降低患某些严重疾病的风险，比如癌症。在研究中，科内利斯（Cornelis）和她的团队发现，一种基因变体可能解释了为什么有些人喜欢每天喝很多杯咖啡，而另一些人则不喜欢喝咖啡。具有该基因的人代谢咖啡因的速度更快，因此刺激效果会更快消失，他们也就需要喝更多的咖啡。这可以解释为什么有些人喝很多咖啡都似乎没问题，而另一些人可能会紧张或变得非常焦虑。

科内利斯说："当他们想到咖啡时，他们会想到苦苦的味道，所以他们也喜欢黑巧克力。这些人可能不只是对咖啡因的影响非常敏感，而且他们对其他具有苦味的食物也有这种习得行为。"

未来的研究将尝试解决对其他苦味食物的遗传偏好，这些食物通常与更多的健康问题有关。

Week Five

Monday【A 完形填空】
● 参考译文

对我们许多人来说，新冠肺炎疫情揭示了谁是我们最亲密的朋友。许多孩子想念他们的社交圈，尤其想念他们最好的朋友，因为由于出现了新冠肺炎疫情，孩子们没有足够的社交机会与更广泛的群体交流。这些朋友不只是我们喜欢和他们一起出去玩的人。相反，他们是我们完全信任的人。拥有"健康的"友谊通常被视为孩子拥有的一项重要技能。童年时期的亲密友谊有助于孩子练习他们在一生的亲密关系中所需要的技能，比如应对孤独、恐惧和失败等情绪的能力。

通常，孩子们通过一起做有趣的事情结交朋友，所以家长们可能需要考虑一下孩子的爱好，然后找出他们可以与其他孩子们共同做的活动。家长们也可以教孩子如何加入游戏和活动。

另外，拥有亲密的朋友可以帮助孩子走出困境。在整个童年时期，友谊一直在变化。当最好的朋友离开时，对于年幼的孩子来说（接受这一情况）会非常困难，因为他们还不习惯于结束一段关系。重要的是，家长要和孩子们讨论这个问题并支持他们。

对于那些还没有找到那个特别的朋友的孩子来说，以后还有很多机会。结交新朋友永远不会太迟，但早点开始是个好主意。

Tuesday【B 阅读理解】
● 参考译文

7岁时，彭霖倩因发烧而失聪。她记得，那时她的世界完全陷入了沉寂。听力障碍影响了她自我表达的能力，这导致她陷入自我孤立。当她长大后，因为知道自我表达的重要性，她一直致力于为听力受损人发声。

后来，她参加了一个为有听力障碍的儿童设立的表演讲习班项目。每天，他们设计许多写作、讲故事和戏剧活动，旨在让孩子们锻炼他们的想象力，发出自己的声音，最后用手语和肢体语言来表演这些故事。在彭霖倩的建议下，他们也设计了一些活动，如让大家摘下助听器或扯着嗓子大喊。

然而，他们遇到了各种各样的困难。孩子们要么过于害羞，要么就是不太愿意参加这些活动。其中一个女孩花了一整天时间练习折纸。后来，团队成员改变了他们的计划，带着孩子们去了一个有创意的地方，孩子们的任务是找到一家他们喜欢的商店，并观察里面的人和物。最后，他们在一起度过了愉快的一天，甚至那个喜欢折纸的女孩还在她选择的明信片商店里留了言。她写道："今天，我过得很愉快。"

通过这个项目，他们最终与孩子们建立了友谊。

Wednesday【C 任务型阅读】
● 参考译文

"城市之花"是一个非营利组织，其目标是把自然带给那些可能没有绿色空间的孩子。该组织已经在华盛顿特区的7所小学、2所高中和18个幼儿教育中心帮助创建了绿色空间。

"城市之花"的课程以生态环境科学、烹饪等健康生活技能和艺术表达为中心。在花园里，学生们可以学习植物生命周期或生态系统等环境理念。但教师也可以通过阅读与园艺相关的书籍或学习与自然相关的词汇来利用绿色空间进行阅读教学。儿童和老年人已经参与了社区的绿色空间活动，例如，在烹饪课上，人们会讲述他们文化中特有的食物。社区花园代表了华盛顿特区的多样性。就像把许多不同的人、文化和社区等放在一起。

在华盛顿特区的一些地方，特别是在较贫困地区，很难找到健康的食物。在华盛顿特区，大约15%的地区是"食物沙漠"。该组织的部分任务是在可能没有绿色空间，也可能没有新鲜、健康食品的空间中进行种植工作。对于学校里高年级的学生来说，他们通过"城市之花"项目的组织来学习如何种植和收割作物。他们还可以在当地的农贸市场出售蔬菜和草药。

人们已经意识到绿色空间在我们的社区中是非常重要的。并且，他们想花更多的时间在户外体验大自然。

Thursday【D 任务型阅读】
● 参考译文

年轻一代似乎变得更乐意接受国内品牌，更愿意为产品的设计和质量付费。年轻人不会只为写着"意大利制造"的大牌买单。

鸿星尔克付出的巨大的努力给我留下了深刻的印象。去年7月，该公司为河南省郑州市抗洪救灾工作提供了支持。尽管之前亏损了2.2亿元，但该体育和生活用品公司还是捐赠了价值5 000万元的物资。这种慷慨的行为给了其他国内品牌一个机会，可以让中国消费者知道，他们也有优质的产品和对国家深深的爱。

我曾经是偏爱国外品牌的人之一，尤其是化妆品。我一直认为使用外国货让我看起来很时尚。我也担心国内产品设计过时、质量低劣。后来，当我尝试了一些中国设计师设计的国产服装后，我放下了偏见。其质量与外国货一样好，但价格要实惠得多。

我认为，人们对国家发展的信心，以及国内产品设计和质量的改进，是这些新的民族产品发展起来的主要原因。这种态度的变化在年轻一代中更为明显，他们是在中国经济蓬勃发展的环境中成长的。

Friday【E 任务型阅读】
● 参考译文

女性的安全问题再次成为公众关注的焦点，她们害怕晚上步行回家。去年在爱丁堡开通的名为Strut Safe的热线电话可以在人们独自步行回家时陪伴他们。

22岁的爱丽丝·杰克逊（Alice Jackson）和她的朋友雷切尔·钟（Rachel Chung）想出了（开通）电话求助热线的主意，如果人们晚上独自步行回家，那么他们可以拨打该热线电话。爱丽丝说："我们买了一部便宜的手机，请志愿者接听电话，并将号码发布到社区团体中。"

接听电话的志愿者们与来电者聊天并提供安慰，但有时来电者会担心自己的安全。

如果来电者认为她不安全，那么她可以提供她的姓名、年龄、生日、地址信息，以及对她的长相和所穿的每一件衣物的完整描述。像爱丽丝这样的志愿者会随时准备通知警察或在需要时叫救护车。

爱丽丝说："每当打来电话的人安全到家，我就松了一口气。他们会说'我现在能看到我的房子了'，或者'我只需要一分钟就能到了'，但我总是说'别担心，没事的，我不会挂断电话。你进了家门就告诉我一声'。"

她会听到钥匙开锁的咔嗒声，听到有的人的妈妈在喊"你去哪儿了？"或者听到狗叫声。

Strut Safe免费服务热线的工作时间为周五和周六晚上7点至凌晨3点，周日晚上7点至凌晨1点。

Saturday【F 短文填空】

● 参考译文

如果你在办公楼被隔离48小时该怎么办？

这听起来很可怕。但艾伦（Allen）——一名被困在位于上海的公司大楼内的公司主管——很心平气和。"没有恐慌；我们的第一反应是往办公室拿日常用品。"她回忆道。"我们被告知我们所在的大楼里有一个阳性病例，我们需要在早上进行核酸检测。然后我们在办公室被封控了48小时。"她说。有人在网上订购了东西，其他人则打电话让家人给他们送东西。政府和公司购买了床上用品，并在被困人员睡前送达。被困人员点餐时可以获得餐补。

和同事睡同一个房间会不会很尴尬？艾伦说，大家被分成好几个小组，并且办公室被分成了好几个区域。"所以我们有足够的空间来摆放床具。唯一的问题是在48小时的隔离期间我们不能洗澡。"所需的食物都被送到了办公室，所以隔离就变成了一场另类的晚宴。

大多数处于隔离状态的办公人员都对此表示理解，并对相关人员作出的快速反应和行动竖起大拇指。

Week Six

Monday【A 完形填空】
● 参考译文

2022年北京冬奥会可爱的吉祥物"冰墩墩"十分畅销。为什么这只"熊猫"这么受欢迎呢?它的设计理念是什么呢?广州美术学院教授、吉祥物设计团队负责人曹雪讲述了这个故事。

曹雪清楚地记得2019年9月17日这激动人心的一天。这一天,冬季奥运会组委会宣布,由广州美术学院设计的吉祥物为北京冬季奥运会吉祥物。经过许多专家的讨论,吉祥物有了一个新的名字——"冰墩墩"。

"冰墩墩"是一只具有高科技感的熊猫。它全身的"壳"由冰制成,吸引了人们的注意。曹雪表示,这一设计灵感来自中国传统美食"糖葫芦",而外壳也类似于航天服。为了让熊猫看起来更讨喜,曹雪和他的团队成员乘飞机前往中国卧龙大熊猫博物馆进行实地观察。

对于冰墩墩的受欢迎,曹雪表示:"它的冰壳是冷的,但形象看起来温暖又可爱。我相信这种温暖可以让每个人都能感受到。我希望它能成为奥运历史上令人印象深刻的记忆。"

Tuesday【B 阅读理解】
● 参考译文

从古至今,无论主体是谁,肖像画向我们讲述了关于人性和身份的基本事实。通过观察肖像画中的人物以及绘画方式,我们能对社会和文化历史了解得更多,这些是其他类型的绘画不能提供的。

卡萨琳娜·范·赫姆森(Catharina van Hemessen)《自画像》	卡萨琳娜·范·赫姆森这幅著名的自画像的侧重点在她的艺术家身份。当然,自画像也是艺术表现的重要部分,它有记录、庆祝的功能,并展示了过去和现在的我们。
梵高(Van Gogh)《割耳朵后的自画像》	梵高在与高更(Gauguin)争吵后割下了自己的一部分耳朵,这幅《割耳朵后的自画像》就是在此之后创作的,展示了他不顾伤痛、继续作画的强大决心。在考陶尔德美术馆最近举办的梵高自画像展览上,这幅画是核心作品。
爱丽丝·尼尔(Alice Neel)《詹姆斯·亨特黑人新兵》	尽管爱丽丝·尼尔的独特的肖像画直到她的职业生涯后期才获得赞同,但这些画的纪实性和民主性展现了肖像画可以发挥的许多功能。在过去,肖像画实际上是等级、地位或名人的标志。

欢迎您在线对文章发表评论,也可以给我们留言,说出您的意见。

Wednesday【C 阅读理解】
● 参考译文

在中国文化中,老虎象征着力量和活力。但笔名为"不二马"的漫画家创作的这种大型猫科动物却并非如此。他创作的老虎又胖又懒,总是带着有趣又笨笨的表情。这使得不二马画的可爱的胖虎在网络上大受欢迎,尤其是在今年这个虎年。

"我看到动物园里的老虎的照片,它们真的真的很胖。"他回忆说,"我看到它们时就把它们画了下来,然后把它们发布在网上。我没想到它们会这么受欢迎。"不二马最受欢迎的作品之一是《喊妈小老虎》。在这幅画中,一只耳朵小而扁平的小老虎紧闭双眼,大声喊着"妈!"。另一幅画叫作《猛虎下山》。不二马画的老虎不是传统的猛虎,而是胖胖的,带着一副搞笑的鬼脸的老虎。他说:"这些作品是新冠肺炎疫情在中国暴发不久后创作的,当时人们处于疫情封锁期,需要通过一些可爱的东西来获得安慰。我想这就是胖虎走红的原因。"

"我现在最大的问题是,胖虎太受欢迎了,我没有足够的时间学习新东西,提升自己,这对我来说是一个危险的信号。"他说,"我希望自己能在这个虎年做出一些积极的改变。"

Thursday【D 任务型阅读】
● 参考译文

纽约地球屋的地板上铺着约 250 立方米的肥沃泥土,是纽约市最不寻常的艺术景点之一。1977 年,迪亚艺术基金会邀请当地艺术家沃尔特·德·玛利亚(Walter De Maria)创建纽约地球屋。经过三年的建设,其于 1980 年向公众开放。

艺术爱好者可以参观这个不寻常的景点,欣赏这堆泥土,体味泥土的芬芳。但是,他们被禁止踩踏泥土,甚至连触碰都不可以。不管你信不信,40 多年来保持 140 吨泥土处于原始状态比听起来要困难得多。他们会不时地给土壤浇水、耙土,并确保去除从土里冒出来的蘑菇。

地球屋的看护人比尔·迪尔沃思(Bill Dilworth)自 1989 年以来一直在回答访客的问题。他每天坐在桌子旁,登记访客,答疑解惑,看起来很神秘。"人们总是想知道这到底意味着什么,但艺术家从来没有赋予其任何意义。所以我认为,我真正想要人们知道的是,他们不必了解与这一作品有关的任何事情。"本身也是艺术家的迪尔沃思说。

你可能认为,很少有人欣然去参观一间充满泥土的大型阁楼,但是你错了。地球屋对外开放时,每天参观这一独特的艺术品的访客多达 100 人。

Friday【E 任务型阅读】
● 参考译文

你知道萝卜干也可以变成一朵美丽的"花"从而用来装点头冠吗?摄影师兼设计师王平就拥有这种变萝卜干为花的"魔法"。

26 岁的王平拥有两家摄影工作室,2020 年他开始对制作头冠产生兴趣。王平发现没有能与工作室的服装搭配的头冠。作为一名工艺美术专业的学生,王平擅长绘画,因此他决定自己动手制作头冠。制作头冠有三个步骤。"首先,我画出设计图纸。然后,准备好需要的所有材料来构建头饰的框架,"王平说,"最后一步是组装所有的材料,并涂上颜色。"令人惊讶的是,几乎所有材料都是"废品",因为这些材料取自废弃的衣物。王平说:"我决定充分利用这些'废料'。我尽自己最大的努力去设计、制作环保的头饰。"

王平更热衷于制作中国传统的凤冠。制作一顶凤冠通常需要一周至几个月的时间,因为凤冠会用到 30 多种材料。现在,王平正在制作以龙为主题的服装。王平说:"大约需要一年的时间才能完成。"

随着人们欣然接受"国潮"风的兴起,王平的作品深受大众喜爱也就不足为奇了。王平说:"我会坚持将中国传统文化与时尚元素相结合,制作更精美的头冠"。

Saturday【F 短文填空】
● 参考译文

德米特里·布拉金（Dmitry Bragin）是一位乌克兰艺术家，他擅长制作蒸汽朋克面具，这种面具让佩戴者看起来更像机器而不是人类。

尽管布拉金大部分造型惊艳的面具从技术上来讲并不是蒸汽朋克，因为它们没有活动部件，但是很明显，科幻风格是它们主要的灵感来源。这位才华横溢的艺术家首先用一个容易塑形的轻薄塑料面具打基础，然后添加各种装饰元素，以便将它变成你看到的可穿戴的奇迹。他的地下室里的材料包括摩托车零件、没有用的相机镜头、儿童金属玩具，等等，尽管你无法从成品中分辨出来。

布拉金的蒸汽朋克面具看起来 100% 是金属的，但这只是在金属涂料的帮助下产生的错觉。说实话，面具中的许多零件实际上都很轻，让佩戴面具更为容易，也更舒适。我们可以看到，涂料赋予了这个令人印象深刻的配饰厚重而复古的外观。

德米特里·布拉金在社交媒体平台上向对这种设计感兴趣的粉丝们分享他最新创作的面具。

Week Seven
Monday【A 完形填空】
● 参考译文

上海的艺术和文化中心的一处新场所今潮8弄（The INLET）经过三年的翻新后向公众开放了。这个地方位于上海主要的商业街之一四川北路附近，由一个有着六十幢海派石库门房子和八幢独立建筑的百年建筑群改建而成。

历史上，这里曾是许多著名人物的家，比如翻译家瞿秋白、作家和诗人鲁迅。四川北路也曾经是中国第一家电影院和私立的上海美术学院的所在地。

该建筑群将被修复用作公共的艺术和文化空间，这从一开始就是很清楚的。该项目的另一个重点是结合传统与现代设计，展示海派文化。使用旧砖来修复建筑物，因为开发商们想要保持其原来的样子。开发商还用与原来相似的石头来修复老房子的大门。

上海国际艺术节是在今潮8弄举办的第一个艺术活动，将有来自歌剧、爵士和现代舞等不同领域的艺术家一直表演到周日。艺术节的目的是让艺术更贴近大众。崇邦集团的首席执行官郑秉泽负责本次翻新项目，他说他希望上海的年轻人能参加当地的文化活动。

Tuesday【B 阅读理解】
● 参考译文

在过去的50年里，迪拜已经成为一个神秘的成功故事——从一个沉睡的渔港变成了一个活力满满的大都市。但这座城市面临着一个重大挑战：荒漠化使剩余的肥沃土地变得危险。随着人口和粮食消耗量的增加，荒漠化正变得极其严重。

荒漠化是土地退化的一种类型，会使干旱地区的肥沃土地变得贫瘠。它通常发生在水和土壤等自然资源负担过重的时候。尽管荒漠化会自然发生，但由于过度放牧、现代农业和建筑开发等人类活动，迪拜和世界各地的荒漠化都越来越严重。科学家威廉·H·施莱辛格（William H. Schlesinger）说："当肥沃的土地（通常是位于沙漠边缘的肥沃土地）负担过重时就会发生荒漠化。"

找到实用的解决办法变得非常重要。目标不是征服沙漠，而是要恢复土地的生产力。一个古老的环境解决方案就是种植更多的树。树木能固定土壤，吸收碳，提高土壤肥力，还能改善地下水的补给。选择正确的树木，尤其是本土树木，对干旱地区的植树项目十分重要。2010年，谢赫·穆罕默德（Sheikh Mohammed）开启了"一百万棵树项目"，旨在种植一百万棵树来阻止荒漠化。

Wednesday【C 任务型阅读】
● 参考译文

对于中国秦朝的建立者，中国第一位皇帝秦始皇来说，兵马俑是不寻常的陪葬品。秦始皇帝陵于1974年被发现，1987年被列入《世界遗产名录》。

内有秦始皇墓地的秦始皇帝陵博物院位于中国西北部的陕西省，以被称为"世界奇迹"的兵马俑而闻名。在这个著名博物院的一号坑中新发现了25件陶俑。在这些文物中，有一件是将军俑，另一件是中级军吏俑。这25件彩绘陶俑保存状况良好，为确保安全，目前被存放在保护室。中国考古学家表示，它们对于了解和研究坑内的军阵排列非常重要。

目前，考古学家已经修复了一些文物，包括三辆二轮战车、马匹和多件金、银、铜制的俑，所有这些都展现了秦朝贵族的奢华生活。

Thursday【D 任务型阅读】

参考译文

通过摄影，我们能够对过去以及已知的地点产生新的了解。你将看到位于巴黎的巴黎圣母院的第一张照片。这张照片是路易·达盖尔（Louis Daguerre）在 1838 年或 1839 年拍摄的，该照片显示的教堂与如今这座历经 2019 年大火的教堂的样子很相似：没有塔尖。

2019 年烧毁的塔尖以及巴黎圣母院的整个屋顶和阁楼在 1839 年时还没有出现。它是在 1844 年开始的长达 20 年的教堂修复工程中建成的。在伟大的建筑师欧仁·埃马纽埃尔·维欧勒-勒-杜克（Eugène Emmanuel Viollet-le-Duc）的领导下，（对巴黎圣母院的）首次修复是历史保护的先锋体现。

今天，巴黎圣母院正在重建。巴黎摄影师托马斯·范·霍特里夫（Tomas van Houtryve）在二月的封面故事中记录了这一事件，他从著名摄影师纳达尔（Nadar）拍摄的一幅肖像中获得了灵感。"我想要使用相同的技术拍摄现代建筑师和工作团队，连接所有这些不同时空的巴黎圣母院的守卫者们。"范·霍特里夫说。他选择使用过去的技术，这不仅是对当前工作人员的尊重，也是对他们的项目精神的尊重。

Friday【E 短文填空】

参考译文

当从巴黎出发的火车向南部区域行驶时，我想起了马赛，它与法国的其他地区不同。无论是在地理上还是在文化上，它都是一个大都市。它的居民是由一批又一批的移民组成的，这使得它不仅是法国最古老的城市之一，也是最具多元文化的城市。

到达马赛-圣-查尔斯车站后，游客可以从其奢华的、高高的站前广场欣赏到美景。我的目光注视着雅典大道，这是一条倾斜的街道。在那里，圣母加德大教堂——这座城市的最高点——像一座伸向大海的神圣灯塔，闪闪发光。马赛旧港仍然是这座城市的中心。湖面上的游艇好似一只天鹅。

这座城市每年有 300 天都沐浴在阳光中。为了避暑，我前往加泰罗尼亚海滩。在傍晚的阳光下，海滩浸透在神秘的琥珀色中。我走过一群打排球的人，当地人在晒日光浴和闲聊。很容易就能感受到这座城市的"好脾气"。正是在这里，我才明显地注意到马赛的"法国风情"。这让我想起了一些夹在国家和海洋之间的大港口城市，如上海或纽约。

关于马赛，我是这样认为的：这座城市只是一个国家的另一种表达方式，它的文化比它自己往往承认的更与众不同。

Saturday【F 短文填空】

参考译文

根据中国考古学家近年来的研究，中原地区与西藏高原地区的文化交流可以追溯到旧石器时期。国家文物局发表了对西藏历史和西藏人民具有重要意义的最具代表性的考古遗址的最新研究成果。

在第一个遗址——西藏嘎尔县的切热遗址，已经发现了 500 多件主要由石头和泥土制成的文物。这些文物和各种各样的石器表明，古代的西藏人与其他地区有着文化交流。同时，该遗址为研究古人类的起源和迁徙路线提供了宝贵的资料。

此外，在康马县的玛不错遗址还发现了火坑、墓葬和陶器等人类活动的考古证据。

札达县的格布赛鲁遗址拥有相对独立的文化。有趣的是，该遗址中的古墓与新疆维吾尔自治区同时期的古墓相似。

这份工作报告表明，西藏的历史和文化不是独立的，而是形成于不同的地区和丰富的文化背景。

Week Eight

Monday【A 完形填空】

● 参考译文

作为一家微型陶瓷工作室的创始人，王文化从未想到他的作品会让海内外观众感到如此惊讶。他的短视频在抖音——中国版的 Tik Tok——上获得了超过 4 500 万的播放量和 420 万个赞。

王文化说他曾经见过世界上最大的陶瓷，但从未见过最小的，所以有一天他下定决心，要尝试一些不同的东西——制作微型陶瓷。

一开始，事情进行得并不容易，许多人质疑他。然而，王文化并没有放弃。最终，他想出了一个依靠自己让这个新想法变成现实的办法。

据王文化所说，制作微型陶瓷作品的关键在于专注。无数次的尝试之后，王文化发现他能做出的最小号的作品在 2 毫米左右，否则他就要用显微镜了。

"有时候，我的关注者或粉丝会告诉我一些很好的创意。我们的关系非常好。"王文化说。他经常在直播的时候和粉丝聊得火热。

目前，王文化每天可制作大约 100 个迷你花瓶，但更有创意的作品可能需要一到两天的时间。

"我创作的作品就像我的孩子一样。除非买家也是陶艺爱好者，或者他们真的很喜欢我的作品，否则我不愿意把它们卖掉。"王文化说。

Tuesday【B 阅读理解】

● 参考译文

大寒是二十四节气中的最后一个节气，通常是在每年的 1 月 20 日前后到来，标志着冬天的结束。

在大寒期间，天气会非常寒冷。尽管在中国的某些地区，大寒期间的天气没有小寒那么冷，但是在一些沿海地区，全年最低气温仍然出现在大寒期间。

在大寒时节，北京人有吃"消寒糕"的习惯。消寒糕是一种年糕。汉语中的"年糕"与"年高"发音相同，象征着好运和不断高升。在安徽省安庆市，人们在大寒期间有吃炸春卷的传统。春卷里包着肉和蔬菜等馅料，口味可咸可甜。江苏南京人则喜欢在大寒时节喝鸡汤。鸡汤可以让我们保持温暖，预防感冒。

在中国各地，大寒还是开展滑雪和滑冰等冬季运动的最佳时节。

Wednesday【C 阅读理解】

● 参考译文

在中国文化中，老虎被视为百兽之王。它们象征着活力、守护、慷慨和难以捉摸。人们认为老虎是无所畏惧的动物，所以在中国你能在寺庙和房屋的墙壁上看到老虎图像，人们以此来抵御灾祸和危险。

不仅在中国，老虎在整个亚洲都有重要的文化意义。

由于老虎大多分布在亚洲，对许多西方人来说，老虎已经成为东方国家的文化象征。例如，东方的强大经济体——新加坡、韩国、中国香港和中国台湾——被称为"亚洲四小龙"。在《少年派的奇幻漂流》一书中，加拿大作家扬·马特尔（Yann Martel）选择了一只孟加拉虎作为印度男孩派（Pi）在太平洋历险的伙伴。

在西方，公认的百兽之王不是老虎，而是狮子。人们称呼勇敢的战士为"狮子"。在欧洲，狮子出现在英国以及其他 13 个国家的国徽上。但在西方，老虎也被视为一种非常强大的动物。在英语中，如果你想让某人冷静下来，你可以说"放松点儿（easy tiger）"。

老虎也是我最喜欢的动物之一。年轻时，作为一位动物爱好者，我因老虎是濒危物种而感到十分难过，想为保护老虎出一份力。

Thursday【D 任务型阅读】
● 参考译文

丽江古城位于中国西南部的云南省，拥有古建筑和丰富的民族文化。它也是中国少数民族纳西族的家园。

丽江流域水资源丰富，气候宜人。纳西族的祖先决定在此地居住，并开展农业。定居后，纳西人建立了城镇并通过建造水井将水运入村庄。水井有三个出水口。它们有不同的用途，以此来节约水资源。高处第一个井口的水来自泉水，因此被指定为饮用水；流入第二个井口的水是干净的，专门用于清洗蔬菜、水果和厨房用具；而流入第三个井口的水则专门用于洗涤衣物等日用品。

如今，多年来，每个家庭都已经安装了现代自来水设施，不再需要从井中取水来满足日常需要。然而，古老的传统却仍然留存在每个当地人的记忆中。你永远不会看到年轻或年长的纳西人在第一个井口洗菜。

Friday【E 任务型阅读】
● 参考译文

在中文里，农历十二月被称为腊月。农历十二月的第八天是腊月初八，或腊八。这一天也被称为腊八节。

腊八节的三大习俗是祭祖、吃腊八粥和做腊八蒜。

在古代，中国人把祭祀祖先的行为称为"腊"。他们也把祈求平安、丰收和健康的祭祀日称为"腊日"。因为腊八节是在农历十二月，所以这个月就被称为"腊月"。

关于在腊八节吃腊八粥的起源，有这么几个故事。有人说吃腊八粥起源于佛教徒；有人说这种由红豆制成的粥可以帮孩子驱邪。还有人说，这粥是为了纪念一对穷苦的夫妇。

腊八粥的主要食材是白米和糯米。人们还会加入糖、核桃、红豆、花生和其他各种各样的食材，使粥变得特别。

在中国北方，人们喜欢制作腊八蒜。他们将蒜浸泡在醋中，并密封在玻璃瓶中。醋使大蒜变得翠绿，而醋本身也充斥着大蒜的美味。

Saturday【F 短文填空】
● 参考译文

在过去的三个周日，无论是在高温天还是在雨天，悉尼蔡李佛（Choy Lee Fut）舞狮队都坚持表演，以宣传唐人街，吸引人们回来。

"由于新冠肺炎疫情，唐人街上少了很多人，不少店铺都已经关门了，大家的心情也都因为去年（的疫情）有些低落，"负责人保罗·纳木钟（Paul Nomchong）说，"所以，这是提振大家的精神，把人气带回唐人街的一种方式。"

蔡李佛开设了中国功夫和舞狮课程，40多年来一直是唐人街社区的一分子。

纳木钟说，很多人是先来他们这里学习中国功夫，然后开始喜欢上舞狮的，因为这两者是相关的。

安娜·拉蒙特（Anna Lamont）是舞狮队的一名成员。"从我还是个孩子起，我就一直想学功夫……我是从2017年开始在这所学校训练的，后来几乎是立刻就开始舞狮了。"她说。拉蒙特发现，学习舞狮既有挑战性，也能收获满满。

"一开始，舞狮很有挑战性，因为你的身体还不习惯那样移动。除了要记舞步，还要学着如何承受狮头的重量。"她说，"但你可以通过舞狮学到很多技能……而且这会让你觉得自己是一个大家庭的一员。"

Week Nine

Monday【A 完形填空】

● 参考译文

奶牛已经进化到可以隐藏自己跛足的程度。当 2073 号奶牛走出挤奶棚,经过附近的摄像头时,计算机会观察它的每一步。

它只在屏幕上短暂地出现了一下,但它的步态出现了轻微的不平衡,这是它正试图隐藏的。人类可能不会注意到有什么问题,但机器可以识别出来。

CattleEye 公司的联合创始人兼首席执行官泰瑞·坎宁(Terry Canning)说:"人工智能可以取代人类去监控奶牛。"他公司的技术可以自动检测牛早期的跛足迹象。目前,这项技术只适用于挤奶棚,但已经在奶牛场进行推广。目前约有 20 000 头奶牛处于该系统的监控之下。跛足的奶牛产奶较少,如果它们不能及时获得治疗,最终会被淘汰。

然而,还有很多农场尚未采用这些技术。莎拉·劳埃德(Sarah Lloyd)博士、她的丈夫和她的家人经营着一个大约有 400 头奶牛的农场。它们产出的所有牛奶都用于奶酪生产。

"我们的牛奶价格根本不够这项技术的成本。"莎拉说。她的丈夫更喜欢"卷起袖子"工作,而不是依赖机器。

其他人则持不同观点。杰弗里·布雷(Jeffrey Bewley)博士说,奶牛天生就想要隐藏跛足,因为它们已经演变成了猎物。因此,帮助农民发现早期跛足迹象的技术可能是有用的。

Tuesday【B 阅读理解】

● 参考译文

您是否正在寻找一些新的应用程序?我们为您提供了 2 月最好的安卓新款应用程序!

Auto Redial 价格:免费/最高 3.49 美元 ★★★★☆ 3.3 7516 个评分	推荐理由:如果您要呼叫的号码占线或未能接听,它基本上会自动重拨该号码。该应用程序会保存您已重拨的号码,您也可以随时停止重拨。它所占的内存大小不会过于离谱。
Celebrations Passport 价格:免费/每年 19.99 美元 ★★★★☆ 3.7 45 个评分	推荐理由:Celebrations Passport 是一款新的应用程序。它可以让您为母亲节等不同场合准备礼品篮或其他礼品。您可以添加鲜花、饼干和其他精致的物件。该应用程序通常是免费使用的。但是,每年 19.99 美元的订阅费可为您提供免费送货服务和其他福利。
Magic Photo Editor 价格:免费 ★★★★☆ 3.4 5 个评分	推荐理由:Magic Photo Editor 是一款基础的照片编辑器。它可以让您在手机上编辑各种照片内容。但是,该应用程序的广告策略确实比较激进,很多人都不喜欢这一点。如果开发人员能让人们选择付费删除广告,这可能会是一个相当不错的照片编辑器。

如果我们遗漏了任何不错的安卓新应用,请在评

论区告诉我们！您也可以点击这里查看我们最新的安卓应用和游戏列表！

感谢您的阅读！

Wednesday【C 阅读理解】
● 参考译文

日本的一个科学家团队研发出了一款新型口罩。如果佩戴者感染了新型冠状病毒，这款口罩就会在紫外线下发光，并且显示病毒的踪迹。

京都府立大学的科学家们称，他们制作出的这款口罩内部有一层额外的过滤片。用含有抗体的荧光染料喷洒后，如果出现新型冠状病毒的踪迹，这层过滤片就会在紫外线下发光。

该团队首先往鸵鸟体内注射灭活的新型冠状病毒，然后从这些鸵鸟产的蛋中提取抗体，并将这些抗体放入荧光喷雾中，从而开发出了这种方法。

日本的一位研究人员表示，他的团队对 32 名新型冠状病毒感染者展开了试验。他们发现，这 32 名测试者戴的口罩在喷上抗体喷雾后，在紫外线下发出了亮光，并显示出新型冠状病毒的踪迹。他的团队还注意到，随着患者病情好转，病毒载量降低，这种光慢慢消失了。

这位研究人员计划在下一轮测试中让 150 名参与者试用这种口罩，并希望日本政府能批准这款口罩在 2022 年上市。

Thursday【D 阅读理解】
● 参考译文

小岩石无时无刻不在撞击（地球）。美国国家航空航天局称，一辆小型汽车大小的东西大约每年会撞击地球大气层一次，但这些东西会在大气层中燃烧，而且在撞击地面之前就爆炸了。当这种情况发生时，没有人会真正注意到。有些人甚至可能会认为这种景象真的很酷，因为这些岩石形成了我们在漆黑晴朗的夜晚喜欢观看的所谓的流星。

美国国家航空航天局正在测试一项名为"双小行星重定向测试"的新技术，又称 DART。如果大型小行星将要撞击地球，它就可能派上用场。人们用它来测试在时间充足的前提下，采用航天器撞击的方式能否使小行星改变轨道，从而避免与地球发生碰撞。

一位美国科学家比较了美国人死于各种原因的风险。死于小行星撞击的概率大约为七万五千分之一。然而，被小行星撞击致死的概率不应该让你夜不能寐。美国人死于飞机失事的概率为三万分之一，死于龙卷风的概率为六万分之一。与小行星撞击相比，这两种命运中的任何一种都更有可能成为你死亡的原因。

Friday【E 短文填空】
● 参考译文

变化无常的全球气候对交通运输构成了越来越大的威胁。昆士兰 2010 年暴发的洪水损毁了 19 000 千米的道路，其中包括供紧急救援车辆行驶的通道。

从那时起，昆士兰就一直在使用泡沫沥青。将少量空气和冷水注入热沥青中，然后沥青会膨胀并形成防水层，最终路面会变得坚固而柔韧，能够更好地抵御洪水。

道路最大的问题之一是它们容易被高温损毁。极端高温会软化路面，导致出现更多裂缝或表面凹陷。有一种解决方案是加铺隔热层。它们可以让街道的颜色变浅并反射太阳辐射。有些隔热道路可以使地面温度最多降低 10 摄氏度。

在举办 2020 年奥运会之前，东京尝试了防晒涂料。到 2020 年年底，防晒涂料已应用于日本境内近 300 万平方米的路面。虽然这种涂料可以保护路面，但它可能会使行人的生活更加不舒适。

Saturday【F 短文填空】
● 参考译文

如果你不想为家人做圣诞节晚餐，那么现在你可以让机器人厨师来做所有的事情。许多科技公司正在开发可以用于商业和家庭厨房烹饪的机器人。

为了帮助开发这款机器人，莫雷（Moley）公司聘请了专业厨师蒂姆·安德森（Tim Anderson），他在 2011 年赢得了 BBC《厨艺大师》电视比赛的冠军。安德森演示他如何做菜，机器人则被设计程序来模仿他的动作。

"我会在一个布局与莫雷公司的厨房相同的厨房里按照食谱烹饪，我的动作会被记录下来，然后转移到机器人的手和手臂上。"安德森先生说。

"接下来，这些动作会被机器人团队简化，最后，我们得到了一个一致的程序，每次都能做出同样的菜。"

米凯拉·皮萨尼·莱尔（Mikaela Pisani Leal）是机器学习领域的科学家。她说机器人厨师可以为餐馆提供许多好处。"这些机器人可以减少食物中的病毒，改善清洁和卫生状况……它们可以颠覆整个行业。"但她也警告说，机器人厨师可能会导致失业。

高级餐厅老板兼主厨韦斯利·斯莫利（Wesley Smalley）表示，虽然厨房机器人提供了便利，但高端市场不会对它们感兴趣。

然而，对于我们当中许多不愿在圣诞节在家做饭的人来说，厨房机器人是一个好的想法。

Week Ten

Monday【A 完形填空】

● 参考译文

徐诗晓出生在江西省山区的一个小县城。因家乡四面环山,徐诗晓在成为皮划艇运动员之前甚至连游泳都不会。

2005年,一位皮划艇教练来到徐诗晓就读的学校,想寻找一些有潜力的皮划艇运动员。当时13岁的徐诗晓个子比她的朋友要高得多,引起了这位教练的注意。回忆起第一次皮划艇运动训练,徐诗晓说:"我的皮划艇每天都要翻倒很多次,我喝了好多河里的水。"

2013年,女子皮划艇仍未被列入奥运会比赛项目,这个消息给了徐诗晓重重一击。没有奥运会,也没有比赛。徐诗晓的教练建议她要么换个运动项目,要么就退役。对彼时已经21岁的徐诗晓来说,换运动项目是不可能的。于是,她放弃了皮划艇运动,找到了自己的第一份工作——在家具公司做销售。

五年前,徐诗晓意外地接到了前教练的电话,前教练询问她是否有意愿重返皮划艇赛场,并参加东京奥运会。徐诗晓很快就做出了决定,三天后她就重返训练场了。

2021年8月7日,徐诗晓和搭档孙梦雅获得了东京奥运会女子500米双人划艇金牌,这也是中国在该项目上获得的首枚奥运金牌。

Tuesday【B 阅读理解】

● 参考译文

三班学生:

英语写作测试将于6月22日上午8:30至10:00举行。本次测试基于第二单元的第一篇文章。

文章一:

毕比安·蒙特尔-斯皮(Bibian Mentel-Spee)是一名单板滑雪运动员,于2021年3月去世,享年48岁。她也是一位先驱,是单板滑雪运动被纳入冬季残奥会的推动主力之一。

蒙特尔-斯皮成为残奥会传奇人物的旅程始于她取得2002年盐湖城冬季奥运会的比赛资格。当她在29岁被诊断出右小腿骨癌时,她已经是一名成功的单板滑雪运动员,并且正准备参加奥运会。但他们不得不给她截肢。

当时单板滑雪运动还处于起步阶段,基础设施很少,没有通用规则,也没有全球性赛事。于是蒙特尔-斯皮与来自世界各地的其他残疾单板滑雪运动员们一起开始工作。他们共同组织了世界杯巡回赛,安排了赞助,游说官员,并努力让这项运动处于公众视野中。她下决心要证明单板滑雪运动属于顶级赛事。在长达八年多的活动之后,她接到一个电话,电话里说单板滑雪运动将被列入2014年索契残奥会的比赛项目中。

在你完成写作任务之后,你将有5~10分钟的时间阅读你写下的文章并检查错误。你要尤其注意:

时态误用;

表达错误

Wednesday【C 阅读理解】

● 参考译文

拉斐尔·纳达尔(Rafael Nadal)赢得的大满贯冠军数达21次,其中有16次比赛是他的叔叔托尼(Toni)担任他的主教练。从托尼·纳达尔扔给他三岁的侄子的第一个球开始,他就看到了这个孩子的不同之处。"通常情况下,当我给一个小孩扔球时,他会站着等球被送到他身边。但我的侄子主动去接球了。这一点很特别。"托尼将纳达尔塑造成了一位球员，并对他的人格塑造影响很大。正如拉斐尔常常承认的那样，如果没有他的叔叔托尼，他不一定会取得成功。

"我对拉斐尔的要求很高，因为我太在乎了。"托尼说。拉斐尔说他的叔叔过去常常会大声喊叫并试图吓唬他。如果这个小男孩在球场上走神了，托尼会用球敲打他。训练结束时，托尼会要求拉斐尔捡起所有的球并扫除红土。如果拉斐尔忘了带水瓶，他就不得不在烈日下不喝水进行训练。拉斐尔在他的书中写道："（尽管）托尼让我很紧张，但我知道我和他相处得很好。托尼是对的。他虽然经常让人生气，但从长远来看，他是对的。"

当拉斐尔赢得他的第10个法国网球公开赛冠军时——托尼最后一次担任拉斐尔的法国网球公开赛教练——这位叔叔来到球场颁发奖杯。他的脸上洋溢着自豪之情。当他们紧紧相拥时，两人（的眼神）之间流露出爱意。

Thursday【D 阅读理解】

● 参考译文

来自越南的年轻发型师阮发知（Nguyen Phat Tri）因其引人注目的花卉发型设计而备受关注。

28岁的阮发知在2015年毕业于安江大学，获得了生物技术学位。由于他一直对艺术有浓厚的兴趣，他决定去胡志明市学习化妆和美发。凭借一些非常有创意的技术和设计，阮发知很快在越南发型设计界出了名。

阮发知的设计在社交媒体上有数百万的浏览量，但很少有人能意识到每一个造型背后要付出多少努力。完成最简单的造型需要耗时一到两天，而最复杂的造型可能需要两到三个月才能完成。

尽管利润丰厚，阮发知通常拒绝的请求比他接受的要多，因为他更愿意把时间花在研究新的设计和技术上。他说："我想激发与我有相同热情的人们的创造力，我希望帮助越南的美发业发展壮大，并走向世界。"

当被问及他会给年轻的造型师什么建议时，这位越南艺术家表示，对他们来说最重要的是评估他们的天赋，因为这是一个需要"艺术的眼光"的领域。此外，他们需要有追求梦想的激情、毅力和决心。

Friday【E 阅读理解】

● 参考译文

拉塔·曼吉茜卡（Lata Mangeshkar）于2022年2月6日去世。她成名于宝莱坞，是印度的文化标志和国家宝藏。几十年来，这位"宝莱坞的夜莺"一直都是印度最受欢迎的歌手。每位顶级女演员都希望拉塔来演唱她们的歌曲。

拉塔·曼吉茜卡于1929年出生在印度中部城市印多尔市。她从未接受过正规教育。由于20世纪40年代初期的电影中没有那么多的歌唱片段，年轻的拉塔转向演戏来谋生。到1947年，她一直靠拍电影谋生，但她并不快乐。"我从来都没有喜欢过这些——化妆、灯光。人们总是命令你做事，说这段对话，说那段对话，我觉得很不舒服。"她后来对某位采访者说道。1949年，拉塔在电影《钟声梦蝶》中演唱了她的第一首完整歌曲，并立即受到人们的关注。在接下来的40年里，她在许多电影中演唱了令人难忘的流行的歌曲。

拉塔优秀到足以挑战顶级男歌手。"我是一个白手起家的人。我学会了如何战斗。我无所畏惧。但我从来没有想过我会得到这么多。"她曾经这样说道。她永恒的音乐无疑给数以百万计的印度人带来了快乐，并成为他们生活的配乐。

Saturday【F 任务型阅读】

● 参考译文

我是一名专业的自由式滑雪运动员。在我 18 年的人生的后 10 年里，我一直在追寻并爱上恐惧。

正如所有那些迷人的恋人一样，这个重要的另一半可能会……反复无常。实际上，"恐惧"是三种不同感觉的总称，这三种感觉即兴奋、不确定和压力。我了解到，当你注意到这些迹象并积极运用这些感觉时，它们能够帮助你成功。

从事极限运动的运动员很容易被认为是无畏且任性的。把自己置于风险之中，这从生物学上来说是违反直觉的。我们不会逃离恐惧，而是会培养自我意识，并做好风险评估，从而与恐惧建立起一段独特的关系。

作为一个长大成人的女孩，我对自己为应对"证明自己"这一压力所做的努力而感到自豪。我增强自尊，并减少自己对于外界的期待的需求，以此来应对这种压力。我专注于这一运动带给我的快乐。

虽然我对自己和对世界的看法一直在变化，但有一件事是不会变的：无论时间过了多久，在恐惧面前的我都会是一个无可救药的浪漫主义者。

Week Eleven
Monday【A 完形填空】
● 参考译文

意大利，基奥贾（Chioggia）

基奥贾建在威尼斯潟湖的一群岛屿上，沿河矗立着拥有数百年历史的古老建筑。如今，基奥贾深受意大利和德国游客的欢迎。他们都被历史中心的建筑美景和索托马里纳（Sottomarina）适合家庭欢聚的海滩深深吸引着。这座城市是自行车旅行的完美基地。

纽约，皇后区

皇后区希望你能饿着肚子出现。这可能是唯一一个能让你在这么小的空间里品尝到150多个不同国家的家常菜的地方。皇后区的餐饮业虽然受到了新冠肺炎疫情的影响，但现在情况正在好转。

墨西哥，芝华塔尼欧（Zihuatanejo）

这个海滩小镇毗邻太平洋海岸的度假胜地伊斯塔帕（Ixtapa），和周围的社区已经开发出了一些游客可以参与其中的环保项目。非营利性保护组织"格雷罗鲸鱼"帮助培训渔民成为观鲸向导。Campamento Tortuguero Ayotlcalli 则给游客提供加入海龟巢巡逻和放生小海龟的机会。你还可以入住南边50英里的普拉雅维瓦（Playa Viva）。这个采用太阳能的度假村通过提供自然保护、观光方面的教育和就业机会拯救了附近的朱露楚卡（Juluchuca）村。

Tuesday【B 阅读理解】
● 参考译文

据报道，在2021—2022年的冰雪季，中国冬季休闲旅游人数将达到3.05亿人次。冰雪旅游已经从一种新的"时尚生活方式"转变为中国人民日常生活的重要组成部分。

哈尔滨	张家口
1. 哈尔滨国际冰雪节：雪地足球赛、冰雕展览。 2. 主题公园"哈尔滨冰雪大世界"：大型冰雪雕塑。	1. 拥有中国北方地区最大的天然滑雪场。 2. 2022年北京冬奥会的主要比赛场馆之一。 3. 崇礼冰雪旅游度假区：国家级旅游度假区。
呼伦贝尔	乌鲁木齐
1. 被称为"冰雪之城"。 2. 多项冰雪运动设施：提供速滑和短道速滑训练场地。 3. 那达慕大会：综合骑马、射箭等多种活动和冬季主题活动。	1. 丝绸之路国际滑雪场：位于天山山脉，有造雪系统。 2. 冬季运动场景：赛马。 3. 乌鲁木齐丝绸之路冰雪风情节：新年音乐会、雪景灯光秀、民族歌舞表演。

Wednesday【C 阅读理解】
● 参考译文

"世界上有很多我喜欢的地方，但达拉纳（Dalarna）完全偷走了我的心。"米尔卡·马蒂（Mirka Mati）告诉我们。

达拉纳是瑞典中部的一个省。"达拉纳"一词意为"山谷"。这个地区是南方的瑞典人的度假胜地，他们夏天经常去那里度假，那里的钓鱼湖、露营地和森林吸引着他们。

越野滑雪是探索达拉纳山脉的完美方式！位于达拉纳北部的格勒韦尔申（Grövelsjön）能提供瑞典最好的越野滑雪。你可以入住一间舒适的小屋、一家青年旅舍或四星级酒店，然后起床享用早餐，再次出发。

户外烹饪是一项典型的瑞典式体验。在冬天无所畏惧地进行户外烹饪让你更像当地人！你可以在越野滑雪休息时烤一些香肠，或者挖一个雪坑，这样你就可以放松身心，享受烹饪食物时火的"噼啪"声。你也可以尝试狗拉雪橇。达拉纳北部的许多地方都提供狗拉雪橇之旅。

偶遇驯鹿是另一个极具吸引力的选择。驯鹿在达拉纳北部的伊德勒（Idre）周围的乡间自由行走。伊德勒是瑞典最南端的萨米村庄的所在地，也是体验和了解萨米文化的理想场所。

让我们一起探索达拉纳所提供的一切，充分利用瑞典的这个冬天吧！

Thursday【D 阅读理解】
● 参考译文

这条漫长而孤独的登普斯特高速公路（Dempster Highway）被认为是加拿大最难驾驶的道路之一。道路未铺砌，不能打电话，中途还只有一个加油站。正如我自己发现的那样，任何行驶在这条道路上的人都需要为不幸做好准备。

当我向南行驶时，碎石从我的车轮下飞出。让我担心的不是饥饿或口渴。我害怕的是雷雨引起的野火，这种野火在加拿大北极地区的夏天越来越常见了。

开始下雨了。接着，雨点噼里啪啦地打在车窗上，变成了倾盆大雨。没过多久，汽车因为泥浆向侧面打滑了。

"这已经发生好几次了。"汽车旅馆餐厅的女服务员环视了一下几乎空无一人的餐厅，说道，"司机在泥里开得太快，车子会从侧面打滑，就像在冰上行驶一样。"

现在，我在返回道森市（Dawson City）的路上。在位于道森市以东约 40 千米处的克朗代克高速公路（Klondike Highway）上时，我的车抛锚了，可能好几个小时都不会有救援人员开车经过。但是，不久就有一位好心人载我一程。在他送我去道森市的这段路上，我意识到这一直是登普斯特魅力的一部分：每当我接近灾难时，幸运就会向我微笑。

或许加拿大最艰难的道路并没有那么艰难。

Friday【E 任务型阅读】
● 参考译文

西藏自治区去年接待游客超过 4 100 万人次，旅游收入超过 440 亿元。多年来，西藏以其丰富的历史遗产、自然风光和传统文化成为深受国内外游客欢迎的旅游胜地。

近年来，该自治区一直忙于为游客提高服务质量，现已推出游客和商户都能从中受益的各种文化产品和奖励措施。从 2016 年至 2020 年，该地区接待的游客超过 1.5 亿人次。据新华社报道，旅游业带来了近 2 130 亿元的收入，是 2011 年至 2015 年的两倍多。

西藏自治区旅游发展厅厅长王松平表示，旅游业为了解该地区的独到之处提供了一个窗口。"旅游部门应重点关注西藏的文化和自然资源，特别是在农村地区，要让更多的农村居民从旅游业中受益。"他说。

林芝市拥有美丽的湖泊、山脉、森林和许许多多的文化活动，是西藏的主要景点。林芝拥有 700 家农村居民旅馆，去年接待了 400 万人次。

Saturday【F 短文填空】
● 参考译文

沙斯塔湖（Shasta Lake）

沙斯塔湖位于加利福尼亚州北部，距旧金山三个半小时的车程。拥有 370 英里长的海岸线，租船屋成为一项热门活动也就不足为奇了。游客还可以欣赏沙斯塔山的景色，那里山顶终年积雪。

卡斯泰克湖（Castaic Lake）

卡斯泰克湖位于洛杉矶的东北部，因此这里是远离雾霾城市的完美户外场所。湖区分为上湖区和下湖区两个主要区域，每个区域都有自己的一系列活动。下湖从5月中旬到9月中旬专门用于划独木舟和非机动船，以及游泳。上湖可乘坐汽艇，还可进行其他活动，如钓鱼和骑摩托艇。

大熊湖（Big Bear Lake）

对于那些想要从洛杉矶来个一日游的人来说，大熊湖是一个不错的选择。从洛杉矶市中心到大熊湖只需两个小时。动物爱好者可以去大熊高山动物园逛逛，那里能近距离观察熊。湖附近还有许多登山步道、自行车道和很多钓鱼的地方。游客在湖边的六个码头都能租用船只。

Week Twelve
Monday【A 完形填空】
● 参考译文

在最近一次的欧洲之行中,我们将一半以上的时间都花在了西班牙。在我看来,西班牙是世界上食物最美味的国家之一。我在菲律宾长大,非常熟悉西班牙菜。许多菲律宾菜肴要么是由西班牙引进的,要么是西班牙菜改良的。

现在我要跟大家介绍一些西班牙小吃(Tapas)。Tapas 是指在西班牙美食中流行的开胃菜或小吃。它们是最著名的西班牙美食之一。

1. Tortilla Española

Tortilla Española 指的是传统上用鸡蛋、土豆和橄榄油制成的西班牙煎蛋饼。它们通常用作小吃或配菜。在制作中可以添加洋葱,但添加洋葱经常会引起争议。一些人认为洋葱在正宗的西班牙土豆煎蛋饼中是没有立足之地的。

2. Calcot

Calcot 是流行于西班牙加泰罗尼亚的菜肴中的一种大葱。它们类似于韭菜,却比常见的大葱更大,口感更温和。在西班牙,食用这种大葱的最佳时间是在它生长的当季,也就是 2 月和 3 月左右。大葱通常放在明火上烤,并用报纸包裹以使其保持柔软。

除了西班牙食物本身,我发现最有意思的是西班牙人的饮食习惯。他们吃晚饭的时间较晚,在晚上 9 点到 10 点左右,这是因为他们的午餐时间很长,随便在哪都需要花两到三个小时。

Tuesday【B 阅读理解】
● 参考译文

弗拉明戈舞是一种表现力极强的西班牙舞蹈形式。它也是一种有着拍手、优美的步法和肢体动作等特征的独舞。舞蹈通常由歌手和吉他手伴奏。

弗拉明戈最伟大的明星——洛拉·弗洛雷斯(Lola Flores)——使这种艺术形式在国际上成为一种典型的西班牙风格。

弗拉明戈有四种不同的元素:歌唱声、舞蹈、吉他演奏和哈来奥舞(即拍手和踩脚)。但也许最有趣的弗拉明戈词语要数"duende"了。在普通语言中,它的意思是"精灵",但在弗拉明戈的语境中,它指的是一种神秘而有力的情感和表达状态,只有最有天赋的弗拉明戈表演者才具备这种状态。

大多数门外汉熟悉的是弗拉明戈那种快节奏的西班牙吉他演奏,但拍手在这种艺术形式中也起着重要的作用。在热爱弗拉明戈舞的家庭中长大的孩子会学习拍手的艺术,并学习区分硬拍手和软拍手。换句话说,如果他们不会唱歌、跳舞或弹吉他,他们至少应该知道如何拍手。

Wednesday【C 阅读理解】
● 参考译文

亲爱的游客:

我们很高兴地宣布世界著名的威尼斯狂欢节于今年回归。由于疫情防控措施仍在实施,如果您计划前来参观,这里有一些您需要知道的事项。

时间

按照惯例,2022 年威尼斯狂欢节于 2 月 12 日(周六)开始,将持续到 3 月 1 日。主要活动在 2 月 19 日至 20 日的周末举行。

今年的庆祝活动将以音乐会和儿童戏剧节目开始,狂欢节于周日晚上正式开幕。

活动

1. Venice Wonder Time

这一活动的形式为一系列的音乐、马戏、木偶、小丑和戏剧表演，于周末（2月12日至13日和2月19日至20日）以及从2月24日（周四）到3月1日（周二）在城市的各个地点举行。

2. Nebula Solaris

这是一场灯光秀和马戏表演，将在威尼斯军械库举行。

新冠肺炎疫情防控

1. 须与他人至少保持一米间距。

2. 须佩戴FFP2类别口罩。

3. 观看Nebula Solaris表演秀，以及进入其他活动和展览区域须出示疫苗接种证明或可以表明持有者在过去6个月内已从新冠肺炎中康复的证明。

祝您玩得愉快！

2022年威尼斯狂欢节主办方

Thursday【D 阅读理解】
参考译文

次仁·施特丹（Tsering Stobdan）将一块小石头装进牦牛绒制成的吊索中，挥动着手腕，让吊索在干旱的土地上空飞舞。他告诉我，他就是这样来保护他的羊群并将它们唤回的。这只是他在过去60年中学到的技能之一，这些技能使他能够在如此艰难的条件下饲养他的牲畜。次仁·施特丹来自一个游牧群体，几个世纪以来，这个群体在印度北部地区饲养了牦牛、绵羊和山羊。那里是地球上最美丽的地方之一——即使当地环境恶劣，荒凉不堪。

该游牧群体曾经十分繁荣，而现在正在衰退。年轻一代被送往附近的城市，在那里他们可以找到更好的医疗和教育机会。他们的生活终年都很艰难。在春季和夏季白昼较长的日子里，人们会在清晨几个小时的时间里挤奶和剪牲畜毛，然后赶着它们出门。通常他们每天都要在高海地行超过12英里。晚上则是新一轮的挤奶和剪毛。但工作并没有就此结束，他们还必须烹制食物，修缮棚屋，以及收集粪肥。

该地区最令人担忧的问题之一就是他们的游牧智慧将在未来几年消失。面对世代的人口外流，他们数百年来积累的丰富文化可能会很快消失殆尽。

Friday【E 任务型阅读】
参考译文

用面包吓跑对你有害的恶灵

过去，爱尔兰人会在午夜前用面包用力敲打门和墙，以驱赶怨灵。据说用面包敲打墙面还能保佑家人在新的一年不会挨饿。

切勿在新年当天洗衣服

有些人相信，如果你在1月1日这天洗衣服，那么你是"为亡者洗衣服"，而那个你爱的人将会在新一年的某一刻去世。

切勿在1月2日之前扔东西

这种关于新年的迷信说法是，在过完元旦之前不能扔家里的任何东西。如果你在1月1日这天扔东西，你身边的人和物都会在这一年离你而去。

在新年前夜制造大量噪声

依照菲律宾人的传统，12月31日这天越吵闹越好，因为人们认为吵闹声可以赶走恶灵。

打扮成魔鬼

在日本的一些小村落，年轻男子会扮成魔鬼然后挨家挨户去吓懒人。据说这些可怕的鬼怪形象可以祛病消灾，还能保佑丰收，一年到头都有充足的食物。

Saturday【F 短文填空】

参考译文

排灯节是为期五天的灯光节，是印度最受欢迎的节日之一。为了庆祝排灯节，人们会点燃小油灯，以庆贺光明战胜黑暗、善良战胜邪恶。

排灯节得名于梵文"万灯节（deepavali）"，其意思是"一排黏土灯"。许多印度人会在家门口点上这些灯，象征着保护他们远离精神黑暗的内心之光。

为期五天的节日进程包括打扫房子、购买新家具和与所爱的人交换礼物。重点庆祝活动也包括传统的庆祝方式，如购买新的厨房用具，以求带来好运，以及吸引神灵的善意的其他做法。

在印度北部的城镇阿约提亚（Ayodhya），当局在节日当天沿着河岸点燃了大约100万盏灯。阿约提亚被认为是印度神罗摩的诞生地，而排灯节据说是他摧毁恶魔后回家的那一天。印度各地的庆祝活动包括烟花和音乐。但在活动庆祝期间，人们也担心在排灯节燃放的鞭炮造成空气污染。

Week Thirteen

Monday【A 完形填空】
● 参考译文

在冰雪覆盖的北冰洋中部,很难在海底找到食物。然而在2011年,当科学家们正在采集样本的时候,他们发现了类似北极熊的东西。据安特耶·波提乌斯(Antje Boetius)回忆,它是一块几乎令人惊讶的海绵。"在这个地区,大约每一平方千米就有一块海绵。"

海绵正在以曾经活跃的管状蠕虫群落的化石残骸为食。这是科学家们第一次发现吃化石的动物。科学家贾斯伯·德·胡耶(Jasper de Goeij)说:"这一发现非常酷,因为海绵能利用其他生物不能利用的食物来源。"

它们大多向山上移动,在那里可能更容易赶上携带小型管状蠕虫化石的局部水流。向山上移动也可以为下一代腾出空间,让较小的海绵在更不受水流影响的地方生活。

"这些海绵的新陈代谢非常低,"一位科学家说,"所以我不明白它们怎么可能在这里吃完它们的食物。"

Tuesday【B 阅读理解】
● 参考译文

我们呼吸的空气、喝的水和吃的食物都依赖着生物多样性——也就是地球上所有动植物的多样性。

最新数据表明,生物多样性正在迅速缩减,其中,英国在(所有)国家中属于最差的10%,在由主要的工业国家组成的七国集团(G7 Group)中排在最后。

研究人员指出,英国有如此多的土地长期以来用于建筑或集约型农业,留给大自然的空间所剩无几。他们警告说,世界失去了太多的生物多样性,我们面临着生态崩溃的危险,未来我们可能将无法依赖自然提供能源、食品和木材。

该研究发表于联合国生物多样性大会前夕,世界各国领导人届时将在线上讨论未来十年的自然保护计划。

过去十年中定下的目标全都没有实现,科学家指出,现在是实现可持续未来的最后良机。

Wednesday【C 阅读理解】
● 参考译文

在新西兰,南露脊鲸在大约一个世纪前被捕杀至濒临灭绝。但自那时起,其数量就已缓慢回升。

艾玛·卡罗尔(Emma Carroll)博士说:"我是一个研究项目的首席科学家。我们发现在2009年约有2 000头鲸鱼。"艾玛的团队正在追踪这些鲸鱼的觅食地,并关注气候变化是否影响其行为。

"我们知道,新西兰南露脊鲸向来会在春夏月份迁徙到新西兰的北部和东部。然而,没有任何一头被我们追踪的鲸鱼显示出这种迁徙模式。相反,它们中的大多数其实是向西迁徙的。"艾玛说,"所以,这些结果非常重要,并让我们生出希望——即使海洋不断变化,这些鲸鱼寻找大量食物的方法也不止一种。"

科学家们正在使用所有的现代工具来获得鲸鱼真正的全貌,不仅了解它们数量上的回升,还了解它们利用海洋的方式。

Thursday【D 任务型阅读】
● 参考译文

受人喜爱的海牛再次以惊人的数量死亡。饥饿和寒冷的天气是首要原因。大多数死亡事件发生在印第安河潟湖。在这里,数十年的农业化肥污染以及住宅开发已经杀死了大片的海草——它们是海牛的主要食物来源。

去年11月，帕特里克·罗斯（Patrick Rose）给予了警告。今年冬天对于海牛来说可能更加艰难：海牛将不得不做出重要的关于生与死的选择——要么不得不外出觅食，在寒冷中早早死去，要么待在温暖的地方挨饿。在过去，海牛很容易在严寒中生存下来。但是现在，许多海牛由于数年的食物短缺而变得虚弱，并且正达到崩溃的边缘。

为了度过寒冷的时刻，海牛将寻找可停留的温暖水域。在污染得到解决和海草恢复之前，海牛将继续遭受痛苦和死亡。

Friday【E 任务型阅读】
● 参考译文

研究人员最近发现了一处不同寻常的珊瑚礁——它是在南太平洋塔希提岛（Tahiti）附近被发现的。该珊瑚礁被认为是在这样的深度所发现的最大的珊瑚礁之一。而且它似乎没有受到气候变化或人类活动的影响。这处珊瑚礁比其他的更深——深度在35米到70米之间。

在这样的深度很难进行探索。潜水队配备了特殊的氧气罐，进行了200小时的潜水，以便对该珊瑚礁进行研究。他们给珊瑚拍照。珊瑚是一种微小的动物，在世界各地的海洋中生长并形成珊瑚礁。

莱提莎·海都因（Laetitia Hédouin）说她第一次看到这些珊瑚是在几个月前。那时她正和当地的一个潜水小组一起潜水。当她第一次到那里的时候，海都因想："哇——我们需要研究一下那个珊瑚礁。它有些特别。"她希望科学家们能更好地了解它在海洋中的角色。未来几个月还会安排更多的潜水活动。

在世界各地，珊瑚礁因过度捕捞和污染而遭到破坏。气候变化也在伤害珊瑚。

Saturday【F 短文填空】
● 参考译文

这是马赛马拉（Masai Mara）中心的一个傍晚，此时光线非常适合拍摄。在地平线上，国家公园的平原上都是动物。我坐在第一排的座位上，看着这趟历史性的旅程——成千上万头角马和斑马成群结队地从肯尼亚的马赛马拉自然保护区穿越到坦桑尼亚的塞伦盖蒂国家公园。这是平静、安宁的时刻，可能是我一生中最好的经历之一。

有超过200万头角马总是在肯尼亚和坦桑尼亚之间循环迁徙。斑马、羚羊和角马群全年都在肯尼亚和坦桑尼亚之间迁徙，其唯一的目的就是追随雨水。由于降雨量是由季节和气候变化决定的，所以没有办法预测降雨的准确时间和这些兽群的活动。

在坦桑尼亚的塞伦盖蒂国家公园，雨季是在3月、4月和5月。而在马赛马拉，我们见到角马的最好时机是从8月到11月月初。

Week Fourteen

Monday【A 完形填空】

● 参考译文

年轻人在应对环境挑战中发挥着带头作用。20岁的程浩生来自澳门,现就读于清华大学,他就是其中之一。他轻而易举地回想起去年年底在全球青年大会上的经历。

这次峰会旨在成为一个跳板,让全世界的青年在面对紧迫的环境问题时发挥更积极的作用,展示集体精神。

程浩生还积极参与撰写会议期间每一项活动的媒体报道,并将其发布在网上。"我又一次意识到了区域和全球合作对于应对气候变化的重要性。来自世界各地的许多学者、学生、年轻人和公民正致力于解决这一问题。"程浩生说。

"我仍然记得街道上到处都是倒下的树木,破碎的窗户几乎碎成碎片(的情景)。"程浩生说。他补充道,澳门每年遭受五到六次台风是很正常的,但台风造成的损失巨大。"这是我第一次意识到全球气候变化对我们生活的影响。"他说。

与此同时,他还和其他同学一起组织多项环保活动,比如在清华大学举办的回收和清洁活动。"通过这些活动,我们希望能激励人们在行动上做出改变。"他说。

Tuesday【B 阅读理解】

● 参考译文

节假日是与朋友和家人庆祝的时候,并且在节日期间人们会赠送礼物。不幸的是,这可能会导致大量的废弃物,例如节日贺卡、圣诞树、宴请(用具)和礼物包装。使用可以被回收的东西来庆祝节日是一种很好的方式。

礼物包装	由于担心纸张浪费,许多人开始考虑其他包装礼物的方式。 你可以使用可重复使用的礼物袋。建议使用旧地图、杂志页面和美术纸。收到礼物的人可以把包装用作别的用途。你也可以用颜色鲜艳的围巾或桌布来包装礼物。
节日贺卡	对许多人来说,寄节日贺卡是一项传统。然而,现在许多人使用数字贺卡或电子贺卡。人们更容易接受电子节日贺卡。那些想送传统贺卡的人可以选择用可回收纸张印制的贺卡。
圣诞树	更环保的选择应该是从当地农场买一棵真正的圣诞树。如果你真的买了一棵假树,那么你应该考虑一下它是由什么材料制成的。它是用可回收材料制作的吗?或者它能被回收吗?
宴请(用具)	举办庆祝活动时,避免使用一次性塑料制品,可以使用平常的盘子和杯子。

Wednesday【C 阅读理解】

● 参考译文

大多数年轻人喜欢在业余时间刷刷智能手机,但李如雪不一样,经常要到森林里才能找到他。这位27岁的年轻人在采访中表示:"虽然这种生活方式有点累,但很有意义。"

大学毕业后,李如雪加入了一个保护天行长臂猿的组织,其主要工作内容之一就是捡猿粪。天行长臂猿是国家一级保护动物,其数量比野生大熊猫还要少。通过分析猿粪中的DNA,研究人员可以弄清不同种群之间近亲繁殖的情况，从而更好地保护它们。因此，在过去四年半的时间里，李如雪整天追猿、捡猿粪。但是李如雪从不后悔自己的选择，也没有感到孤独，因为他发现参与自然保护的年轻人更多了。

同李如雪一样，初雯雯也一直致力于动物保护工作。由于其父亲从事野生动物研究工作，初雯雯和河狸、雪豹等野生动物一起度过了很长时间。毕业后，初雯雯追随了她父亲的脚步。蒙新河狸是国家一级保护动物。为了保护河狸，初雯雯在2018年发起了"河狸食堂"项目，最终吸引了一百多万名网友捐钱。由约四十万棵灌木柳苗的巨型"食堂"被建立了起来，而捐款大多数来自年轻的网友。

新华社指出："年轻人是世界的未来，也是全球生物多样性保护的未来。"

Thursday【D 任务型阅读】
● 参考译文

长期以来，中国人民是创造更绿的土地、更蓝的天空的主力军。从多年前发起的造林运动到如今的在手机上种植"虚拟树木"，多亏了中国人民的努力，中国的森林覆盖率已经从早期的8.6%增加到2020年的23.04%。

在这些奇迹背后，生动的故事和创新的措施体现了中国为改善空气质量和生态环境所做出的努力。

"沙尘暴一年刮一次，一次刮半年"曾经是形容中国北方生态的一句习语。在过去，由于过度放牧，草地在雨季到来之前就被羊吃掉了，这使得农田变成了沙土。

目前，像"蚂蚁森林"这样将网络和现实植树项目结合起来的项目在中国越来越受欢迎。截至2020年，参与"蚂蚁森林"的总人数超过5亿，线下植树（面积为）3.9万公顷。

中国政府还筹集了100多亿元的林业经营补贴。

"十三五"规划（2016-2020）期间，中国全面禁止天然林商业性采伐，建立了一支约700万人的国家管理和保护队伍，充分利用技术手段加强对森林资源的保护。

Friday【E 短文填空】
● 参考译文

"如果有一天世界末日来临，这些种质资源将为地球上的生灵带来新开始的希望。"中国西南野生生物种质资源库的工作人员李培说。中国西南野生生物种质资源库于2007年建成，是一个研究、保护珍稀濒危动植物的综合设施。

由于五分之二的植物物种濒临灭绝，保护国内那些神秘植物的生命是在与时间赛跑。那么，这个种质资源库是如何运作的呢？首先，科学家们采集濒危的、有用的野生物种，并将种子送到种质资源库。然后，为了将来的研究，采集人员必须记录这种植物的详细信息，包括采集地点、种子的体积、周边地区中单株植物的数量等。

该种质资源库坐落于云南，与国际合作伙伴开展样本的收集、交流和研究。该种质资源库拥有来自45个国家和地区的2 176组种子，每组包含数千粒单独的种子。李培说："中国拥有丰富的生物资源，我们旨在进一步加强种质资源保护，开展更深入的研究，期待为中国乃至世界的生物多样性保护做出贡献。"

Saturday【F 短文填空】
● 参考译文

18岁的邓肯·尤尔曼（Duncan Jurman）来自美

国佛罗里达州，现在是佛罗里达州戴维市诺瓦东南大学的一名学生。他是一个名为"让蝴蝶回归，激励青年为了后代保护蝴蝶"的环境项目的创始人，该项目旨在让蝴蝶的数量回升。

尤尔曼说："我认为我真正爱上蝴蝶的原因之一是它们非常容易接近。例如，如果你想吸引一只蝴蝶，你就种植很多花。"尤尔曼在家里建立了一个蝴蝶花园，多年来他在那里饲养和放生了5 000多只蝴蝶。为了让其他学生也能接触到蝴蝶，他在学校里建立了一个蝴蝶花园。"每当一只蝴蝶落在他们身上，或者我把一条毛毛虫放在他们手中，这些年轻学生马上就会爱上它们。他们对昆虫产生了新的兴趣。"他说。

"蝴蝶对环境真的非常重要，主要有两个原因。"尤尔曼说，"第一，蝴蝶像蜜蜂一样给花授粉，是世界上最重要的传粉者之一。另一个重要原因是，蝴蝶是鸟类等许多物种的食物。"

尤尔曼的环境项目"让蝴蝶回归"帮助当地学校打理花园，并帮助进一步开展外展服务工作。

官方微信　　更多福利及售后

时文速递
新闻速递

云图分级阅读研究院·编著

强化篇

北京理工大学出版社

Live letter

ENGLISH READING

Contents 目录

新闻速递

		主题	
002	Week One	生活成长	24岁小伙迎接艰巨挑战，为环球帆船赛启航
003	Week Two	校园生活	丰富多彩的劳动课程走进校园
004	Week Three	家庭教育	读书沙龙助力为孩子营造健康的家庭成长环境
005	Week Four	健康饮食	斯里兰卡的风味小吃——扁豆馅饼
006	Week Five	社会人际	为成功而着装是否重要？
007	Week Six	文学艺术	北京大学考古学：中国考古学家的摇篮
008	Week Seven	历史地理	英国古运河焕发新气象
009	Week Eight	文化风俗	半山立夏节：送春迎夏
010	Week Nine	科学技术	巅峰使命：中国将架设全球海拔最高气象站
011	Week Ten	人物传奇	64岁滑雪教练开启新的人生
012	Week Eleven	旅行交通	英国知名度假城堡推荐
013	Week Twelve	异国风情	阿肯色州的绝美风景与乐趣
014	Week Thirteen	自然生态	倾听鸟鸣：你听到的就是鸟类听到的吗？
015	Week Fourteen	环境保护	2022选举：英国地方政府如何应对气候变化？

参考译文   016

新闻速递

Week One

体　　裁	记叙文	题　　材	生活成长	词　　数	219
难　　度	★★★☆☆	建议用时	6分钟	实际用时	＿＿＿

　　Britain's James Harayda, displaying the natural steeliness (刚毅) of a sailor (水手), is aiming to become the youngest competitor in the 2024 Vendee Globe (旺代环球帆船赛).

　　The 24-year-old young man may never have experienced sailing in the Southern Ocean but sailor Dee Caffari, who competed in the 2009 Vendee Globe, believes he has the qualities to succeed in perhaps the most difficult challenge in yachting (帆船运动). Caffari has been competing with Harayda in the Double-Handed Offshore class (双人离岸组比赛), and they have been British champions twice. Their aim to compete in the 2024 Paris Olympics ended when the International Olympic Committee decided last year to remove (移除) the event from the program.

　　Under the guidance of the extremely experienced Caffari, Harayda is aiming to take on the very difficult challenge of the Vendee Globe, which half of all competitors fail to finish due to rudders (船舵) smashing (撞击) or capsizing (倾覆). As Caffari says, you need certain qualities such as resilience (韧性), commitment and the courage to overcome a challenge and face disadvantages. "Stepping into the Vendee Globe you are changed from being an adventurer to a professional sailor," Caffari said.

　　Harayda is very self-sufficient (自立的). He is also quite calm when things are difficult to deal with. Caffari says it is Harayda's eagerness (渴望) to learn that gives her confidence he will be up to the task.

(From *China Daily*, May)

词汇碎片

quality *n.* 品质；质量　　succeed *v.* 成功　　professional *adj.* 职业的；专业的

重难句讲解

　　Under the guidance of the extremely experienced Caffari, Harayda is aiming to take on the very difficult challenge of the Vendee Globe, which half of all competitors fail to finish due to rudders smashing or capsizing. 在经验丰富的卡法里的指导下，哈拉伊达的目标是挑战极具难度的旺代环球帆船赛，其中一半的参赛者会因为船舵被撞碎或翻船而无法完成挑战。

　　本句是复合句。which引导非限制性定语从句，修饰the Vendee Globe；Under the guidance of... 意为"在……的指导下"；fail to 意为"未能，没做成"；due to rudders smashing or capsizing 作原因状语。

Week Two

体 裁	说明文	题 材	校园生活	词 数	171
难 度	★★★☆☆	建议用时	6 分钟	实际用时	

The Ministry of Education recently released a new curriculum (课程) standard for labor education in compulsory education (义务教育), which will be carried out in the fall term of this year.

Labor courses cover mainly household chores (家务), productive (生产的) labor and services. The goal is to encourage students to form positive values, good character and key abilities.

Schools can choose to decide the number of task groups to learn in different school stages based on the actual situation. "Our school responded (回应) actively to the new standard. We are finding new ways of driving students' passion (热情) in labor courses and guiding them not only to simply complete the work but also to learn and enjoy the process of labor," said a teacher.

By cooking, sewing (缝纫), knotting (打绳结), planting trees and vegetables and volunteering, students can try out different options (选择) in extracurricular (课外的) classes. Wang Zhenlin, a student, joined the knotting class. "From ancient times, there have been books about knotting. I tried out different methods in the class and found a way to knot fast and beautifully," Wang said.

(From *China Daily*, May)

词汇碎片

labor *n.* 劳动   positive *adj.* 积极的，乐观的   character *n.* 品质，性格   task *n.* 任务

重难句讲解

We are finding new ways of driving students' passion in labor courses and guiding them not only to simply complete the work but also to learn and enjoy the process of labor. 我们正在寻找新途径来激发学生对劳动课的热情，不仅仅要引导学生完成任务，还要引导他们学习和享受劳动的过程。

本句是 and 连接的并列句。are finding... in labor courses 和 (are) guiding... of labor 为并列的谓宾结构，主语都是 We。find new ways of doing sth. 表示"寻找新途径来做某事"，guide sb. to do sth. 表示"引导某人做某事"。

Week Three

体 裁	记叙文	题 材	家庭教育	词 数	253
难 度	★★★☆☆	建议用时	6分钟	实际用时	

"Come on, time to go to school," Tan Xiangying, 70, would once urge (敦促) her two grandchildren, but now it is the other way around—the kids remind Tan about her classes.

Thanks to a unique (独特的) education model that is slowly accepted in the rural areas of southwest China's Chongqing, children are enjoying a healthy family environment. Organized by a primary school in Shizhu Tujia Autonomous County, the weekly salon (沙龙) focuses on family education, emphasizing (强调) the important role of the parents in children's growth.

In 2019, Tan began attending a reading salon at the local primary school with her grandchildren. Tan's son and daughter-in-law work far away from home. To learn how to get along better with her two grandchildren, Tan joined the salon. The reading salon focuses on specific topics for guardians (监护人), such as how to manage their emotions and how to get along with children. The adults read together and exchange their thoughts, while teachers give lectures.

"I had no idea my every small move could have a strong influence on the children. I used to berate (斥责) them. However, I have tried to befriend them now," Tan says. Tan's granddaughter says she has noticed important changes in her grandmother. "She is more gentle now and often praises us," she says.

"Be it theory (理论), or in practice, a good education needs effort from both the school and the family. We hope every child can grow in a healthy environment filled with love," says Tan Lamei, deputy director (副主任) of the county's education department.

(From *China Daily*, May)

词汇碎片 education *n.* 教育 manage *v.* 管理；经营 emotion *n.* 情绪，情感 gentle *adj.* 温柔的

I had no idea my every small move could have a strong influence on the children. 我不知道我的每一个小举动都会对孩子们产生巨大的影响。

本句是复合句。主句为主谓宾结构，I 作主语，had 作谓语，no idea 作宾语，后面接省略 that 的同位语从句，解释说明抽象名词 idea。have a strong influence on 为固定短语，表示"对……产生巨大的影响"。

重难句讲解

Week Four

体 裁	记叙文	题 材	健康饮食	词 数	265
难 度	★★★★☆	建议用时	7分钟	实际用时	

As the train pulled into Peradeniya junction station (枢纽站) in central Sri Lanka (斯里兰卡), the man sitting opposite me jumped out of his seat and leaned (倾斜) out of the window, whistling loudly. A seller soon appeared outside, removed a basket from the top of his head and handed it to the passenger. The man quickly pulled out a fritter (油炸馅饼), leaving money behind, and then passed the basket to other hungry passengers, who did the same before returning the basket back to the seller through the window. As the train moved away, everyone got back into their seats and happily ate what I later learned were lentil patties (扁豆馅饼), one of the most delicious street foods you could ever find on an island.

Lentil patty is beloved throughout Sri Lanka, and it is popular because of its deeply familiar and simple ingredients: lentils and prawns (对虾), together with onions and curry (咖喱) leaves. And it is a cheap and tasty treat for people.

Although lentil patty is sold at every beach, seafront, train station or public space where people might get together, the much-loved street food tells a story about Sri Lanka's history and cooking culture. It is traditionally made of red lentils, which don't grow in Sri Lanka but in India; so, this is a food which crossed the ocean to arrive in Sri Lanka.

Sri Lankans have always adapted (改良) every foreign food that was ever introduced to the island. They like to stamp (印) their own identity (特征) on them. And they are a nation that eats with their hands, so lentil patty is very pleasing to Sri Lankans.

(From *BBC News*, May)

词汇碎片

tasty *adj.* 美味的   treat *n.* 款待   pleasing *adj.* 令人满意的

重难句讲解

Sri Lankans have always adapted every foreign food that was ever introduced to the island. 斯里兰卡人总是会改良每一种传入岛上的外来食物。

本句是复合句。主句是 Sri Lankans have always adapted every foreign food，为主谓宾结构。that 引导定语从句，修饰 foreign food。

Week Five

体 裁	议论文	题 材	社会人际	词 数	239
难 度	★★★★☆	建议用时	7分钟	实际用时	_____

The idea of dressing for success used to be relatively simple: wear formal (正式的) clothes. In traditional offices, most leaders would be found in a suit. The rise of the tech sector (科技行业) changed this style. Picture Silicon Valley's most famous leaders, and what they wear are jeans, hoodies and black turtlenecks instead of the suits of the past.

In 2020, the widespread change to remote (远程的) work upended (翻转) work dress style completely. During the pandemic, workers at home could easily perform well in a meeting of a video call in a T-shirt, sweatpants and slippers. Now, as workers come back into offices, few companies are demanding a return to formal wear. Then is it still possible to "dress for the job you want"?

Studies have shown wearing more formal clothes can make workers feel more self-confident and improve work performance actually. These days, there's another reason to dress for success: showing that you understand and agree with the company culture.

If you're not paying attention to what people can see, then you're missing an opportunity to be remembered. For workers looking for promotion (晋升), it is important to find a way to stand out, especially when you're in that little box on a screen.

Still, the right dress might look very different in different workplaces which can help position you for success. As long as you have to impress somebody directly or indirectly, your appearance really does play a role in that.

(From *BBC News*, May)

词汇碎片   jeans *n.* 牛仔裤   slipper *n.* 拖鞋   appearance *n.* 外表

If you're not paying attention to what people can see, then you're missing an opportunity to be remembered. 如果你不注意别人看到的东西，那么你就错过了一个被他人记住的机会。

本句是复合句。主句是 then you're missing an opportunity to be remembered，opportunity to do sth. 表示"做某事的机会"。If引导条件状语从句，其中包含宾语从句 what people can see，pay attention to 表示"注意；留心"。

重难句讲解

Week Six

| 体 裁 | 记叙文 | 题 材 | 文学艺术 | 词 数 | 273 |
| 难 度 | ★★★★☆ | 建议用时 | 7 分钟 | 实际用时 | |

A new exhibition was held at Peking University on Tuesday to mark the 100th anniversary (周年纪念) of the establishment (建立) of the archaeology discipline (考古学科) at the school.

One hundred years ago, after modern archaeology was introduced to China, Peking University set up an archaeology research room. In 1952, Peking University established the first archaeology major in the country. Over the past 100 years, Peking University has made great contributions (贡献) to the development of Chinese archaeology and the protection of cultural heritage (遗产). Archaeologists from both China and abroad said that the progress made by the School of Archaeology and Museology at Peking University is a mirror reflecting (反映) the rise of modern Chinese archaeology and has allowed it to stand at the forefront of the discipline in the world.

In March, the Piluo Site in Daocheng County, Sichuan Province, a large-scale Paleolithic site that was excavated (挖掘) under the leadership of professors from Peking University, was listed as one of China's top 10 archaeological discoveries of 2021 by the country's National Cultural Heritage Administration. In addition, the Sanxingdui Ruins Site is one of the most visited archaeological wonders in 2021. Many professionals working in the different pits (坑) at the site are graduates from the School of Archaeology and Museology at Peking University.

The level of sophistication (高水平) in archaeology that Peking University has gotten in the past century has also been recognized (认可) by the world. Dorian Fuller, a famous archaeologist, pointed out that the School of Archaeology and Museology at Peking University has continued training archaeologists to the highest standards (标准) over the years. They will continue devoting (奉献) themselves to the development of archaeology with "Chinese features and style".

(From *Global Times*, May)

词汇碎片

major *n.* 专业　　protection *n.* 保护　　continue *v.* 继续

重难句讲解

Archaeologists from both China and abroad said that the progress made by the School of Archaeology and Museology at Peking University is a mirror reflecting the rise of modern Chinese archaeology and has allowed it to stand at the forefront of the discipline in the world. 中外考古界人士表示，北京大学考古文博学院取得的进步是中国现代考古学崛起的一面镜子，使其走在了世界学科的前沿。

本句是复合句。主句为主谓宾结构，Archaeologists 作主语，said 作谓语，后面接 that 引导的宾语从句。宾语从句的主干为 the progress is a mirror and has allowed it to stand；made by the School of Archaeology and Museology at Peking University 为过去分词短语作后置定语，修饰 progress；reflecting the rise of modern Chinese archaeology 为现在分词短语作后置定语，修饰 mirror。

Week Seven

体 裁	说明文	题 材	历史地理	词 数	216
难 度	★★★★☆	建议用时	7分钟	实际用时	

The Leeds-Liverpool Canal (利兹—利物浦运河) has played an important role in history. It is now being revived (复兴) by a project called the Super Slow Way.

While the north, east and west parts of Pendle Hill (彭德尔山) have green and pleasant landscapes popular with hill walkers, the south is densely populated (人口稠密) and poor. The canal provides an excellent calm space. Built to service mills and mines, it has been looking for a new role for more than fifty years—the Super Slow Way might just do the job.

You can walk it, cycle it, or run it. Or a mixture of those. Here's what to look out for on the journey, however fast or slow you go.

Many of Lancashire's mills have been torn down. But in Briercliffe, two miles from the canal, the Grade I listed Queen Street Textile Mill Museum (皇后街纺织厂博物馆) still has working looms (织布机).

Canal Kitchen is a floating laboratory that brings together artists, architects, scientists, engineers, cooks and members of the public to explore the biological (生物的) environment of the canal. Workshops are planned at three places during May and June.

Today, the stretch of canal between Burnley and Accrington is positively pastoral (田园的), but this was once the place of the Burnley Coalfield (煤田). There's a small mining museum at a nearby farm. Coal power has given way to wind farms.

(From *The Guardian*, May)

词汇碎片 floating *adj.* 漂浮的；流动的   laboratory *n.* 实验室   explore *v.* 探索

Built to service mills and mines, it has been looking for a new role for more than fifty years—the Super Slow Way might just do the job. 修建运河原本是为了服务于工厂和矿山，但五十多年以来，运河一直在寻找新的定位——"超慢路"项目或许会起到作用。

本句中的 it 指代上文提到的 The canal，has been looking for 作谓语，a new role 作宾语。Built to service mills and mines 为过去分词短语作状语。破折号后面的 the Super Slow Way might just do the job 对破折号前面的句子进行解释说明。look for 为固定短语，表示"寻找；寻求"。

重难句讲解

Week Eight

| 体 裁 | 记叙文 | 题 材 | 文化风俗 | 词 数 | 189 |
| 难 度 | ★★★☆☆ | 建议用时 | 6分钟 | 实际用时 | _____ |

This may be an age of weather and communication satellites, of mobile phones and online messaging, but old customs and traditions still have a role to play.

On May 5th last year, in Banshan National Forest Park, Hangzhou, Zhejiang Province, some people dressed in *hanfu* and holding lanterns with candles, showed a great spectacle (壮观的场面). They performed the ceremony to "send away the spring and welcome the summer", a custom passed down the generations. The ritual (仪式) celebrates *lixia*, or Start of Summer, one of the 24 solar terms (节气) that often falls on May 5th.

If the four seasons of the year are likened (把……比作) to the four stages of nature, Start of Summer is a ceremony celebrating nature's youth. From this day on, nature has entered a mature and enthusiastic (热情的) period from a green and mild childhood. The temperature begins to gradually warm up.

The Banshan Lixia Festival was started over 10 years ago by a group of locals interested in culture. In 2007, some folk culture enthusiasts held the first festival. Later, the local government helped organize cultural activities, and the festival has gradually become a cultural brand in Hangzhou.

(From *China Daily*, May)

---

generation *n.* 一代 period *n.* 时期 mild *adj.* 温和的 local *n.* 当地人 *adj.* 当地的 **词汇碎片**

If the four seasons of the year are likened to the four stages of nature, Start of Summer is a ceremony celebrating nature's youth. 如果把一年四季比作大自然的四个阶段，那么立夏就是一个庆祝大自然的青少年时期的仪式。

本句是复合句。主句为主系表结构，Start of Summer 作主语，is 作系动词，a ceremony 作表语，celebrating nature's youth 为现在分词短语作后置定语，修饰 ceremony。If 引导条件状语从句，其中 liken 在此处作动词，意为"把……比作"。 **重难句讲解**

Week Nine

体　　裁	说明文	题　　材	科学技术	词　　数	226
难　　度	★★★★☆	建议用时	7分钟	实际用时	

Chinese scientists are mounting efforts to establish a meteorological monitoring station (气象监测站) at an altitude (海拔) of 8,800 meters on Mount Qomolangma, the world's highest peak (顶峰). If the station is established successfully, it will replace the one at an altitude of 8,430 meters set up by the British and US scientists on the south side of the mountain in 2019, to be the world's highest of its kind.

At present, the engineers responsible for establishing the station are still waiting for the perfect weather for mountaineering (登山). The Qinghai-Tibet Plateau (青藏高原) is facing a warming tendency (趋势) along with global warming, and the higher the altitude is on the plateau, the more the temperature has risen. Such a conclusion is only based on the data (数据) of weather stations at sea levels below 5,000 meters and the estimated (估计的) calculation according to the remote sensing data, because weather monitoring data from high-altitude stations were missing in the past.

Including the highest, eight elevation gradient meteorological stations (海拔梯度气象站) will be set up on Mount Qomolangma, one of the main tasks in China's new scientific expedition (考察) on the world's highest peak. The eight stations will collect the wind speed and wind direction data, as well as humidity (湿度) on the north side of Qomolangma, and the elevation gradient meteorological station system is of great importance for monitoring the melting glaciers (冰川) and mountain snow at the high altitudes.

(From *China Daily*, May)

词汇碎片

replace v. 取代，代替　　at present 目前，现在　　conclusion n. 结论

重难句讲解

If the station is established successfully, it will replace the one at an altitude of 8,430 meters set up by the British and US scientists on the south side of the mountain in 2019, to be the world's highest of its kind. 如果该站顺利建成，那么它将取代英美科学家于2019年在珠穆朗玛峰南侧海拔8 430米处建立的监测站，成为世界上海拔最高的气象监测站。

本句是复合句。If引导条件状语从句。主句为主谓宾结构，it作主语，will replace作谓语，the one作宾语。set up by the British and US scientists on the south side of the mountain in 2019 为过去分词短语作后置定语，修饰the one；set up 表示"建立，创建"。

Week Ten

体 裁	记叙文	题 材	人物传奇	词 数	263
难 度	★★★☆☆	建议用时	6分钟	实际用时	

On his most recent course, Andy Walters thought, "Am I too old for this?" At the age of 64, Andy Walters has just taken a further qualification as a ski instructor (教练), reaching a level that makes him teach almost anywhere.

Walters had always had a fascination (着迷) with skiing, even though he was born in Kuwait (科威特), a place "as snowless as you can get". He first skied at 11 on a school trip to Austria (奥地利). "We were allowed to go up the mountain on the second day and I remember, with a friend, being so scared of skiing down that we actually walked down," he says. Yet it didn't put him off. Later, Walters became part of the school's ski team (including just him and another boy).

He now regularly works with a company, teaching groups of children during their school holidays. He is pretty fit, he says, and being a 64-year-old ski instructor isn't too tiring, although, he adds: "You can find yourself out of breath (气喘吁吁) sometimes if you're following a 20-year-old down a run and they refuse to stop. The thing about skiing is, if your skill is very good, it's quite efficient (高效的), so you don't tend to be exhausted."

What has this change of life given him? "Great friends," he says. "I've met a lot of really interesting people, and skied with them." It has been fun to teach children, he thinks, and see them progress. "It's something I didn't anticipate (预料) I would do this late. I like to keep myself interested, and I think it keeps me feeling young."

(From *The Guardian*, May)

---

course *n.* 课程　　　　scared *adj.* 恐惧的，害怕的　　　　exhausted *adj.* 疲惫不堪的

Walters had always had a fascination with skiing, even though he was born in Kuwait, a place "as snowless as you can get". 沃尔特斯一直沉迷于滑雪，尽管他出生在科威特，一个"几乎没有雪的地方"。

本句是复合句。主句为 Walters had always had a fascination with skiing；even though 引导让步状语从句，意为"虽然，即使"，其中 a place "as snowless as you can get" 为 Kuwait 的同位语，起到补充说明的作用；have a fascination with 表示"对……着迷"；be born in 表示"出生于"。

Week Eleven

| 体 裁 | 说明文 | 题 材 | 旅行交通 | 词 数 | 171 |
| 难 度 | ★★★☆☆ | 建议用时 | 6分钟 | 实际用时 | |

Stay at these historic places and you get to experience them after all the tourists have gone home.

Manorbier Castle (城堡), Pembrokeshire

This 11th-century Norman castle is usually open to the public during the day, but you can have it all for yourself if you stay here. There are three holiday cottages (小屋), while Castle House sleeps 12 in great comfort and guests have their own walled garden.

Cardigan Castle, Ceredigion

Overlooking the River Teifi (泰菲河) in Wales, Cardigan Castle is lovely to hang around once it's emptied of visitors. Much fought over in the past, now it's a history-rich community project with medieval (中世纪的) battlements (城垛) and gardens to explore.

Easton Walled Gardens, Lincolnshire

Come to this garden in May to see the fruit trees blossom (开花), or in June when the famous sweet peas of Easton start to bloom—more than 50 different varieties (品种) can be smelled across the garden. There are three holiday cottages that give you space to dip into the gardens in the early mornings and evenings as well as during the day.

(From *The Guardian*, May)

词汇碎片 comfort *n.* 舒适，安逸   empty *v.* 清空   community *n.* 社区

Much fought over in the past, now it's a history-rich community project with medieval battlements and gardens to explore. 这里曾发生过很多次战争，如今，卡迪根城堡是一个历史悠久的社区项目，有中世纪的城垛和花园供人们探索。

本句为主系表结构，it 在句中作主语，is 作系动词，a history-rich community project 作表语。Much fought over in the past 为过去分词短语在句中作状语。

重难句讲解

Week Twelve

体　　裁	记叙文	题　　材	异国风情	词　　数	207
难　　度	★★★☆☆	建议用时	6分钟	实际用时	

No landscape is as closely connected with Arkansas (阿肯色州) as the Ozark Mountains. Arkansas is seen as a natural wonderland (仙境).

Drive the looping (环形的) roads that spiderweb across the area and you'll get into a world of great rock, and deep, dark groves (树丛). From following hiking trails and visiting state parks to having an adventure on the Buffalo River, here are the best things to do in the Ozarks.

You can float down the Buffalo River, which is the first national river in the USA. And it is still one of the most beautiful rivers. Head to a nearby town to connect with adventure outfitters (装备供应商) who can help you set up a "float" adventure into beautiful gullies (沟壑) and sandbars (沙洲), or direct you towards some of the area's hikes. Bring a tent, because camping out here with the river lapping nearby and the stars soaring (升空) overhead is kind of fantastic.

You can also feel the music and folk culture in the town of Mountain View. It is a good place to start this journey. The musical traditions of the Ozarks are both protected and interpreted (诠释) here. Have a walk, ask some questions, and sit for a while on someone's porch (门廊) if they invite you around—it happens a lot around here.

(From *Lonely Planet*, May)

---

area *n.* 区域　　　direct *v.* 指导　　　for a while 一会儿；暂时

词汇碎片

Bring a tent, because camping out here with the river lapping nearby and the stars soaring overhead is kind of fantastic. 带上一顶帐篷，因为在这里露营的话，附近有河水拍打，头顶有星星闪动，这是无与伦比的。

本句是复合句。主句 Bring a tent 为祈使句，表示建议。because 引导原因状语从句，其主干为 camping out is fantastic。kind of 为固定短语，表示"有点儿"。

重难句讲解

Week Thirteen

体　　裁	说明文	题　　材	自然生态	词　　数	188
难　　度	★★★★☆	建议用时	7 分钟	实际用时	

When we humans hear birdsong, we can't help but think about parallels (相似特征) to human music and language. Recent research has shown that birdsong sequences (序列) do not sound to birds like they do to us. Then how does birdsong sound to them?

　Birds appear to listen most closely not to the melodies (旋律) that catch our ears but rather to fine acoustic (声音的) details in their songs that lie beyond the range of human perception (感知). That is to say, birds hear song differently than we might expect. Studies have found surprising differences between the abilities of birds and humans to hear sequences of sounds and acoustic details. Birds perform surprisingly poorly on recognizing a melody changed up or down in pitch (音高). This is something humans do naturally. So, the melodies we hear when we listen to birdsong may be very different from the birds' perceptual experiences.

　The next time you hear a birdsong, try thinking of it less like a catchy (朗朗上口的) melody and more like a fast-moving, coordinated (协调一致的) dance of the syrinx (鸣管)—one that is as rich in emotion and meaning as human language or music but expressed in a different way.

(From *Scientific American*, May)

词汇碎片

birdsong *n.* 鸟鸣　　fine *adj.* 细微的　　expect *v.* 预料；期待

重难句讲解

　Birds appear to listen most closely not to the melodies that catch our ears but rather to fine acoustic details in their songs that lie beyond the range of human perception. 鸟类似乎不是在听我们听到的旋律，而是在听鸟鸣中人类无法感知的细微之处。

　本句是复合句。主句是 Birds appear to listen most closely not to the melodies but rather to fine acoustic details in their songs，not... but... 为固定搭配，表示"不是……而是……"，连接的前后内容在意义上表示转折，结构上表示并列。that catch our ears 和 that lie beyond the range of human perception 都是定语从句，分别修饰 melodies 和 acoustic details。

Week Fourteen

| 体裁 | 说明文 | 题材 | 环境保护 | 词数 | 203 |
| 难度 | ★★★★☆ | 建议用时 | 7分钟 | 实际用时 | |

Local elections (选举) are taking place in the UK on Thursday, and environmental questions may play a large part in people's voting (投票) decisions. The UK has a national ambition (追求的目标) to be net zero by 2050. Local governments have great control over emissions (排放). Andy Gouldson, Professor of Environmental Policy at Leeds University says that local governments should reduce emissions from transport and buildings.

Less driving and more walking are important. In the UK, local governments have the power to influence how people move around their area, and to push greener ways of travel. For example, local governments can help people change to electric cars by increasing the number of public chargers (充电桩) on the street. They can also develop more space for pedestrians (行人) and cyclists.

In the UK, households spend 70% of their energy on heating and cooling. Local governments should introduce energy-saving measures. These measures could not only reduce emissions by 6 million tons by 2030, but also save households up to £300 per year on their energy bills.

Governments can help reduce emissions by supporting the development of wind turbines (涡轮机). They can also encourage local green networks—small energy generation systems—to provide low carbon (低碳) energy and reduce the cost of energy for local people.

(From *BBC News*, May)

---

electric *adj.* 用电的　　　cyclist *n.* 骑自行车的人　　　energy *n.* 能源；能量

These measures could not only reduce emissions by 6 million tons by 2030, but also save households up to £300 per year on their energy bills. 到2030年，这些措施不仅可以减少600万吨排放量，还可以为家庭每年节省高达300英镑的能源费用。

not only... but also... 意为"不仅……而且……"，在本句中连接 reduce 和 save 两个并列谓语。up to 为固定短语，表示"高达"。

参考译文

Week One

英国的詹姆斯·哈拉伊达（James Harayda）展现了水手与生俱来的刚毅，他的目标是成为2024年旺代环球帆船赛最年轻的参赛者。

这位24岁的年轻人可能从来没有在南大洋航行过。但是，曾参加2009年旺代环球帆船赛的水手迪·卡法里（Dee Caffari）认为，在或许是最艰难的帆船运动挑战中，哈拉伊达有能力取得成功。卡法里一直与哈拉伊达进行双人离岸组比赛，他们曾两次获得英国冠军。他们参加2024年巴黎奥运会的目标由于国际奥委会去年决定取消该项赛事而落空了。

在经验丰富的卡法里的指导下，哈拉伊达的目标是挑战极具难度的旺代环球帆船赛，其中一半的参赛者会因为船舵被撞碎或翻船而无法完成挑战。正如卡法里所说，你需要某些品质，比如韧性、投入性和克服挑战、面对逆境的勇气。"参加旺代环球帆船赛，你就从一个冒险家变成了一个职业水手。"卡法里说。

哈拉伊达非常自立。遇到棘手的事情时他也非常冷静。卡法里说，正是哈拉伊达对学习的这种渴望给了她信心，让她相信他能胜任这项任务。

Week Two

教育部最近发布了新的义务教育阶段的劳动课程标准，这一标准将于今年秋季学期实施。

劳动课程主要包括家务劳动、生产劳动和服务性劳动。其目标是鼓励学生形成积极的价值观，塑造良好的品格，以及培养关键能力。

学校可结合实际，在不同学段自主确定任务小组的数量。"我们学校积极响应劳动课新课标。我们正在寻找新途径来激发学生对劳动课的热情，不仅仅要引导学生完成任务，还要引导他们学习和享受劳动的过程。"一位老师说。

烹饪、缝纫、打绳结、植树、种蔬菜、做志愿者，学生们可以在课外课堂上尝试不同的选择。学生王真林（Wang Zhenlin）参加了绳结班。他说："自古以来，就有关于打绳结的书。我在课堂上尝试了不同的方法，最终找到了一种又快又美观的打结法。"

Week Three

"来吧，该上学了。"70岁的谭祥英曾经这样敦促她的孙子孙女，但现在情况正好相反——孩子们提醒谭祥英上课。

在中国西南部的重庆农村地区，由于一种独特的教育模式正在慢慢得到接受，孩子们正在享受一个健康的家庭环境。石柱土家族自治县的一所小学每周举办沙龙，关注家庭教育，强调家长在孩子成长中的重要作用。

2019年，谭祥英开始和她的孙子孙女一起参加当地小学的读书沙龙。谭祥英的儿子和儿媳在离家很远的地方工作。为了学习如何更好地与两个孙子孙女相处，谭祥英加入了沙龙。读书沙龙关注与监护人有关的特定话题，例如，如何管理自己的情绪，如何与孩子相处等。大人们一起读书，交流思想，老师们则进行授课。

谭祥英说："我不知道我的每一个小举动都会对孩子们产生巨大的影响。我过去经常斥责他们。然而，我现在试着和他们成为朋友。"谭祥英的孙女说，她已经注意到奶奶身上的重大变化。她说："她现在温柔多了，还经常表扬我们。"

"无论是理论还是实践，良好的教育需要学校和家庭的共同努力。我们希望每个孩子都能在充满爱的健康环境中成长。"县教委副主任谭腊梅说。

Week Four

当火车驶进斯里兰卡中部的佩拉迪尼亚（Peradeniya）枢纽站时，坐在我对面的男子从座位上跳了起来，身子探出窗外，大声吹着口哨。很快，一个小贩出现在外面。他从头顶上取下一个篮子，递给了这位乘客。这名男子很快（从篮子中）拿出了一个油炸馅饼，付了钱，然后把篮子递给其他饿着肚子的乘客，这些乘客也拿了饼，付了钱，然后通过窗口把篮子还给了小贩。火车开走后，每个人都回到自己的座位上，开心地吃了起来。我后来才知道他们吃的是扁豆馅饼——岛上最美味的街头小吃之一。

扁豆馅饼在斯里兰卡深得喜爱，广受欢迎，因为它的原料十分常见和简单：扁豆和对虾，再加上洋葱和咖喱叶。对人们来说这是一种实惠又美味的款待。

尽管扁豆馅饼在各个海滩、海滨、火车站或人们可能聚集的公共场所都有出售，但这种深受喜爱的街头小吃讲述了斯里兰卡的历史和饮食文化。传统的扁豆馅饼是用红扁豆做的，这种东西种植于印度，而不是斯里兰卡。因此，这种食物是漂洋过海来到斯里兰卡的。

斯里兰卡人总是会改良每一种传入岛上的外来食物。他们喜欢在这些食物上印上自己的特征。因为斯里兰卡的人们吃东西时都是手抓，所以扁豆馅饼令斯里兰卡人非常满意。

Week Five

过去，为了成功而着装的概念相对简单：穿正装。在传统的办公室里，大部分领导者都会穿西装，但是科技行业的崛起改变了这种风格。想象一下硅谷最知名的领导人的着装，他们穿的是牛仔裤、连帽衫和黑色高领毛衣，而不是过去的西装。

2020年，远程办公的广泛普及彻底颠覆了工作着装风格。疫情期间，居家的员工穿着T恤衫、运动裤和拖鞋，就可以轻松地在视频会议上有出色表现。现在，随着员工重返办公室，很少有公司要求回归正式着装。那么是否还有可能"为心仪的工作而着装"呢？

研究表明，穿更正式的服装可以让员工感到更自信，实际上还能提升工作表现。如今，为了成功而着装还有另一种解释：表现出你了解并认同公司文化。

如果你不注意别人看到的东西，那么你就错过了一个被他人记住的机会。对于寻求晋升的员工来说，想办法脱颖而出是很重要的，尤其是当你出现在屏幕上的一个小小方格中的时候。

尽管如此，在不同的工作场所，合适的着装可能看起来非常不同，这有助于你走向成功。不管是以直接还是间接的方式，只要你想给别人留下好印象，你的外在形象都会起到一定的作用。

Week Six

一场新的展览于周二在北京大学拉开帷幕，以纪念该校考古学科成立一百周年。

一百年前，现代考古学传入中国，随后北京大学设立了考古研究室。1952年，北京大学开设了全国第一个考古学专业。这一百年来，北京大学对中国考古事业的发展和文化遗产保护做出了重大贡献。中外考古界人士表示，北京大学考古文博学院取得的进步是中国现代考古学崛起的一面镜子，使其走在了世界学科的前沿。

今年 3 月，在北京大学教授的带领下发掘的大型旧石器时代遗址——四川稻城皮洛遗址——被国家文物局列为 2021 年中国十大考古发现之一。另外，三星堆遗址是 2021 年参观人数最多的考古奇观之一。在遗址各个坑道工作的许多专业人士都毕业于北京大学考古文博学院。

北京大学近百年来的高水平考古也得到了世界的认可。知名考古学家道瑞安·富勒（Dorian Fuller）指出，北京大学考古文博学院多年来持续以最高标准培养考古学家。他们将继续致力于发展具有"中国特色和中国风格"的考古学。

Week Seven

利兹—利物浦运河在历史上发挥了重要作用。如今它正通过一个名为"超慢路"的项目得到复兴。

彭德尔山的北侧、东侧和西侧都拥有绿色宜人的景观，深受登山者的喜爱，而南部则是人口稠密、经济落后的地区。运河则提供了一个极好的宁静空间。修建运河原本是为了服务于工厂和矿山，但五十多年以来，运河一直在寻找新的定位——"超慢路"项目或许会起到作用。

你可以沿着运河步行、骑自行车或者跑步。这几种方式也可以同时进行。无论你走得快或慢，以下是在旅途中要留意的事情。

兰开夏郡的许多工厂都被拆除了。但是在距离运河两英里的布里尔克利夫（Briercliffe），被列为一级建筑的皇后街纺织厂博物馆仍然可以运行的织布机。

运河厨房是一个漂浮的实验室，它将艺术家、建筑师、科学家、工程师、厨师和民众汇集起来，探索运河的生态环境。研讨会计划于 5 月至 6 月期间在三个地点举办。

如今，连接伯恩利（Burnley）和阿克宁顿（Accrington）的这段运河完全是田园风光，但这里曾经是伯恩利煤田的所在地。在附近的农场有一个小型采矿博物馆。煤电已经被风电所取代。

Week Eight

这也许是一个气象和通信卫星、移动电话和网络信息的时代，但古老的习俗和传统仍然发挥着作用。

去年 5 月 5 日，在浙江省杭州市半山国家森林公园，一些人身着汉服，手提蜡烛灯笼，呈现出一派壮观的场面。他们举行了"送春迎夏"的仪式，这是一种代代相传的习俗。这一仪式是为了庆祝立夏。立夏是二十四节气之一，通常在 5 月 5 日这一天。

如果把一年四季比作大自然的四个阶段，那么立夏就是一个庆祝大自然的青少年时期的仪式。从这一天起，大自然从青涩而稚嫩的童年时期步入了成熟而热情的时期。气温也开始回升。

十多年前，一群对文化感兴趣的当地人发起了"半山立夏节"。2007 年，一些民间文化爱好者一起举办了首届节日。后来，当地政府协助组织文化活动，这一节日逐渐成为杭州市的一个文化品牌。

Week Nine

中国科学家正努力在世界最高峰珠穆朗玛峰上的海拔 8 800 米处建立一个气象监测站。如果该站顺利建成，那么它将取代英美科学家于 2019 年在珠穆朗玛峰南侧海拔 8 430 米处建立的监测站，成为世界上海拔最高的气象监测站。

目前，负责建站的工程师仍在等待可以登山的好天气。随着全球变暖，青藏高原正面临变暖趋势。高原海拔越高，气温上升越多。过去因为缺少高海拔气象站的监测数据，所以这样的结论只是基于海拔5 000米以下的气象站的数据和根据遥感数据进行的估算。

包括最高的监测站在内，中国将有8个海拔梯度气象站在珠穆朗玛峰建成，这是中国对世界最高峰进行新的科学考察的主要任务之一。这8个气象站将采集珠穆朗玛峰北侧的风速、风向以及湿度数据，并且这一海拔梯度气象站系统对监测高海拔地区冰川融化和山体积雪具有重要意义。

Week Ten

安迪·沃尔特斯（Andy Walters）在他最近的课程上想："我是不是太老了？"在64岁时，安迪·沃尔特斯才获得滑雪教练的高级资格，达到了几乎在任何地方都可以执教的水平。

沃尔特斯一直沉迷于滑雪，尽管他出生在科威特，一个"几乎没有雪的地方"。他第一次滑雪是在他11岁的时候，当时学校组织去奥地利旅行。他说："第二天我们获得允许上山，我记得，当时我和一个朋友非常害怕滑雪，所以我们实际上是走着下山的。"但这并没有让他却步。后来，沃尔特斯成了学校滑雪队的一员（滑雪队只有他和另一个男孩）。

沃尔特斯现在定期在一家公司工作，在学校放假期间给孩子们上课。他说自己很健康，而且成为一名64岁的滑雪教练并不太累，不过，他补充说："如果你跟在一个20岁的青年后面跑，而他们又拒绝停下来时，那么有时你会发现自己上气不接下气。滑雪的关键在于，如果你的滑雪技巧很棒，那么你学起来会很有效率，这样你就不会疲惫不堪。"

这种生活的变化带给了他什么呢？沃尔特斯说："好朋友。我遇到了很多非常有趣的人，还和他们一起滑雪。"他认为教孩子们滑雪并看着他们进步是很有趣的。"我没想到自己会这么晚才做这件事。我喜欢让自己有一兴趣，这让我感觉很年轻。"

Week Eleven

在所有游客都回家后，你可以留下来，体验一下这些历史古迹。

马诺比尔城堡，彭布罗克郡

这座11世纪的诺曼城堡通常白天对公众开放，但如果你留在这里，你就可以欣赏城堡里的一切。这里有三间度假小屋，而城堡别墅可以容纳12人，非常舒适，且客人们有自己的围墙花园。

卡迪根城堡，锡尔迪金郡

卡迪根城堡俯瞰威尔士的泰菲河，游客一走空，你就可以在城堡周围闲逛。这里曾发生过很多次战争，如今，卡迪根城堡是一个历史悠久的社区项目，有中世纪的城垛和花园供人们探索。

伊斯顿围墙花园，林肯郡

5月份来伊斯顿围墙花园观赏果树开花，或者6月前来，那时伊斯顿远近闻名的甜豌豆开始开花，在花园里可以闻到50多种不同品种的花的香味。伊斯顿围墙花园有三间度假小屋，可以让你在清晨、傍晚以及整个白天畅游花园。

Week Twelve

奥沙克山脉（Ozark Mountains）是阿肯色州最具代表性的景观。阿肯色州被视为一个自然仙境。

沿着蜘蛛网般的环形道路穿越这片区域，你将进入一个由壮观的岩层、茂盛而昏暗的树丛组成的世界。

徒步旅行到州立公园参观,再去布法罗河(Buffalo River)上来一场冒险,这是在奥沙克可以做的最好的事情。

你可以沿着布法罗河漂流,布法罗河是美国第一条国家河流,也是最美丽的河流之一。你可以前往附近的小镇,与探险装备供应商取得联系,他们可以帮助你在绝美的沟壑和沙洲之间策划一场"漂流"冒险,或者指导你前往该地区进行徒步旅行。带上一顶帐篷,因为在这里露营的话,附近有河水拍打,头顶有星星闪动,这是无与伦比的。

你也可以感受山景城的音乐和民俗文化。山景城是开始这段旅程的好地方。奥沙克的音乐传统在这里得到了保留和诠释。闲逛一下,请教别人一些问题,如果有人邀请你的话,就在门廊上坐一会儿——这在这里经常发生。

Week Thirteen

当我们听到鸟鸣时,我们会不由自主地想到鸟鸣与人类的音乐和语言的相似之处。最近的研究表明,鸟类听到的鸣声序列不像我们听到的那样。那么鸟类听到的鸣声是怎样的呢?

鸟类似乎不是在听我们听到的旋律,而是在听鸟鸣中人类无法感知的细微之处。也就是说,鸟类听到的鸣声可能与我们想象的不同。研究发现,鸟类和人类在听到声序和声音细节的能力上存在惊人的差异。鸟类在识别音高上下变化的旋律时的表现差得出奇。而这是人类天生便会做的事情。因此,当我们听到鸟鸣时,我们听到的旋律可能与鸟所感知的存在很大差异。

下次你听到鸟鸣的时候,试着不要把它想象成朗朗上口的旋律,而要把它想象成快速移动、协调一致的鸣管在跳舞——一种像人类语言或音乐一样富有情感和意义,但表达方式不同的舞蹈。

Week Fourteen

英国将于周四举行地方选举,环境问题可能对人们的投票决定起着重要作用。英国的国家目标是到2050年实现净零排放。地方政府对排放进行严格控制。利兹大学环境政策学教授安迪·古尔德森(Andy Gouldson)表示,地方政府应该减少交通业和建筑业的排放。

少开车多走路很重要。在英国,地方政府有权力影响人们在当地的出行方式,并促进绿色环保出行。例如,地方政府可以通过增加街道上公共充电桩的数量来帮助居民转向驾驶电动汽车。他们还为行人和骑自行车的人规划更多空间。

英国家庭将70%的能源用于供暖和制冷。地方政府应该推行节能措施。到2030年,这些措施不仅可以减少600万吨排放量,还可以为家庭每年节省高达300英镑的能源费用。

地方政府可以通过支持风力涡轮机的开发,从而帮助减少排放。他们还可以鼓励当地的绿色网络——小型能源发电系统——为当地居民提供低碳能源,降低能源成本。

官方微信　　更多福利及售后